WITHDRAWN

Gramley Library
Salem Academy and College
Winston-Salem, N.C. 27108

Florida A&M University, Tallahasse
Florida Atlantic University, Boca Rat
Florida Gulf Coast University, Ft. My
Florida International University, Mia
Florida State University, Tallahasse
University of Central Florida, Orlan
University of Florida, Gainesville
University of North Florida, Jacksonv
University of South Florida, Tampa
University of West Florida, Pensaco

Rhetoric and Resistance
in Black Women's Autobiography

Johnnie M. Stover

University Press of Florida
Gainesville/Tallahassee/Tampa/Boca Raton
Pensacola/Orlando/Miami/Jacksonville/Ft. Myers

Copyright 2003 by Johnnie M. Stover
Printed in the United States of America on recycled, acid-free paper
All rights reserved

08 07 06 05 04 03   6 5 4 3 2 1

ISBN 0-8130-2676-8
Cataloging-in-publication data are available at the Library of Congress.

The University Press of Florida is the scholarly publishing agency
for the State University System of Florida, comprising Florida A&M
University, Florida Atlantic University, Florida Gulf Coast University,
Florida International University, Florida State University, University
of Central Florida, University of Florida, University of North Florida,
University of South Florida, and University of West Florida.

University Press of Florida
15 Northwest 15th Street
Gainesville, FL 32611-2079
http://www.upf.com

Contents

Acknowledgments

Let me take a moment to thank those who have given me the spiritual, emotional, and intellectual support I required to complete this project. First and foremost, I thank the members of my family for their constant, unconditional love and encouragement. Any project of this magnitude requires adequate "focus" time away from other professional and economic considerations, and I thank Dr. William Covino, former chair of the English Department and now dean of the College of Arts and Letters, for instituting a program of research release time for junior faculty at Florida Atlantic University. From the initiation of this project through its various draft stages, I have received immeasurable insightful comments and suggestions from a number of colleagues—Bonnie Braendlin, Dennis Moore, Tom Martin, and especially Carol McGuirk.

I also offer thanks to Marlene NourbeSe Philip for permission to reproduce excerpts from her text, *She Tries Her Tongue: "Her Silence Softly Breaks."* These excerpts were vital in representing my own thoughts and in linking those thoughts together.

Last but not least, I must acknowledge the graduate students in my African American autobiography courses for their enthusiasm toward the subject of life-writing, keeping me sharp and on track; I particularly want to name Erika Rosiers, for it was her excitement about and research into the work of Elizabeth Keckley that provided me with so much valuable information.

Portions of this text appear in the *College English* article "Nineteenth-Century African American Women's Autobiography as Social Discourse: The Example of Harriet Ann Jacobs" and in the *a/b: Auto/Biography Studies* article, "African American 'Mother Tongue' Resistance in Nineteenth-Century Postbellum Black Women's Autobiography: Elizabeth Keckley and Susie King Taylor."

Thank you all.

Introduction

Life-Writing and Subversion

Slip mouth over the syllable; moisten with tongue the word.
Suck Slide Play Caress Blow—Love it, but if the Word
gags, does not nourish, bite it off—at its source—
Start again
—**Marlene NourbeSe Philip**, *She Tries Her Tongue*

On June 2, 2000, the *Chronicle of Higher Education* reported on the National Association of Scholars' (NAS) critique of an alleged reduction of "fundamental" English courses.[1] "Losing the Big Picture: The Fragmentation of the English Major Since 1964" surveys the English curriculum at twenty-five colleges and universities, concluding that few "'still encourage undergraduates to take the "big picture" or foundational courses emphasizing broad periods, the greatest writers, and the most important literary genres'" (Leatherman A19). The NAS report further suggests that the quality of the English education curricula has declined since 1964. But rather than consider what writers and genres those earlier curricula include, I prefer to consider which they exclude—any substantial representation of American literary works by women and people of color, and especially those works produced in nineteenth-century America. If we were to use those pre-1964 curricula as defining markers of the "greatest writers" and the "most important literary genres," we would have to conclude that there were no great African American women writers in the nineteenth century and that slave narratives and African American autobiography do not constitute important literary genres.[2]

Neither of these conclusions would be accurate. In the 1960s and 1970s, American college students, the NAACP, and women's rights groups demanded more representative curricula from the various humanities departments within colleges and universities, including English departments. As they saw it, the "big picture" had to be more than just "big"; it had to include the literary contributions of Americans who had traditionally been excluded—placed outside the white-male-heterosexual-middle-class paradigm. Slave narratives and the autobiographical texts of nineteenth-century African American women had been rendered invisible, along with their writers, and would have remained so had we settled for the narrow vision of those who believe that the 1964 English department curricula presents an acceptable model for the study of American literatures. In citing Mrs. N. F. Mossell's 1894 listing of African American publications, Carla L. Peterson notes that slave narratives joined "sociological texts, fiction, journalism, history, religious studies, poetry, and spiritual autobiographies" on Mossell's list (*Doers* 5). Not only does this list represent the tendency of African American writers to blur the lines between genres but it also demonstrates, because of Western society's need to establish clear genre distinctions, why the literary works of African Americans were summarily dismissed. Peterson writes that Mossell's list includes "genres and texts that would be considered either 'nonliterary' by modernist criteria, and thus more appropriate to the fields of history or sociology, or 'minor' by historical standards, and thus unworthy of serious attention," resulting in "the erasure from scholarly investigation of 'minority' texts considered insufficiently 'important' or 'beautiful' by dominant cultural standards" (*Doers* 5).

The late-twentieth-century critical and theoretical interest in historically situating American literatures has not only opened the doors for revisiting and re-reading canonical texts (such as Twain's *Huckleberry Finn*, Hawthorne's *The Scarlet Letter*, Melville's *Moby Dick*, and others), but has also breathed life into texts previously ignored, minimized, or marginalized. Russell J. Reising notes that previous generations of literary scholars have been guilty of working within a limited canon and guilty of "deny[ing] or minimiz[ing] American literature's status as a social discourse" (229). He goes on to suggest that such theorists limit the possible range of social discourse by "positing a homogeneous . . . tradition of New England literature and by defining literature so as to exclude texts and genres of a frankly social cast" (234). By approaching texts from their historical contexts in this book, I specifically and intentionally apply social perspectives to American literatures because "literary analysis can no longer merely focus on texts as pure objects but must examine how these were shaped both by a politics of publication . . . and by a politics of reception" (Peterson, *Doers* 5). I wish to give appropriate credit to nineteenth-century African American women autobiographers, whose texts represent a new and distinct American literary form.

In this study, I primarily apply my theories to four nineteenth-century African American women autobiographers as examples of black women using their personal narratives to engage the systems of enslavement and disempowerment perpetrated against them: Harriet E. Wilson, *Our Nig: or, Sketches from the Life of a Free Black, in a Two-Story White House, North. Showing that Slavery's Shadows Fall Even There* (1859); Harriet A. Jacobs, *Incidents in the Life of a Slave Girl, Written by Herself* (1861); Elizabeth Keckley, *Behind the Scenes. Or, Thirty Years a Slave, and Four Years in the White House* (1868); and Susie King Taylor, *Reminiscences of My Life in Camp With the 33rd United States Colored Troops, Late 1st S.C. Volunteers* (1902).[3] Although I have chosen to apply my theory in depth to only these four autobiographical texts, I submit that it is relevant to most if not all personal narratives written by nineteenth-century black women struggling against sociopolitical enslavement and that these communicative techniques and characteristics continue to shape the works of twentieth-century black women autobiographers. I will also show that because Wilson and Jacobs published their texts prior to the Civil War while Keckley and Taylor wrote postbellum narratives, the state of America's social and political positions is reflected in the structures and themes of their nineteenth-century stories.

I acknowledge that using a historical approach to the writings of people of color can lead to the marginalization of such writings by focusing on their historical rather than their literary value. Yet the chapters that follow are going to challenge that idea of mutual exclusivity. These autobiographers and their texts are significant both on historical and literary grounds: a discussion of the historical context of autobiography does not preclude a recognition of its literary merits as well. I am in agreement with the conclusions reached by Frances Smith Foster and Henry Louis Gates Jr. in their respective works. Foster wrote the following statement about the analysis of spiritual autobiographies: "Although the autobiographical details may vary, these narratives present female protagonists who can enrich our concepts of history and literature and thus of our notions of selfhood" ("Neither Auction Block" 145). In proposing the notion that the autobiographical self is an "attempt to recreate or represent a historical self in language," Gates argues that we must "insist upon the recognition and identification of the black autobiographical tradition as the positing of fictive black selves in language" (*Figures in Black* 123).[4]

The power and influence of the black woman's autobiography that emerged out of nineteenth-century America was sociopolitical as well as literary. And of all the literary genres, autobiography is the one that best lends itself to historical as well as literary approaches. As creative nonfiction, autobiography suggests the importance that place and time have on the development of the author; writers of autobiography re-interpret "self" for the reading of others. Unlike the poststructuralist or textual critique that is appropriate to a purely creative, fictional work, the historical self of the author is very much a part of any autobiography. We as readers need to know out of what social, spatial, and temporal location(s) that self emerged. Autobiography, especially the African American woman's autobiography, rejects critical efforts to categorize the genre merely as literature or merely as history; instead, this autobiography took on hybrid characteristics as a merger of literary writing and personal history that grew out of and reflects the world that shaped both it and its writer.

Despite many constraints—historical, sociological, and political—nineteenth-century African American women writers of autobiographical texts assumed literary power over their personal narratives and left written records of their struggles for freedom. They wrote at a time when the literary circles that dominated nineteenth-century American writing (and as a result, American reading) were predominantly close-knit, white-male bastions of power and authority. The result was that these women, excluded from "high" literary realms, infused their autobiographies with the flavor of social discourse—both in shaping their texts and in presenting their contexts. Their uses of literate resources have, in the words of Jacqueline Jones Royster, "been . . . evidence of a full and flowing stream of creativity and productivity" (77). They drew from various literary styles to create their personal narratives, relying heavily on the sentimental, the gothic, the adventure, the historical, and the slave narrative structures. The slave narrative that Northern abolitionist leaders initiated for fugitive slaves to use was characterized by a focus on the humanity of the slaves, the hardships they had suffered, their determination to achieve freedom, and their escape to free, Northern soil; the result of their flight was to be a new life in which they could pursue the American dream. The slave narrative, as such, became an important tool of propaganda for the movement to abolish slavery and fed the fires of that movement.

Another important avenue of expression for African American women in the 1800s was the spiritual autobiography, but few of these autobiographers used the slave narrative format. They appeared to be less concerned with earthly issues of state and country (that is, the American dream) and more focused on issues of the soul, on spiritual freedom. Also, the "I" in the slave-narrative type of autobiography was more difficult to establish and maintain than the "I" of African American women's spiritual autobiographies, such as Jarena Lee's *Life and Religious Experience* and Rebecca Cox Jackson's spiritual journals, *Gifts of Power*. This spiritual "I," as Katherine Clay Bassard notes, presents a picture of a self that is comfortable, empowered, and able (4). This "I" need not address the earthly standards and demands of man; this "I" only needs to be accountable to the higher power of God. Bassard writes, "It is within these *private* encounters with Spirit that African American women often experienced a conferral of personhood denied by larger social constructions of African American and female subjectivity" (3; my emphasis). However, establishing a presence was problematic for black women autobiographers who were objects of enslavement and who chose or felt compelled to move from the "private" arena into public places. I address in this text the particularly literary and sociopolitical struggles of some of those autobiographers, specifically Wilson, Jacobs, Keckley, and Taylor.

I do not intend my statements to be a dismissal of the relevance and contributions of black women's spiritual autobiographies (or black women's speeches—another avenue that African American women claim in expressing their voices). Spiritual autobiographies occupy a special place in the development of black women's expression in the American literary arena. Foster notes that "Lee's narrative is especially important because it controverts the tendency to consider nineteenth-century black autobiography as synonymous with the slave narrative" in which "with the notable exception of a handful of slave narratives written by women, female characters are objects of pity" ("Neither Auction Block" 144). When I refer to "nineteenth-century black women autobiographers" in my analysis, however, I am primarily engaging those black women who wrote public life stories that represented their resistance to enslavement. My focus in *Rhetoric and Resistance in Black Women's Autobiography*, then, is on nineteenth-century African American women who chose to share their personal and secular life experiences and hopes, staking their claim to literary and historical significance. While other scholars—such as Bassard, Joanne Braxton, Hazel Carby, Carole Boyce Davies, and Foster, among others—have engaged in varying degrees the hegemonic oppressions that limited the voices of nineteenth-century black women autobiographers, no prior study has fully investigated both the linguistic and sociopolitical ways in which these presumably silenced women spoke up and challenged the American literary consensus that sought to exclude them. Nineteenth-century African American women's autobiography is significant as social discourse in its structure (text) as well as in its content (historical context).

In *Rhetoric and Resistance in Black Women's Autobiography* I demonstrate the ways in which African American women autobiographers thwart attempts to keep them silent and invisible. To that end, I introduce a unique series of communicative techniques that I define as a black woman's "mother tongue." Joanne M. Braxton in *Black Women Writing Autobiography*, Carole Boyce Davies in *Black Women, Writing and Identity*, and Marlene NourbeSe Philip in *She Tries Her Tongue*, among others, use the term "mother tongue" in referring to a woman's subversive approach to communication, especially the approach of the black woman. An earlier reference to a "mother tongue" appears in Henry David Thoreau's 1854 *Walden, or Life in the Woods*. Thoreau's reference, however, is not complimentary as he elevates the written discourse (which he sees as man-made) above the spoken discourse (which he sees as the product of woman): "[T]here is a memorable interval between the spoken and the written language, the language heard and the language read. The one is commonly transitory, a sound, a tongue, a dialect merely, almost brutish, and we learn it unconsciously, like the brutes, of our mothers. The other is the maturity and experience of that; if that is our *mother tongue*, this is our father tongue" (108–9; my emphasis). As I see it, the black woman's mother tongue embodies the characteristics of the nineteenth-century African American woman autobiographer's voice as it responds to the metaphorical places, spaces, and gaps of the "traditional," white-male autobiography.[5] First she challenged, and then she subverted that "tradition."

Am I suggesting a deliberate, planned act on the part of these women to create a new type of personal narrative? Did each conclude that existing genres were too restrictive and that she would, therefore, create a new one? The answer, of course, is "no" to both questions. The development of this new style of writing was, for the most part, an accident, a happy accident that produced something unique, creative, and unexpected. In her attempt to re-create and re-present the experiences of her black woman's self, by shaking, twisting, and sometimes breaking the existing types of life-writing, each of these black women autobiographers created a new literary form. Developed out of emotional need and not out of deliberate forethought, these autobiographies reflect the fragmented self of each writer, as I will show as I analyze the narrators' purposes for writing, their uses of mixed genres, their sometimes confusing or conflicted points of view, and their uses of both conciliatory and chastising rhetoric within the narratives.

Nineteenth-century African American men also exercised subversive communicative means for resisting oppression, but their tongue was not a mother tongue; they were not subjected to the gender-based oppressions that women in nineteenth-century America (both black and white women) experienced, specifically the oppression of sexual abuse. The mother tongue approach is indeed gendered, and both European American and African American women defined and employed communicative techniques that best served their needs in resisting stereotypical oppressions from their respective positions in society. There was and is a special woman's way of approaching language and communication. This is not to suggest the existence of a biological essentialism. The uniqueness is not a result of biology; it does not exist because a woman is female. Rather, it exists because she is a woman, a product of a specific cultural, sociopolitical environment. Her mother tongue has developed over time—changing, shifting, and adjusting in accordance with a woman's need to find outlets for her voice in a male-dominated society. I will demonstrate that this mother tongue is a combination of words, rhythms, sounds, and silences that women have encoded with veiled meanings. And it is more. There is a physicality to the mother tongue ways of communicating—a look, a set of the lips, a positioning of the hand, hip, and head. It is a stance, an attitude of resistance that includes secrets, misdirection, irony, song, humor, and lying, among others. The nineteenth-century African American woman autobiographer used her special way of communicating, her mother tongue, to write her life and to shape her text; she also demonstrated its importance as a mainstay in the African American community and in African American literary tradition.

While I assert that all nineteenth-century African American women autobiographers probably made use of mother tongue techniques in resisting oppression,[6] I have chosen to focus on Wilson's *Our Nig*, Jacobs's *Incidents*, Keckley's *Behind the Scenes*, and Taylor's *Reminiscences* for two reasons. First, they embody a range of communicative characteristics that can be found in virtually all black women's writing to some degree. At the same time, these protean autobiographies show the range of creativity black women writers claim in their disparate (and sometimes desperate) attempts to speak for themselves and for their black communities. I want to take a moment now to establish the publication histories of these four autobiographies, briefly describing them and establishing their literary and historical places in black women's life-writing.

Harriet Wilson's *Our Nig* represents one of the earliest extant, published attempts by an African American woman to use the medium of autobiography in calling attention to the oppression of blacks by whites. This fictionalized personal narrative also exemplifies the power of genre-merging as Wilson's text took the form of a novel and, for years, was regarded as the first novel written by an African American. As Peterson notes, African American women entering the literary realm in mid-nineteenth-century America appropriated novelizing techniques because black Americans "were simply adapting themselves to the economy of the dominant culture in which the novel was fast becoming one of the most popular and lucrative forms of writing" (*Doers* 149). In other words, Wilson used a literary medium that was easily recognizable, that was popular during her time, and that might offer the greatest possibility for monetary returns.

Our Nig, as written by "Our Nig," relates the story of Frado (Wilson), the mulatto daughter of a poor white mother and a black father who married and resided in the Northern state of New Hampshire. Placed into indentureship when she was only six years old, Frado struggles to overcome various oppressions and obstacles, including abandonment by her mother, loneliness and isolation, physical brutality at the hands of Mrs. Bellmont, Northern racial bigotry, lameness, and extreme poverty. Wilson notes in her preface that she made the decision to write her story so that she could raise enough money to reclaim her sickly young son from what she identifies later as the foster care of "a kind gentleman and lady [who] took her little boy into their own family" (136).[7] Wilson did not have an editor for her text; she registered the copyright herself with the District Court of Massachusetts on August 18, 1859. Less than a month later, on September 5th, *Our Nig* was printed by the Boston firm of George C. Rand and Avery. In his 1983 introduction to the second edition of the autobiography, Henry Louis Gates Jr. writes that a notation of the death of Wilson's son, George, appeared in the Amherst, New Hampshire,

Farmer's Cabinet on February 29, 1860, "just five months and twenty-four days after the publication of *Our Nig*" (xii). The narrative received a short, limited run at the time of its release, arousing little public interest. With its re-issue in 1983 by Random House, accompanied by documentation from Gates verifying its autobiographical nature, *Our Nig* was finally acknowledged as an important nineteenth-century African American autobiography.

The early chapters of Wilson's autobiography highlight the social/ sexual struggles of Mag, the white woman who would become the protagonist's mother; Mag's rejection by her community because of her "fall" from virtue; the later impoverished Mag's unusual marriage to a black man, Jim; the birth of two children from this union, including Frado; Jim's death; and, because of continuing poverty and shunning by the white community, Mag's eventual abandonment of Frado, later called Nig. The remainder of the narrative follows Frado's life after being abandoned by Mag.

From the age of six until she receives her freedom at the age of eighteen, Frado works as an indentured servant for the Bellmont family, experiencing the same kind of inhuman treatment at the hands of Mrs. Bellmont that was suffered by the slaves of the South. In addition to relating the harsh beatings that Frado receives, Wilson records intimate details of interactions within the family, including those surrounding Frado that lead to her education and her Christian training. By the time Frado reaches her eighteenth birthday, she is lame and generally in poor health. The final few chapters of the narrative trace the poverty she faces as a result of her physical disabilities, ending with her marriage, a second abandonment, the birth of her son, the death of her husband, and her attempts to provide for her child and herself both physically and financially. Throughout the autobiography, Wilson peppers her text with a chastising of the North for its poor treatment of free blacks, attempting at the same time to avoid making statements that would lessen Northern white efforts to aid her Southern brothers and sisters still laboring under the lash of slavery. Her mother tongue techniques of blurring of narrative styles, merging literary forms (fiction and nonfiction), and using a variety of literary genres (sentimental, gothic, and slave narratives) are all characteristic of Wilson's reflection of the African American woman writer resisting the oppressions that weighed upon her "in a Two-Story White House, North."

The second antebellum autobiographer that I discuss, Harriet Jacobs, assumes the pseudonym of Linda Brent in *Incidents*. *Incidents* has become a much-cited slave woman's narrative because it is the first and only autobiography that focuses on two specific evils of slavery: how it degraded the black female slave and how it separated the members of black families. As is characteristic of writers fluent in mother tongue, Jacobs subverts an existing literary genre—the sentimental novel—in order to enlist the sympathies and support of the Northern white women who were readers of such narratives. To this select audience, Jacobs relates her story of sexual oppression, the dissociation of black family units, and her fight for and flight to freedom, attempting to build a bond of sisterhood between herself and these women readers—a bond that she hoped would inspire Northern white women to take action against the "patriarchal" institution of slavery.

Encouraged by her Quaker friend, Amy Post, Jacobs first considered publication of her life story in 1852, stating in a letter to Post that "if it could save another from my fate it would be selfish and unchristian in me to keep it back."[8] Jacobs's Northern employer, Mrs. Willis (the Mrs. Bruce in her narrative), initially suggested approaching Harriet Beecher Stowe to edit the work, an avenue that Jacobs then pursued through Post. However, Jacobs soon learned that Stowe planned to incorporate these autobiographical notes into her own forthcoming narrative, *Key to Uncle Tom's Cabin*, rather than crediting the accounts to Jacobs (Yellin, introduction xix). Jacobs then determined to publish the story herself. In 1853, eight years before *Incidents* was actually published and a year after receiving the gift of her freedom from slavery, Jacobs began sending bits and pieces about her life to various "newspapers in the form of letters from a fugitive slave" (Doriani 201). She wrote late at night after completing her regular duties as a servant to Mrs. Willis, and she wrote in secret. She shared copies of her work only with her daughter, Louisa, and with Post.

Jean Fagan Yellin writes in her introduction to *Incidents* that Jacobs tried unsuccessfully for several years to get her story published in the United States as well as in England (xxii). After securing Lydia Maria Child as her editor, Jacobs finally succeeded, through the negotiations of Child, in finding a publisher in Boston—Thayer and Eldridge (September 1860). Although that company went bankrupt before it was able to print the book, Yellin notes the following publication history for *Incidents:* "Arrangements were somehow made enabling Jacobs to buy the plates from the Boston Stereotype Foundry and to have a Boston printer publish the book 'for the author.' The following year an English edition was published in London by W. Tweedie under the title *The Deeper Wrong; Or, Incidents in the Life of a Slave Girl*. This edition was evidently printed from Jacobs's plates; only the page bearing the new title is different" (xxiv). The publication information on the title page of the first American edition reads "Boston: Published for the Author. 1861."

In *Incidents,* Jacobs traces her life experiences as "Linda Brent" from her early days of childhood innocence when she did not realize what it was to be a slave, through her sexual harassment at the hands of Dr. Flint and other brutalities of slavery, to the purchase of her freedom by Mrs. Bruce. While documenting the attempts of Linda's master, Dr. Flint, to sexually exploit her, Jacobs also gives much attention to the struggles of the entire African American community that she knew and to the general, pervasive abuses suffered by all blacks under the oppressive yoke of slavery. Using an African American mother tongue approach to shape and tell her story, Jacobs showcases the literary power of subversive communicative tools as they are employed by African American women autobiographers. *Incidents* traces the various acts of resistance used by Linda and other slaves to nullify the oppressions of enslavement; it reveals her act of claiming her own sexuality as a weapon against her master by voluntarily giving herself to another white man; it details her attempts to secure freedom for herself and her children; it shows the strength of her determination to survive the mental and physical oppressions of slavery, even during the seven-year period in which she was self-confined to the garretlike space above her grandmother's house; it outlines the incidents of disappointment Linda experiences after arriving in the North to find that racism was not limited to the Southern states; and it ends with a limited freedom over which the shadows of enslavement, oppression, and marginalization still hang—those same "shadows" that darken the life of Wilson's Frado, as Wilson notes in the extensive title of *Our Nig*. The pattern, tone, and structure of Jacobs's narrative (its text) mirror the incidents (the context) that she shares with her readers.

Elizabeth Keckley's postwar *Behind the Scenes* combines incidents of her life in slavery with her memoirs as a modiste to Mrs. Jefferson Davis and, especially, as a modiste and confidante to Mary Todd Lincoln during and following the Lincoln years in the White House. Keckley's narrative focuses primarily on the years after she secured freedom from slavery, describing her entrepreneurship, her attempts at self-reliance, her belief in the future of America, and her place in it as an African American. Yet, her narrative also contains incidents of various oppressive acts committed

Gramley Library
Salem Academy and College
Winston-Salem, N.C. 27108

against her during her years of slavery and details the methods she used to resist these acts. Like the personal narratives of other nineteenth-century African American women autobiographers, hers is untraditional in its unique use and manipulation of literary and linguistic styles, reshaping existing literary genres to accommodate a very untraditional and, at times, antitraditional personal experience.

Like Wilson, Keckley registered her own copyright: "Entered according to Act of Congress, in the year 1868, by Elizabeth Keckley, In the Office of the Clerk of the District Court of the United States for the Southern District of Pennsylvania."[9] *Behind the Scenes* was published in that same year by the New York publishing company of G. W. Carleton. It was republished by Oxford University Press in 1988 with an introduction by James Olney.

Keckley devotes the larger section of her narrative to a memoir of the political activities taking place in the Capitol and, after the assassination of Abraham Lincoln, to her continued involvement with the destitute and emotionally unstable former First Lady. This early "tell-all" publication, through its conflicted use of form and literary style, also gives us a telling glimpse into Keckley's own conflicts in trying to attain the American dream. As a postwar, postslavery narrative, *Behind the Scenes* brings to the literary arena new emphases on self-reliance, economic security, class structures, and nationalism as they affected African Americans—especially this African American woman. Keckley's narrative is an important addition to the African American women's autobiography canon because it is published at the crossroads of a new political, social, and literary America, a crossroads that sees the continuation but modification of the use of an African American mother tongue and its techniques.

In *Reminiscences,* the final personal narrative that I analyze in depth, Susie King Taylor focuses on the efforts of both black men and black women during and after the Civil War in the cause of freedom and advancement. Despite the amount of time that elapses between Keckley's 1868 and Taylor's 1902 narratives, Taylor's text provides a valuable link to the previous three. It serves as a continuum that demonstrates the connective nature of black women's autobiographies, temporally and spatially; through her status as a slave, her participation in the Civil War, and her experiences in both the Reconstruction and post-Reconstruction periods of American history, Taylor embodies important nineteenth-century characteristics of the Wilson, Jacobs, and Keckley texts while simultaneously ushering us into the twentieth century. Although Taylor begins her narrative by noting her own early status as a slave, tracing her blood-line through the maternal side of her family and describing her theft of literacy while living in the Southern slave state of Georgia, she is chiefly concerned with presenting a historical account of the black men and women who fought for an American freedom that was, in her opinion, still too slow in coming. *Reminiscences* is more documentary in tone and in style than the earlier autobiographies of Keckley, Jacobs, and Wilson. Her gaze is more confrontational. Her positions as laundress, nurse, and teacher for the first Southern, black volunteer unit of the Civil War to-tally composed of former Southern slaves (except for the white officers sent to lead them) put her in position to observe and later record military, political, and social developments within an emerging, changing America. Her text, devoted to recording the involvement of African Americans in the preserving of the Union and in the making of America, pays particular attention to the nation's failure to honor the promises of freedom and equality made to this large group of "Americans."

With the support of a number of her friends and Thomas Wentworth Higginson (the white commander of her former regiment and later an important figure in the business of American literature), Taylor wrote her story to remind white and black Americans about the slave effort during the war and to bring to light the injustices still being perpetrated against her black brothers and sisters. Published just after the turn of the century, *Reminiscences* represents the voice of an African American woman who cleverly balances her sense of patriotism with her outrage at the inhuman treatment inflicted on America's black citizens; it explicitly offers a his-torical and political commentary. Like Wilson, Jacobs, and Keckley, Taylor blurs the usual boundaries between literary genres; she merges elements of the historical narrative, the memoir, and the adventure novel to create a form for her story. The flexible, versatile African American mother tongue gives her story and its form literary uniqueness.

As with the other narratives, the copyright for *Reminiscences* is in the author's name; the publication information on the title page reads, "Bos-ton; Published By The Author; 1902."[10] *Reminiscences* has been repub-lished three times since this first printing: 1) in 1968 through Arno Press and the *New York Times* as part of a series: *The American Negro—His History and Literature;* 2) in 1988 by Markus Wiener Publishing under the title *Reminiscences of My Life: A Black Woman's Civil War Memoirs;* and 3) through the Oxford Schomburg series edited by A. G. Barthelemy.

There are traits in common among these women autobiographers and the text that each produced. Each attempts to assume authority by manipulating the language and literary traditions of the dominant white culture, a culture that has minimized her as a person. Each woman attempts to reconcile the writing of an "I"-centered text, despite belonging to a community-based tradition derived from West African heritage. Each woman expresses her rejection of racism, sexism, and classism as these constructs attempt to limit her black woman's voice. Finally, each woman struggles with conflict as she negotiates the distance between the oral traditions of nineteenth-century African Americans and the written traditions of nineteenth-century European Americans. I will also note the differences in the literary styles and approaches of Wilson, Jacobs, Keckley, and Taylor, especially differences between the two antebellum and the two postbellum narratives. Primarily, I focus on the relevance and power of African American women autobiographers' voices in late-nineteenth-century America and on the similar and dissimilar ways in which Wilson, Jacobs, Keckley, and Taylor literally and figuratively use an African American mother tongue to operate within an American literary tradition, turning aside sociopolitical oppression as they embrace writing as an act of resistance.

It is generally accepted that the majority of the linguistic practices that characterize the use of mother tongue techniques by nineteenth-century African American women autobiographers grew out of the slavocracy of the American Southern states—a balance of African, European, and African American techniques. European American women and African American male slaves of the nineteenth century also had distinctive discursive techniques by which they challenged white-male oppression. Nineteenth-century European American women primarily used secrets, silences, hesitations, and whispers, techniques that had special meaning for other women but that confounded interpretation by their male counterparts.[11] African American male slaves, likewise, were masters of the use of secrecy, to which they added feigned misunderstanding, lying, masking, guile, mumbling, and double entendre in empowering themselves.[12] Nineteenth-century African American women—slaves, former slaves, and freewomen alike—laid claim to all of these techniques. But in addition to the techniques named above, they developed other ways to communicate that were distinctly their own—sass, invective, dissembling, and sexually suggestive impudence, among others.[13]

Silence, or absence of language, was often a tool and weapon for African American women's particular type of discourse. In discussing the various ways in which African Americans have traditionally veiled their communications from those outside of the community, Gates asserts that the tradition of African American folklore produced a culturally distinct aspect of signifying.[14] Roger Abrahams adds that signifying within the African American community involved "speaking with the hands and eyes, and in this respect encompasses a whole complex of expressions and gestures" (quoted in Gates, *Signifying* 54). Abrahams also notes that in this same tradition, African American women use "more indirect methods of signifying," such as an "unexpected pronoun," usually "we" when the expected pronoun would be the more accusatory "you" (77). While such evasive techniques are visible in the works of many writers—regardless of race, culture, or gender—I will argue in this book that they appear more intensely, more consistently, and on a much larger scale in black women's personal narratives. Their importance and prominence give credence to the idea of a distinctive idiom—an African American mother tongue that resisted nineteenth-century European American oppressions. African American women autobiographers' resistance led them to create a new form in autobiography—not so much a subgenre as a countergenre. Life-writing for nineteenth-century American black women does not merely constitute a subcategory of traditional autobiographical forms. These autobiographers challenge those forms and their limitations. In its expression of a counterculture, the mother tongue is so far removed from the existing paradigms that it stands outside of and away from them.

Wilson, Jacobs, Keckley, and Taylor each, in her own way, introduces a unique communicative text that expresses resistance. No one has fully addressed to date the contributions these black women, individually and collectively, have made to American literature. Gates, Claudia Tate, and Ronna Johnson all note that textual irregularities in *Our Nig* are deliberately structured to enhance meaning in the narrative, but none extends this brief observation or conducts an analysis of textual and contextual elements—what I call mother tongue techniques. Gates refers to the text's "silences and lacunae" in addressing gaps in the content that are represented by structural inconsistencies (introduction to *Our Nig* xxxv); Tate notes that *Our Nig* contains "deliberately constructed double-voiced representations" as she also discusses the idea of silences within the text mirroring the disruptions of the text itself (*Domestic Allegories* 36); and Johnson, focusing specifically on the unspoken sexual abuse in *Our Nig*, suggests that this unspoken white-male threat is presented "by means of the author's [Wilson's] and the narrator's [Frado's] interventions and narrative elisions," further noting that these various silences, elisions, and lacunae "provide conjunctions that unify the otherwise disjunctive narrative of the tale" (96). Just as there are no in-depth developments of these textual-contextual relationships, likewise, no other scholar has probed deeply into the style and historical contexts of nineteenth-century African American women's autobiography. I intend to explore the links between autobiography and social discourse, showing how use of their mother tongue serves these black women writers in challenging nineteenth-century sociopolitical and literary norms.

In chapter 1, "Autobiography, Authorship, and Authority," I show how the historical, social, literary, and political conventions of autobiography tended to minimize the life stories of women and nonwhites. Some of this will be familiar to scholars of nineteenth-century American literary development, especially as it pertains to the writings of women and African Americans. But it is important to establish a sense of overall nineteenth-century American literary contexts so that African American women autobiographers' deviation from that "norm" can be appreciated. I address the oppressive systems that worked to place nineteenth-century women in general, and nineteenth-century African American women in particular, on the fringes of American society and consequently of American literary traditions. I also show how and with what degree of success nineteenth-century African American women confronted and surmounted such oppressive and silencing systems as white-male patriarchy and American "exceptionalism," a belief based on the assumptions of American superiority grounded in gender, racial, and cultural prejudices.

Chapter 2, "Black Women Autobiographers' Encounter with Gender, Race, and Class," explores the impact of gender, race, and class on nineteenth-century African American women and on African American women autobiographers. As I revisit the unique African American woman's position in both the gender and the race wars, I argue the question of why she is neither a woman who is *also* African American nor an African American who is *also* a woman, but must be viewed as "an African American woman"—the issues of gender, race, culture, and class in her case interlocked.[15] I also evaluate the fluctuating relationship between nineteenth-century black women and nineteenth-century white women in their respective struggles for selfhood, examining the impact of this relationship as it manifests itself in the lives and autobiographies of black women.

In chapter 3, "A Patchwork of Cultures: Journeys of African American Women Autobiographers," I examine temporal, physical, and metaphysical factors affecting black women's eventual emergence as a force in nineteenth-century America. Although all four of the women I discuss are several generations removed from Africa, I find it helpful to situate the beginning of their journeys—physical, cultural, and emotional—in the Yoruba culture of West Africa, the locus for many of the linguistic practices, traditions, and beliefs that survived the Middle Passage and found their way into the oral traditions of the American slave.[16] I consider the circular, recursive characteristics of West African tradition as they relate to oral storytelling traditions, the African diaspora, and the development of written literary traditions. My evaluation takes into account select aspects of Yoruba myths, beliefs, traditions, and practices; American slavery and the birth of African American folklore (with its characteristic use of signing, masking, and concealing); and finally, black women's acts of writing themselves into American literary history.

Chapter 3 further argues that the concept of time in these narratives is intertwined with that of the journey of the enslaved from childhood innocence to painful awareness, placing African American women's autobiographies in the tradition of the Bildungsroman as they recount the trauma inherent in the discovery and understanding of what it meant to be enslaved and what it meant to be black women in nineteenth-century America. I consider the physical and emotional shifts embodied in the cultural experience of African American movements—abduction from Africa (a place of relative freedom), to the American South (a place of slavery), to the American North (a conflicted place of both freedom *and* racism). I also consider the elements from each of these places (and the displacements within) that African American women autobiographers used in their search for voice and freedom. Finally, borrowing a phrase from Jacobs's *Incidents*—"loophole of resistance"—I look at the private and domestic places that all nineteenth-century American women, black and white, occupied. I then consider the methods that African American women autobiographers employed to claim, subvert, and re-cast these places as their own. I take into account not only the historically social places of domesticity (kitchen, bedroom, nursery, sewing room) but also the literary places of American literature (both marginal and classically centered). I then look into the shadows to find the "loopholes" (those special spaces and interstices into which women fell or climbed) where nineteenth-century African American women autobiographers would situate themselves. The dominant culture was aware of these loci but thought it could control the spaces and the women who occupied them. Like those who were disciples of the Bentham Panopticon Penitentiary school of thought, nineteenth-century white men believed that their prisoners—women and people of color—were so conditioned by the fear of the white man's gaze that these prisoners remained victims, unsure of when and whether the gaze was upon them. White men believed that all was within their power and within their vision.[17] But nineteenth-century African American women autobiographers surprised them by looking back at and challenging that gaze.

In chapter 4, "The Emergence of an African American Mother Tongue," I concentrate on the unique "gaps"[18] that mid- to late-nineteenth-century American women writers (both black and white) created for themselves in American literary society. I then note the special development of black women's communicative approaches—returning to the autobiographies of Wilson, Jacobs, Keckley, and Taylor. Wilson's and Jacobs's prewar narratives describe obstacles and oppressions particular to that situation. The post-Emancipation works of Keckley and Taylor describe very different factors. Therefore, I will address how the tone, scope, and direction of their autobiographies were in many ways driven by the reason(s) they chose to write and publish their personal narratives. Chapter 4 further considers the literary spaces that Wilson, Jacobs, Keckley, and Taylor—as African American women—occupied and how they exploited those spaces to create special gaps from within which they alone could assume authority through self-validation and self-representation. I categorize the types and degrees of linguistic resistance that black women and black women autobiographers employed—the mother tongue techniques with which these women operated. Although some overlap will occur, I have established three main groupings of mother tongue communicative techniques. The first category includes tools of subtle resistance—here, the resistance is noted by the oppressor, but it is so mild in nature that punishment is minimal, if there is punishment at all. The tools in the second category represent the act of saying or suggesting one thing but meaning something entirely different—a masking of intent that generally goes undetected by the oppressor. The third category includes the tools of flagrant resistance, techniques that are obviously and boldly resistant wherein the user does not care about the punishment their use might bring.

Having established relevant historical, sociopolitical, and literary groundwork in nineteenth-century black women's autobiographies, I show in my next three chapters how these three categories of African American mother tongue techniques play out in their application to *Our Nig, Incidents, Behind the Scenes,* and *Reminiscences.* By analyzing these four black women's autobiographies and by demonstrating the historical, literary, and sociopolitical factors that necessitated their uses of an African American mother tongue, I submit that a paradigm develops which is applicable to all black women's autobiographical writing (and perhaps black women's writing in general)—a connection that has not as yet been analyzed in depth.

The autobiographies that Wilson, Jacobs, Keckley, and Taylor wrote are representative—in their mother tongue communicative approaches and in their engagement of sociopolitical issues—of the personal narratives produced by most black women in mid- to late-nineteenth-century America and are forerunners of black women's autobiographies that emerge in the twentieth century. In chapter 8, "Linkages: Continuation of a Tradition," I offer closure to my argument by paradoxically showing that there is no closure to the tradition of black women's writing, by showing that the threads that link black women's autobiographical writing continue from generation to generation. Here, I briefly review some basic communicative and social discourse characteristics of other select nineteenth-century as well as some well known twentieth-century black women autobiographers (Maria Stewart, Anna Julia Cooper, Ida B. Wells, Zora Neale Hurston, Maya Angelou, and Alice Walker) to demonstrate the connection and continuation of the African American mother tongue.

Each of the African American women autobiographers I analyze here presents an account of the obstacles that the (primarily) white, (primarily) male American culture put in place to minimize and control her. Each shows, through textual and contextual development, the actions that she took to overcome these obstacles in order to assume authority over her life and over her narrative. By taking control of language and molding it—shaping it with her mother tongue—and by locating other creative, nonlinguistic ways to communicate, each woman, in claiming sociopolitical and literary agency, creates a new literary form— talking back to the traditional autobiography.

1

Autobiography, Authorship, and Authority

In the New World after the destruction of the native peoples, Africans would be renamed with the name of the stranger. If what the artist does is create in her own i-mage and *give* name to that i-mage, then what the African artist from the Caribbean and the New World must do is create in, while giving name to, her own i-mage—and in so doing eventually heal the word wounded by the dislocation and imbalance of the word/i-mage equation. This can only be done by consciously restructuring, reshaping and, if necessary, destroying the language.
—**Philip,** *She Tries Her Tongue*

The genre of autobiography continues to provoke debate over its place within literary discourse. Because this genre defies our attempts to freeze it into an easily categorized state, we look for possible common threads that might establish specific patterns. Literary scholars who attempt to place autobiography into a historical context trace it back to the European man's first attempt to celebrate his uniqueness; then they try to apply this same pattern of development to attempts at self-writing by "others," that is, by women and by people of color attempting to record their own personal histories. But the original autobiographical mold that established the white man's autobiography is not a one-size-fits-all model.[1] Both black and white women looked at the model of the white-male autobiography and found it—not themselves—wanting. I agree with the conclusion offered by Bella Brodzki and Celeste Schenck, who write that "by denying women writers a place in the historical development of autobiography, critical work in the field, for all its insistence on mirroring universals, has presented a distorted reflection of the history of the autobiographical genre" (2).

Several contemporary feminist theorists have considered the problems nineteenth-century women autobiographers encountered as they tried to privilege themselves in their texts. In "Resisting the Gaze of Embodiment:

Women's Autobiography in the Nineteenth Century," Sidonie Smith points out that whereas the notion of self is embodied by the "I" of the autobiography, "that 'I' is also unabashedly 'white,' Eurocentric, colonizing in its deployment" (80). As a result, black women autobiographers such as Harriet Wilson, Harriet Jacobs, Elizabeth Keckley, and Susie King Taylor faced the task of producing personal narratives despite the accepted notion that the autobiography was male-centered and European. Each had to establish a literary place in a hostile arena, a presence and voice that whites would regard as legitimate and authentic. The members of the dominant white-male culture did not have these women in mind when they used the term "American." Gregory Jay writes that many calling themselves "Americans" did so to "reinforce the illusion that there is a transcendental core of values and experiences that are essentially 'American,'" further noting that "the 'American' of conventional histories of American literature has usually been white, male, middle- or upper-class, heterosexual, and a spokesman for a definable set of political and social interests" (267). In effect, these "spokesmen" assumed the right of calling themselves Americans based on their racial, gender, and class characteristics, successfully eliminating from positions of power (for a while at least) all others who might attempt to call themselves Americans as well.

European settlers in America, as well as those who remained on the Continent, regarded America as the new Garden of Eden. This attitude gave rise to the idea of an American "exceptionalism," the concept by which "successive generations of inhabitants and observers of continental Anglo-America encountered, experienced, examined, evaluated, and explained America."[2] Separation from the Old World invited the early inhabitants of the New World, removed by history and geography from the Continent, to define and interpret what America and what Americans were. Anglo-America established an environment in which the Anglo-American was not only dominant but also superior in all ways to other groups. Although the term "American exceptionalism" did not surface until the 1950s and 1960s, these earlier attitudes clearly helped to shape national sentiment—a sentiment that supported nineteenth-century white-male domination of American society.

American exceptionalism led inevitably to the minimization of texts produced by those outside the white-male circle. Russell Reising argues, for instance, that distinctions made between "major" and "minor" works of literature serve to minimize the minor, "sub-literary," texts that tend to "reflect a direct interest in social and political concerns" (220). Histori-cally, this category of "sub-literary" texts has included the autobiogra-phies of the four writers I consider here—and nonmale or nonwhite writ-ers in general.

The practice of validating and celebrating the self through autobiogra-phy is usually traced back to St. Augustine and his A.D. 397 "*Confessions* of sin and salvation*" (Andrews, *Classic* 7).[3] When Jean-Jacques Rousseau wrote his own *Confessions* between 1764 and 1770, he followed the pat-tern established by Augustine and used the act of telling his life as an opportunity to unburden his soul, simultaneously valorizing his life's contributions to society. Unlike the black women autobiographers that followed, these white men writing autobiography did not have to prove their worthiness as human beings, writers, or citizens.

Political leaders and autobiographers from the eighteenth, nineteenth, and early twentieth centuries in America, including Benjamin Franklin and Henry Adams, produced autobiographies that focused less on the spiritual cleansing of "confession" and more on the individual's earthly, political, and social accomplishments, all celebrated in a memoir format (Andrews, *Classic* 8).[4] Few readers questioned the veracity of these auto-biographers' stories. Critique of this genre, however, has advanced to the point that all autobiographies are now viewed as offering combinations (in varying degrees) of fact, truth, memory, creation, fraud, and dissem-bling. What appears to be contradictory in any autobiography actually emphasizes the limitless shifting and blurring of the boundaries of this genre. Definitions and interpretations of the concepts of truth and lying, according to Mary Field Belenky, have been informed by a history that reflected the thoughts of the white-male dominant culture: "Drawing on their own perspectives and visions, men have constructed the prevailing theories, written history, and set values that have become the guiding principles for men and women alike" (5). As women and people of color began to challenge these white-male perspectives, it became possible for them also to challenge established dichotomies, like fiction versus nonfic-tion, literature versus history, truth versus lying, and so forth. It became possible for them to write their lives.

Citing from the works of Thomas J. Roberts, Timothy Dow Adams sug-gests that "distinctions between fiction, non-fiction, and fraud . . . fre-quently have more to do with the generic contract . . . and the reader's expectations than with the actual contents of the narrative" (13). Stating that "lying in autobiography is impossible because the audience begins with the assumption that the complete truth is not possible," Adams proceeds to examine the concept of the lie and the various shadings attached to it: "That lie can be multiple is demonstrated by the ease with which a list of related terms can be generated: Equivocation, duplicity, deception, manipulation, falsehood, false, distortion, perjury, feign, fakery, sham, evasion, suppression, cover-up, exaggeration, euphemism, fib, and prevarication. In addition to plain lying, we find quibbling, misleading, misinforming, duping, withholding, dissembling, disguising, glossing over, simulating, counterfeiting, embroidering, inventing, fudging, doctoring, and being mendacious" (14–15). Of course, there remain many other terms for not telling the truth. One noticeably missing from Adams's list, for instance, is the *little white lie,* with all of its racial and cultural implications of acceptability—smallness and whiteness suggesting innocence, purity, and harmlessness.

Like the narratives written by escaped male slaves, no work penned by a black woman in nineteenth-century America was accepted at face value by the dominant white society; it had to be authenticated by white voices at the time of its publication through attached letters or introductory statements. Even so, many valuable autobiographical works that black women produced were undervalued and overlooked, lying dormant for years until they were re-discovered. Wilson's *Our Nig* and Jacobs's *Incidents* required twentieth-century research and documentation by contemporary scholars Gates and Yellin, respectively, to establish that they are indeed life stories written by these women themselves. Until Gates published his data-filled introduction to *Our Nig* in 1983, readers and critics had assumed that the text was a work of fiction instead of a personal narrative and that it had been written by a white woman—"white" because of the use of the epithet "nig" and "woman" because of the sentimental language and tone of the narrative.[5] It took the literary detective work of Gates and his research team—the matching of dates, names, locations, and official documents—to establish that Wilson's primarily third-person narrative actually mirrored to a great extent her own life. Gates's act of painstakingly reconstructing the life and times of Harriet E. Wilson effectively places *Our Nig* within the genre of the autobiography.

Yellin is credited for her exhaustive research in verifying that the people, locations, and activities within *Incidents* could be historically placed. At the same time, by using letters that Jacobs wrote and other documents, Yellin was also able to "establish [Jacobs's] authorship of *Incidents,* and . . . identify the people and places she presented pseudonymously in her book" (introduction xv). Suddenly, Linda Brent was no longer a fictional character, but a pseudonym behind which stood Harriet Ann Jacobs, the real ex-slave. While Yellin deserves credit for bringing this information to light, Joanne Braxton notes that Marion Starling, a doctoral student at Howard University, had stated in her 1946 dissertation, thirty-five years prior to the publication of Yellin's 1981 research, that Jacobs had, in fact, authored *Incidents* and that the text represented the progression of incidents in Jacobs's own life.[6] Many critics still insist on asserting that much of *Incidents* was actually written by Jacobs's editor, Lydia Maria Child; I submit that the editorial assistance reflected in Jacobs's narrative is no more than that received by white-male writers (and less than most), as is substantiated by comparing the writing style in the Jacobs letters located by Yellin to the discursive style of *Incidents.* I agree that Child probably had a hand in re-arranging some of the chapters of the narrative, as her introduction asserts, and that she probably suggested that Jacobs develop an extended treatment of the Nat Turner rebellion, but such are editorial tactics commonly used then and now to promote increased sales and circulation. To conclude from this editorial work that Child was the ghostwriter for the narrative is a broad leap.

Elizabeth Keckley experienced the same cloud of doubt regarding her authorship of *Behind the Scenes.* Although James Redpath is documented as being Keckley's editor, there appears to be no substantial, documented proof that he was unduly involved in any significant way in the writing of the text proper.[7] Foster does write that Redpath took literary liberties and "violated [Keckley's] trust by appending, with no attempt to remove personal elements, Mary Lincoln's letters to Keckley" ("Autobiography" 39). Since the narrative was published by Keckley, however, and we can assume that it would not have been published if she had strong objections to materials being included, we might wonder if the inclusion of Mary Todd Lincoln's letters in toto was indeed a violation of Keckley's trust. Regarding Taylor's *Reminiscences,* it seems that there was never any challenge to the fact that Taylor had written a legitimate autobiographical text—by herself.

Another problem that African American autobiographers, both male and female, encountered was the need, as mentioned above, to have members of the dominant white society write authenticating letters and statements to preface or append their narratives, attesting to the "truth" of the words and the "good character" of the author. In the most often cited slave narrative, the 1845 *Narrative of the Life of Frederick Douglass, An*

American Slave, Written by Himself, William Lloyd Garrison was the authenticator, writing in his preface that the narrative was "entirely [Douglass's] own production" and stating his confidence that "it is *essentially* true in all its statements; that nothing has been . . . exaggerated, nothing drawn from the imagination" (234; my emphasis). Note that in his comments Garrison does a bit of dissembling himself by using the term "essentially" when attesting to the truth of Douglass's account, apparently not willing to give unconditional attestation to the validity of the narrative by this black man. In her "Introduction by the Editor" for *Incidents,* Child makes unqualified statements as to the veracity of Jacobs's text, writing, "[T]he author of the following autobiography is personally known to me" and "[T]hose who know her [Jacobs] will not be disposed to doubt her veracity" (3). In this way, Child shows no hesitation in validating Jacobs's text for her white readership. While Taylor includes letters from former white regiment commanders C. T. Trowbridge and Thomas Wentworth Higginson endorsing her text as a "truthful account" (xiii), Keckley makes her own assertions (sans a white authenticating voice) regarding the validity and veracity of her autobiography, writing, "[E]verything I have written is strictly true" (xi). However, as noted earlier, Redpath, apparently with Keckley's consent in part, appends to her narrative an extensive number of documents written by a white hand— letters written to Keckley by Mary Todd Lincoln. True to the nature of nineteenth-century American society, in each of these cases, a white voice authorizes the black voice.

Predictably, European American man resisted these unclassifiable texts of nineteenth-century African American women autobiographers. Their failure to follow the white-male autobiographical tradition or the defining characteristics of the black-male slave narrative tradition smacked of rebellion. And rebellion it was. Despite resistance from both of these literary camps, black women autobiographers forged ahead, appropriating "the English literary tradition to reveal, to interpret, to challenge, and to change perceptions of themselves and the world in which they found themselves" (Foster, *Written* 16). This literary rebellion, by its very nature, functions also as a sociopolitical rebellion. Jacqueline Jones Royster writes,

[W]e must learn to read women's stories . . . between the lines and around the "facts" and artifacts. We must learn to shake out vigorously the observations and propositions that have been and are being set forth about social forces and conditions. . . . The very act of writing, especially for people who do not occupy positions of status and privilege in the general society, is a bold and courageous enterprise rather than simply a demonstration of the ability to express oneself. . . . African American women have consistently included social, political, and economic problems and interests as focal points in their writing. . . . Looking at their written texts, therefore, permits us to articulate the consistent ways . . . in which these women have participated energetically in change processes. (81, 104)

Of course, we now know that the way these women "participated energetically in change processes" was through the use of a distinct African American mother tongue.

Wilson, Jacobs, Keckley, and Taylor manipulated their audiences and encoded their texts with meaning by using a variety of hybrid literary techniques. As Foster notes, the literary tradition as well as the history of the African American woman "is an amalgam, a mixture of diverse elements, some carefully and purposefully created and some a matter of coincidence or convenience" (*Written* 15). But there is no one mixture, no one amalgam. The result is that some stylistic traits are unique to one particular writer or the other, depending upon that writer's social, political, economic, and literary circumstances. Foster writes that the African American woman's literary tradition is "more than the sum total of its parts" (15). Being greater than any one of the genres it appropriates, African American woman's autobiography exists as a separate body of work—as a countergenre—that must be read with a broader vision than that governing other autobiographies.

The patchwork-quiltlike narratives that eventually emerge as black women's autobiographical experiences represent the diverse cultural patterns from which their voices speak. In describing the unique literary texts that evolved from the experiences of African American women writers, Barbara Smith adopts phrasing similar to that used to describe one of the primary genres appropriated by many African American women autobiographers, the sentimental novel. Smith writes, "The use of Black women's language and cultural experience in books by Black women *about* Black women results in a miraculously rich coalescing of form and content and also takes their writing far beyond the confines of white/male literary structures" (164; Smith's emphasis). In asserting the relevance of the sentimental novel, Jane Tompkins likewise argues for the important contributions that the texts of this genre—written for, by, and about women—made to the American literary tradition. She asserts that these sentimental narratives represent "a political enterprise, halfway between sermon and social theory, that both codifies and attempts to mold the values of time" (126). Therefore, one of the primary genres of nineteenth-century African American women autobiographers was itself an amalgamation.

In Elizabeth Barnes's "Affecting Relations: Pedagogy, Patriarchy, and the Politics of Sympathy," she addresses the emergence of sentimental ideology in post-Revolutionary America. According to her theory, "Sentimentalism is a manifestation of the belief in or yearning for consonance—or even unity—of principle and purpose," and because "sympathy complements the work of sentiment," the sentimental novel attempts to create "this relationship between reader and text" (597). When nineteenth-century black women used the paradigm of the sentimental narrative, they were tapping into sympathetic attachment to arouse a response from their target readers. As Barnes further notes, critics of the sentimental novel "believed that, regardless of the author's intentions, the power of sympathetic attachment might provoke uncontrolled and unreasoned responses on the part of readers" (604). We can safely assume that those nineteenth-century critics were white men and that the parties they feared might become uncontrollable and unreasonable (perhaps, hysterical) were white women. This white-male fear speaks to the degree of power black women autobiographers using the sentimental model held in their hands. However, while three of the four autobiographers I address—Wilson, Jacobs, and Keckley—each made extensive use of this sentimental style of writing (Taylor much less so), each also exposes how unsatisfactory this genre is when she applies it to her particular oppressed condition. As a result, the message of each narrative is actually *counter*-sentimental, or perhaps both sentimental and antisentimental within the same text.

Eighteenth- and nineteenth-century black male slave narrators in the United States were more or less guided by Northern abolitionists and took their lead from secular white-male autobiographies in the style of their writing, a style which "emphasized the individual, and for the most part ... reflected the Puritan theocentric society" (Foster, *Witnessing* 44).[8] By contrast, the personal narratives of African American women (and European American women) rarely separated the accomplishment of "self" from the status of their "community." Specifically, the black woman autobiographer usually balanced the self-celebratory aspects of the memoir and self-revelatory aspects of the confession with an attack on the destruction of the family under slavery and human bondage, many times focusing on the importance of establishing and sustaining the black community during and after slavery.

This focus on community distinguishes most black women's autobiographies from those of most black men—black men's autobiographies such as those written by Olaudah Equiano, William Wells Brown, Frederick Douglass, and Booker T. Washington—which were more obviously individual-centered celebrations of heroism and freedom won. I am not suggesting that the black-male autobiographer was unconcerned with the struggles of the black community. Many—Brown and Douglass just to name two—dedicated much of their free lives to elevating the economic, social, and political positions of blacks in American society. I argue simply that the emphasis in their narratives was on the need for the black man to be strong, independent, and heroic in the face of white-male biases. His was a more private struggle, neither especially supported nor hindered by ties to the slave community from which he was escaping. The black woman autobiographer, on the other hand, routinely demonstrates her ties to family and community; her allegiance to the community makes her decision to escape the bonds of slavery more difficult and complex, as demonstrated in Jacobs's *Incidents*. Joycelyn Moody writes that "the American literary tradition of self-effacement, defined by texts in which the autobiographical self is represented by her/his community, is perpetuated in blacks' narratives" (59). For most black women autobiographers, then, the self is secondary to the primary needs of family and/or community.

Notable differences in focus between the black man's and the black woman's autobiographical accounts, differences in style as well as in subject matter, have often led black-male critics to dismiss the less-heroic-sounding texts of black women autobiographers. Houston Baker, in comparing Jacobs's *Incidents* to the slave narratives of Equiano and Douglass, erroneously concludes that an "absence of adventure characteriz[es] the black woman's account" (*Blues* 50). Such a statement appears to equate physical violence with adventure. In fact, Jacobs's *Incidents*, though not violent, does include some characteristics of an adventure narrative. Just as the sentimental novel (typically feminine) was predictable because of its formulaic approach, so was the (typically masculine) adventure novel, its plots always situated in a primitive arena with heroes, enemies, battles, victories, and defeats. I submit that all of these elements are present in *Incidents*, even if they are more personal and intimate. The description of the adventure narrative as it appears in *The Columbia History of the American Novel* has a decidedly masculine tone, stating that it was "noteworthy not merely for its distancing from the domestic zone but also for its immersion in the details and lexicon of work" (Elliott 51). Those defining the genre, then, have attempted to create a cultural literary division between the private feminine sphere of the sentimental narrative and the public masculine sphere of the adventure narrative by specifically aligning the sense of adventure with the labor of man and separating it from the "domesticity" of woman. The adventure narrative, then and now, was a genre from which the narratives of Jacobs and Taylor have tended to be excluded by both black and white men. Like the early white-male autobiographers, the early black-male autobiographers in a more limited way established a paradigm for the slave narrative. When the established patterns were broken and those "others" breaking the patterns were women, challenges to the validity of these women's texts predictably arose. My defense of nineteenth-century black women autobiographers explains how and why their personal narratives took on the characteristics of countergenre.

Black women's break from the male model of the autobiography, while motivated in part by racial/cultural differences, was also inspired by a difference in women's view of the autobiography. A woman's autobiography was not as rigid, as definite, as those produced by nineteenth-century white men. It did not suggest or attempt to imply a completeness, but tended to be open-ended—inviting a dialogue between writer and reader. For instance, women writing autobiographies tend to speak to their readers more often and more directly than do men. Both Jacobs and Wilson address their readers as "O virtuous women" and all four of the principal black women autobiographers I analyze in this text periodically use the second-person "you" to maintain a dialogue with their readers. The autobiographies of white men were closed monologues and admitted to no possibility of incompleteness.[9] However, in the words of Shari Benstock, "autobiography reveals gaps, and not only gaps in time and space or between individuals and the social, but also a widening divergence between the manner and the matter of its discourse" (11).[10]

If this is true, then an autobiography must, by its very nature, exhibit an incompleteness, one that women's autobiography readily accepted but that white men's autobiography staunchly denied. Benstock further notes that it was important to a white man writing an autobiography that his consciousness, his presence in the narrative (the "I" of the autobiography) remain stable and constant. This stability reflects white men's attempt not only to maintain control over their lives but also to control how others might interpret those lives; any sign of weakness or incompleteness would compromise their elevated position of power. Women writing auto-biographies in nineteenth-century America were neither attempting to assert nor to maintain controlling positions, perhaps because they had none to protect. Therefore, their autobiographies are filled with inconsis-tencies, "fissures of discontinuity," as evidence of the incompleteness that these women autobiographers made no attempt to re-configure or to sanitize, but welcomed into their respective narratives as representative of the lives they led (Benstock 29).

Some scholars criticize Wilson's *Our Nig* because of its inconsistent points of view—sometimes it is told in first person, sometimes in third person. Such discontinuities, however, are synonymous with the flaws in the social structure of Wilson's life as an indentured servant. The "first-person" Wilson in the early parts of the autobiography strives to be a part of society, a part of a community; the "third-person" Wilson, in the body of Frado that dominates most of the narrative, has been forced outside of society and is isolated and alone, disconnected from the bonds, needs, and support of community. In this way, Wilson's narrative clearly exhibits the black woman autobiographer's use of both language and social context to develop her message. Wilson's narrative also illustrates the importance of community for the black woman autobiographer and the destruction that accompanies her disconnection from community.

The typical nineteenth-century black woman's autobiography made the importance of "self" dependent on a relationship with a larger, com-munal body. Baker, who criticizes Jacobs's *Incidents* for its lack of adven-ture, does note that, unlike Equiano's and Douglass's narratives, Jacobs's autobiography "gives a sense of *collective*, rather than individualistic, black identity" (*Blues* 55; Baker's emphasis).[11] A black woman success-fully overcoming bondage depended upon her connection to this larger "collective" for strength and encouragement. When such support was lacking, as it was for Wilson's Frado, the black woman usually became hesitant or unsure. The Frado that we see throughout most of the narrative suffers from isolation and loneliness because of her early abandonment and her later losses (through deaths or departures) of ties that might have offered her a sense of community. Jacobs's Linda Brent passes up an earlier opportunity to escape slavery because of the discouragement she receives from her grandmother, Aunt Marthy, who reminds Linda that she is a mother and, as such, should endure her condition of enslavement for the sake of remaining with her children. Both Keckley and Taylor show a greater focus on the "individual" in their respective postwar narratives, perhaps partially because they no longer feel burdened by the retaliatory possibilities of slave masters or slave hunters; both eventually progress, however, with the help of community—black and white military men for Taylor and white political and business figures for Keckley—in achieving a level of independence.

When Sidonie Smith suggests that the autobiography promotes a very clear conception of the human being, a conception that, in her opinion, "valorizes individual integrity and separateness and devalues personal and communal interdependency" (*Poetics* 39), she cites characteristics that are more applicable to men's (primarily white men's) autobiography than those written by black women. Geoffrey Galt Harpham offers an equally narrow view when he suggests that the autobiography is the result of a conscious attempt by the writer to lead a life that would lend itself to a later recording, that autobiography reflects lives "lived in anticipation ... of their own narratability" (42). This statement may have been true for many white men (and some white women) who eventually wrote autobiographies, but it is doubtful that nineteenth-century black slaves or indentured servants consciously lived their lives in anticipation of making written records of those lives. Obviously, neither a slave nor a black indentured servant in nineteenth-century America had much control over or much advance knowledge of the direction his or her life would take, so the idea of purposefully steering that life to make it more interesting for some future reading public is highly improbable. Furthermore, most enslaved blacks would never entertain the notion of writing their life stories, or anything else, because slaves in Southern states were denied literacy, and the scanty education allowed most black indentured servants would not have led most to entertain the notion of becoming authors. Again, we are dealing with generalized statements about the genre of autobiography where scholars try to apply, unsuccessfully, the practices of white men to the autobiographical works of all "others."

James Olney exhibits the same tendencies to "normalize" white men's narratives at the expense of those produced by women and nonwhites as he tries to define and characterize the genre of autobiography:

> We can understand [the autobiography] as the vital impulse—the impulse of life—that is transformed by being lived through the unique medium of the individual and the individual's special, peculiar psychic configuration; we can understand it as consciousness, pure and simple, consciousness referring to no objects outside itself, to no events, and to no other lives; we can understand it as participation in an absolute existence far transcending the shifting, changing unrealities of mundane life; we can understand it as the moral tenor of the individual's being. Life in all these . . . senses does not stretch back across time but extends down to the roots of the individual being; it is atemporal, committed to a vertical thrust from consciousness down into the unconscious rather than to a horizontal thrust from the present into the past. ("Versions" 239)

In this scenario, a "vertical" thrust denies the "horizontal" extension necessary for black women autobiographers who serve as integral parts of a collective and ongoing support system; that is, as members of a larger community. Such a definition of autobiography effectively denies the importance of ancestral connections, another aspect of community rootedness that characterizes African American women's autobiography. Royster uses the term "cultural imprinting" in accounting for "continuities from continent to continent, from Africa to North America" that led diasporic Africans in America to remake themselves by establishing a "black culture, here defined as African cultural elements reworked and expanded" (84, 87). Royster elaborates: "Cultural imprinting would explain not just a general continuity in terms of remnants and resonances but also a specific continuity in terms of the genesis of African American women's authority as writers and the emergence of what I am naming here 'ancestral voice' . . . [O]ver time, this voice becomes so deeply imbedded in cultural practices that it may be transmitted from generation to generation to generation" (87, 88). We will see that the autobiographies of Wilson, Jacobs, Keckley, and Taylor clearly demonstrate a dependence on community and ancestral networks, networks tied to an oral tradition. However, to enter into and establish a presence in Western society, African American women had to merge their ancestral legacy of oral traditions with the dominant society's legacy of written traditions.

Regardless of the obstacles that nineteenth-century European American women faced, they had obvious advantages over nineteenth-century African American women when it came to writing their personal narratives. Aside from race and class privileges, nineteenth-century white women also enjoyed a higher degree of literacy. Since the majority of early- to middle-nineteenth-century black women in America were slaves, the laws of slavery effectively kept most of them illiterate, denying them the tools with which to record their stories in Western society. The earliest autobiographical texts produced by African American women show that these stories were generally "as told to" accounts: their oral stories were recorded by and entrusted to the interpretations of a white person. Braxton places the beginning of the African American woman's participation in the genre of autobiography—when the black woman took her private voice and projected it onto a public forum—in 1787, with the story of Belinda, a slave who dared petition the New York legislature "for reparations" because she had been taken from her homeland and placed into slavery (2). Belinda learned the language and the customs of her captors and subsequently told her private story on the public stage (a place normally occupied and controlled by white men); although these men were determined to keep her voiceless and confined, Belinda became the first black woman documented as having taken "a political position as spokesperson for millions of transported Africans" (3).

As nineteenth-century African American women began recording their narratives for themselves, they continued to speak for their own needs as well as for those of the other members of their communities. Black autobiographers, men or women, are understandably both conciliatory and confrontational within the same narrative—sometimes unconsciously juxtaposing these tonal effects in an effort to gain the attention and support of those with the power to help or hinder their efforts.[12] This paradoxical struggle is reflected in the language, the structure, and the content of African American women's autobiography. We witness, by reading the personal narratives of nineteenth-century African American women writers, "an important stage of psychological development in the autobiographer's self-awareness and in the formation of her black and female [woman's?] identity, as well as her public voice" (Braxton 205).

As I have mentioned, the earliest African American autobiographers had to use their speaking voices to tell their stories because so few of them had been taught to read and write. When one is denied access to the primary communication tools of the dominant society, acquiring these tools and projecting a voice into that society can be a formidable task. Literacy, in this context, can take on a number of meanings—not only the ability to read and write but also the capacity to deny and oppress. It can take on the power of "a symbolic device exploring issues of cultural inclusion or exclusion" (Babb 39). The connection between literacy and acceptance may be seen in the personal narratives of nineteenth-century African Americans: all see the attainment of literacy as the first step toward acquiring a sense of freedom in the New World.[13] Learning to read and write the English language provided African Americans with that first taste of freedom, giving them a tool—eventually, a weapon—to counteract their total cultural exclusion from "American" society by the dominant white controllers of that society.

Because the ability to read and write also relates to the ability to produce literature within the dominant society (that is, a written document, in its most narrow sense), the two together "have long been linked to equal social and political participation" (Babb 38). As long as black Americans in general were kept illiterate, white Americans entertained no thought of sharing social and political power with them (whites did not see the black demand for social and political power as a threat until after the Civil War). However, more and more free blacks and slaves were finding ways to attain literacy. The next logical step after its attainment was the production of written documents. When literate slaves acquired freedom, many of them used the tool of literacy to connect the oral past with the written present and future. The vehicle that most chose for this process was the autobiography, as exploring self was the first step toward empowering self. Gates writes that "black people . . . had to represent themselves as speaking 'subjects' before they could even begin to destroy their status as 'objects,' as commodities, within Western culture" ("Gronniosaw" 10).

The autobiography then became the African American's way of preserving cultural memory while at the same time challenging their marginalization and oppression by the sociopolitical, economic, and literary establishment. African American autobiographers were always conscious of history and memory. As Braxton puts it, "autobiography, perhaps more than any other literary genre, is a form of symbolic memory, a confluence of culture and consciousness" (208). The oral, private voice found in the slave community was thus joined by a written, public voice as a way for African American autobiographers to preserve past cultural traditions while at the same time taking possession of and claiming the cultural traditions of the dominant white society. Using the tool of literacy, black autobiographers could themselves contradict those members of white society who denied the humanity of blacks. Therefore, nineteenth-century African American autobiographers initially wrote their lives not so much to advance in the art of *humane* letters, but, according to Gates, "to demonstrate her or his own membership in the *human* community" ("Gronniosaw" 9; my emphasis). However, since, in the eyes of the dominant white society, such membership was not possible for blacks, given the absence of their production of conventional "literary" works, human validation could still be withheld.[14]

Once African Americans became literate, how could the members of the dominant white society then ignore the reality that they were not only writing but also were writing themselves into the political and social fabric of America? Logically, they could not ignore that reality, but, illogically, they did exactly that. Blacks were merely mimicking whites, many said; others responded that truly literate and literature-producing blacks were merely exceptions.[15]

In an obvious paradox, the now-literate black women autobiographers must use the language of the oppressor to express their resistance to that oppression. From a theoretical point of view, Maggie Sale writes that language is "a site of struggle between differently empowered groups and is predicated on the notion that meaning cannot be divorced from the cultural and historical context in which these groups interact" (696). The language of Wilson, Jacobs, Keckley, and Taylor is necessarily the language of the dominant white culture, the only site of mutual communication available to them. Each writer uses aspects of existing literary traditions, molding and reshaping the language of her discourse to accomplish several tasks—the personalization of her story from her own cultural experiences; the creation of a text that would be palatable, in most instances, for a predominantly white readership;[16] the building of a common bond, an identification, between black and white women; and an understanding of and appreciation for African American contributions in the formation of America. While the intricate blending of various literary traditions was more than likely not a planned, deliberate act on the part of any of these autobiographers to create a new autobiographical paradigm, this blending does occur, and its occurrence is a direct reflection of the writer's struggle to tell her own story, using the bits and pieces of communicative tools that she consciously and subconsciously adopts.

For nineteenth-century African American women autobiographers, adhering to distinctions between the proper and improper use of language, genres, and styles was not particularly relevant. I doubt that any of them purposefully developed a blueprint of how the various genres and writing styles would play out in her narrative. Each writer's aim was to present a text that represented her voice and the voices of the personae within her narrative, as well as she could recall them. For instance, when Jacobs assures her readers that *Incidents* is "no fiction" (1), I do not believe she is using the term "fiction" as a literary form; she uses it to distinguish between something she recollects as being true (her story) and something that is fabricated, that is, "fictional" meaning a lie in the sense of Timothy Adams's list of lies. Her intent is to establish the veracity of her narrative. For nineteenth-century black women autobiographers, the blurring of language, genre, and style adds potency to their narratives as social discourse and allows them to use a discordant structure in their texts to reflect the discordant lives within their stories.

While various theorists, literary critics, and artists establish distinctions between the historical (supposedly factual) and literary (supposedly fictional) aspects of the autobiography, I prefer to apply Mikhail Bakhtin's dialogic theories of language. Wilson, Jacobs, Keckley, and Taylor all use the malleability and changeability of language to enhance the power of the texts and contexts of their narratives. Michael Holquist, editor of Bakhtin's *The Dialogic Imagination*, writes that Bakhtin blurs the hard line drawn between literary genres when he defines the "novel" as "whatever force is at work within a given literary system to reveal the limits, the artificial constraints of that system" (xxxi). Bakhtin writes that "the separation of style and language from the question of genre has been largely responsible for a situation in which only individual and period-bound overtones of a style are the privileged subjects of study, while its basic social tone is ignored" (259). In reading and assessing the literary value of a text, we must emphasize its historical and social setting. We must not allow the little pictures to be obscured or overwhelmed by the demand for the so-called big picture, that is, the canon. Using Bakhtin's definition of the novel as a text reflective of forces at work that "reveal the limits" and the "artificial constraints" of a particular literary genre, and then applying his theory to the subsequent blurring of literary genres by the four writers I consider here, it is clear that nineteenth-century African American women's autobiography may be viewed "novelistically," in Bakhtinian terms. When the dust has settled, histories, autobiographies, and fictions are all, in effect, just narratives.

Bakhtin's theory introduces the now well-known concept of heteroglossia, "the base condition governing the operation of meaning in any utterance." He expands on this definition by writing that "at any given time, in any given place, there will be a set of conditions ... that will insure that a word uttered in that place and at that time will have a meaning different than it would have under any other conditions" (284). While some contemporary scholars are moving away from the practice of "historicizing" texts, we must respect the impact of historical, political, and social considerations on the life-writing of nineteenth-century African American women. These autobiographers and the texts that they wrote reflect the influence of these conditions, including accessibility to historically specific literary definitions and models. Did these women employ traditional literary conventions? Yes and no. While they may have begun with the established literary models of a particular time and place, those models could not sustain the power of the story or the unique voice of the storyteller. Remaining within the boundaries of a particular form was not important; these autobiographers did not hesitate to pick and choose from whatever literary mode best reflected the tone they wanted to convey at any particular juncture of their story, relying upon oral storytelling techniques as much as the written traditions of the West to capture and hold their audiences.

While I note the impact of Bakhtin's dialogics of discourse, Mae Gwendolyn Henderson suggests that Hans-Georg Gadamer's "'dialectical model of conversation'" may be as relevant as Bakhtin's theory when applied to the discourse of black women writers: "If the Bakhtinian model suggests the multiplicity of speech . . . , then Gadamer's model moves toward a unity of understanding. . . . It is the first as well as the second meaning which we privilege in speaking of black women writers: the first connoting polyphony, multivocality, and plurality of voices, and the second signifying intimate, private, inspired utterances. Through their intimacy with the discourses of the other(s), black women writers weave into their work competing and complementary discourses" (19, 23). This statement reinforces the use of balancing acts that characterize black women's personal narratives—balancing various genres; linking literature and history; engaging self and community; juxtaposing the tones of humility and chastisement; and so forth. I believe that Henderson's astute observation has particular relevance when considered alongside most black women autobiographers' use of humility (the Gadamerian model of intimacy and privacy that works to establish a bond with white women readers) and chastisement (the Bakhtinian model of polyphony that challenges white women readers' assumption of understanding or, in some cases, superiority). Since the intended audience for most nineteenth-century black women autobiographers was a white-female readership, these black women had to vacillate between the sometimes "competing," sometimes "complementary" nature of that relationship. It might well have been Jacobs's act of establishing a complementary relationship with her readers that had an adverse effect on the general reception of her *Incidents* by nineteenth-century white-male readers.

Black Women Autobiographers' Encounter with Gender, Race, and Class

> when the smallest cell remembers—
> how do you
> how can you
> when the smallest cell
>   remembers
> lose a language
> **—Philip,** *She Tries Her Tongue*

Although Jacobs's *Incidents* was widely read by Northern white women, Claudia Tate speculates that the narrative probably fell into "scholarly disrepute" among nineteenth-century white males "due to the fact that [it] does not adhere to the general format of well-known slave narratives, like [Frederick] Douglass's 1845 narrative" (*Domestic* 26). Tate further argues that Jacobs, in the portrayal of her sexual harassment, not only "dared to breach social and literary convention" but also had the audacity "to make the sexual oppression of an adolescent black female a symmetrical paradigm to that of the brutally whipped bondman for the institution's depravity" (26). Such a suggestion was unacceptable to white (and to many black) men, then and now. White men especially felt challenged at the suggestion of equality between the male slave's suffering and that of the female slave, or any suggestion, for that matter, of equality between men and women.

To accept any level of equality between the black man and the black woman was tantamount to admitting the possibility of a similar equable relationship between the white man and the white woman, an admission that would obviously shake the foundation of white-male superiority. Just as telling in assessing the nineteenth-century white man's rejection of Jacobs's text was his reaction to the subject of rape itself, a topic that caused him some alarm. It could be that nineteenth-century white men turned away from Jacobs's *Incidents* and its sexual subplot in part because it threatened, however indirectly, the myth of the purity of womanhood that white men had erected to celebrate the "true woman."[1] This is not to suggest that Jacobs, as the character Linda Brent, had membership in this true woman society in the eyes of white men; of course, she did not. But because Jacobs's appeal to white women suggested a woman-to-woman relationship and implied that Jacobs was the "sister" of white women, it is my opinion that white men felt threatened, rejecting Jacobs and her narrative.

For three of the four autobiographers I treat—Wilson, Jacobs, and Keckley—the woman-to-woman relationship between the nineteenth-century African American woman slave/indentured servant and the nineteenth-century European American mistress is characterized by the mistress's bouts of jealousy and attempts to minimize the black woman. Taylor gives no indication in her narrative that she, at the age of thirteen when the Civil War broke out, had experienced any such conflict with her mistress (although such an omission is not tantamount to nonoccurrence). The typical nineteenth-century mistress, especially but not exclusively the mistress of the Southern plantation, oftentimes victimized the sexually abused woman/girl slave/servant in an effort to relieve her own sense of victimization under the constraints of the "cult of true womanhood," a concept that left her socially, politically, and sexually frustrated in a white-male-dominated society. White men, thus, effectively created a combative situation between white women and black women. While myths of true womanhood appeared to celebrate the white woman's piety, purity, submissiveness, and domesticity, the "cult" in reality proved to be a cage—in claiming to honor, pamper, and protect white women, it actually served to deny them the freedom to find and express their voices in public arenas. One cannot deny the oppressive nature of such confinement. But the bars of most of these cages inhabited by middle- to upper-class white women were padded with velvet, unlike the rougher bars of the cages in which nineteenth-century black women found themselves.

One of several negative aspects associated with membership in the "cult" was its creation of sexual repression in white mistresses. While they felt obligated to repress their own sexual desires for the sake of their pure image, they were often forced to accept in their own homes the promiscuous behavior of their husbands with black servants/slave women. As a result, a white woman often became resentful of a black woman's apparent sexual freedom and "might be expected to react with terrible vengeance and intense sexual jealousy toward a coerced slave woman, seeing in her, perhaps, something of a lost female sexuality which she herself had been denied" (Gwin 40). As Barbara Omolade notes, many nineteenth-century Southern white women appeared to be more inclined to blame and vilify the victim (the black slave woman) than the victimizer (her own white husband), choosing to avoid the emotional strain and social embarrassment that public acknowledgment of her husband's dalliances might cause: "'Under slavery we lived surrounded by prostitutes like patriarchs of old; our men live in one house with their wives and concubines'" (9).[2]

Throughout history, black women situated in white societies have struggled against stereotypes that minimize their beauty while at the same time maximizing their supposed promiscuity in an unfavorable comparison to pure, beautiful, chaste white women. In the mid-1980s, Sander Gilman completed a study of nineteenth-century European art, medicine, and literature, tracking a historical "conspiracy" to create a sexual difference between black and white women. Gilman argues that the Western concept of beauty places "white women at the top of an imaginary hierarchy of beauty and sexual virtue while consistently relegating black women to the lowest order of the female" (231). This European conspiracy was well established in nineteenth-century America, wherein black slave women were often portrayed as "Jezebels." To justify their own violent actions against black women, white mistresses necessarily had to view them as "prostitutes" and to perceive the white masters (at least in public) as unwitting, benevolent gentlemen who were the victims of seduction. So it was that one victim of white-male subjugation, white women, vented their anger and frustration upon another, black women.[3]

Many of the cruelties inflicted on Wilson, Jacobs, and Keckley—at the hands of or on the orders of their white mistresses—were tied to their mixed-race heritage. In these narratives, all three protagonists are depicted as mulattos and, because much of their suffering can be linked directly to their biracial characteristics, they might appropriately be described as "tragic mulattos." Frances Smith Foster characterizes the tragic mulatto as the "earliest and most pervasive image of the female protagonist in Afro-American literature, the epitome of True Womanhood" as it had been defined for the nineteenth-century white woman ("Adding Color" 34).[4] Most of these mulatto women were house servants trained to be pious, pure, submissive, and domestic in the tradition of the "cult." In some cases, they were considered more beautiful than their white mistresses, an acknowledgment that led to many of the tragic circumstances of their lives. The jealousy and resultant cruelty that their white mistresses displayed toward them created many tragic events that Wilson, Jacobs, and Keckley record in their personal narratives. All three present protagonists who "transcend the images of the victimized slave woman and the home-bound True Woman" (35).[5] Evidently, Susie King Taylor was the issue of two dark-skinned African American parents and, therefore, was not a mulatto. As such, it appears that she was neither sexually pursued by her white master nor treated especially cruelly by a jealous white mistress. At least, she makes no direct reference to such treatment in *Reminiscences.*

Wilson, Jacobs, and Keckley all portray their jealous white mistresses as "enraged monsters," and as "specters of slavery itself" (Gwin 45). Wilson wrote her narrative based on her indentureship to a Northern white family, showing Mrs. Bellmont to have all of the characteristics of a cruel and jealous Southern plantation mistress. Jacobs wrote a personal narrative in which "her vivid depictions of [Mrs. Flint] are designed to shock those who believed that the plantation mistress was . . . 'the conscience of the slave south.'"[6] Foster writes that Keckley assumes "the image of the black woman betrayed by her white sister, for it was Mrs. Burwell, a 'morbidly sensitive' and 'helpless' woman, who urged the local schoolmaster to subdue Keckley's 'stubborn pride'" (*Written* 122).

Foster sees Wilson's character Frado as being closest to the typical tragic mulatto, "pious, sensitive, and long-suffering," eager to find a true love who would adore and support her ("Adding Color" 35). However, Foster also notes that when Frado later has to deal with the flawed character of her husband and the failure of her marriage, she does not waste away in the tradition of the tragic mulatto or of the true woman. Instead, she continues her battle to overcome victimization and attempts to achieve independence for herself and for her child.

In *Our Nig*, Wilson provides numerous examples of the physical and psychological abuses heaped on Frado by Mrs. Bellmont and by the oldest Bellmont daughter, Mary. When one recalls that Frado entered the Bellmont household as a six-year-old child, it is difficult to understand the motives behind the ferocious nature of Mrs. Bellmont's attacks. Julia Stern writes that "the female body of the child of color registers a level of maternal fury [in Mrs. Bellmont] that far exceeds purely private conflict; Frado's tortured form bears witness to a political rage as well. Inscribed

within the beatings and attempts at suffocation Frado endures is a convoluted and incestuous history that links patriarchal exploitation of women
with the American exploitation of African American slaves" (441). Again
we see the similarity between Frado's treatment and that inflicted on
slaves in the American South. I would further suggest that Mrs. Bellmont's actions, as well as Mary's, also indicate a fear that their comparison
to this pretty and amiable mulatto might represent a threat to their positions as the true women of the household: "In addition to Frado's ambiguous racial heritage, the child's gender and sexual identities become battle-
grounds upon which Mrs. Bellmont rages her campaign of terror. She
engages in a systematic program to degrade the mulatta physically. Mrs.
Bellmont dresses Frado in motley made up of her son Jack's old clothes
and shaves her glossy ringlets. The meaning of Mrs. Bellmont's attempts
to masculinize her servant are transparent to Jack, who is ever attuned to
Frado's emerging sexuality" (Stern 443). Obviously, Mrs. Bellmont is experiencing feelings of jealousy toward Frado and is probably also aware of
Jack's reactions to Frado's budding womanhood. She thus opts to make
Frado's appearance less appealing and punishes her for being a sexual en-
ticement—a "Jezebel."

Although Wilson's autobiographical text is not a slave narrative, she
clearly highlights the many instances in which Frado is treated just as
brutally as the slaves, a reality that perhaps makes Wilson's text the more
disturbing. In the free North, not only is Frado beaten and mistreated but
she also suffers these cruelties at the hands of the mistresses of the house,
not the masters. Elizabeth Fox-Genovese notes that this woman-as-en-
emy depiction is relevant because "Wilson's enemy represents the world
of female domesticity and, inescapably, underscores the possible adversarial relation between the Afro-American female autobiographer and
her readers" ("My Statue" 192), many of whom Wilson might have
wanted to attract.

In *Incidents*, Jacobs's mulatto protagonist, Linda Brent, catches the eye
of Mrs. Flint, another jealous white mistress. However, Mrs. Flint finds
herself unable to vent her frustration against Linda because her husband,
Dr. Flint, has forbidden his wife to punish this object of his sexual obses-
sion. So, although Mrs. Flint vows at one point to kill Linda, mistakenly
thinking that the slave girl has had sex with her husband and that the
baby Linda is carrying was fathered by Dr. Flint, she knows that she dare
not touch the slave girl because of her husband's edict. Linda is aware of

the combination of jealousy and hatred that Mrs. Flint feels toward her. Jacobs writes that because of the preponderance of rapes and seductions perpetrated by white slave owners, "even the little child . . . will learn before she is twelve years old, why it is that her mistress hates such and such a one among the slaves" (28).

Jacobs even titles one chapter in her narrative "The Jealous Mistress." She continues her description of the attempts by Dr. Flint to seduce Linda Brent and also blames Mrs. Flint, the mistress, for her inability or refusal to protect Linda and other slave girls from Dr. Flint's sexual abuse, noting that Mrs. Flint had long had knowledge of her husband's sexual activities and that she should have "used this knowledge to counsel and to screen the young and the innocent among her slaves" (31). The implication here is that Jacobs, the autobiographer, expected Mrs. Flint, as a fellow woman, to have acted protectively toward these young black girls. Instead, at least in Linda's case, Mrs. Flint vacillates between accusing her husband of licentious behavior (accusations that he merely denies) and accusing the slave girl of harlotry. Mrs. Flint's position would have been pitiable had it not been for Linda's fears that Mrs. Flint would eventually release her anger in a way that would be even more devastating to Linda than any beatings she could have suffered. Her fear is that Mrs. Flint might, through her frustration at being denied Linda as a target, turn her rage against Linda's children. That such jealousy could drive Mrs. Flint to the point of harming these children or selling them away from her is a real concern for Linda and is, eventually, the emotional force that gives impetus to her decision to become a runaway.

While Mrs. Flint is forbidden to strike Linda in Jacobs's *Incidents*, Mrs. Burwell in Keckley's *Behind the Scenes* is not hindered by objections or interference from her husband, just as Mrs. Bellmont in Wilson's *Our Nig* seems to punish Frado with hardly a word or protest from Mr. Bellmont. In both of these narratives, the white mistresses assume aggressive roles in the mistreatment of the young black women. Yet, Mrs. Bellmont brutalizes Frado with her own hand in *Our Nig*. She is both judge and executioner, never wavering in the hatred that she feels for Frado nor in the severity of the punishment that she imposes. Mrs. Burwell, on the other hand, never touches Lizzie herself. First, she orders the schoolteacher, Mr. Bingham, to flog Lizzie in order to subdue her "stubborn pride" (36). When Mr. Bingham later repents and refuses to continue with the beatings, Mrs. Burwell urges her husband, the Reverend Mr. Burwell, to whip

Lizzie, which he does severely. However, as Mrs. Burwell witnesses for herself the bleeding and tormented body of young Lizzie, she relents and begs her husband to stop the beatings, exhibiting a regret for her actions that *Our Nig's* Mrs. Bellmont never displays.

Keckley writes of Mrs. Burwell that the sight of Lizzie's distress "even touched her cold, *jealous* heart" (38; my emphasis). Up to this point in her text, Keckley has not made jealousy an issue in her beatings, making this reference to her mistress's "jealous" heart especially noteworthy. Now that she has opened that door, she writes that she was "fair-looking" and that a white man, whom she refuses to name, "persecuted me for four years, and I—I—became a mother" (39). Although (as was prudent during those times and as we see addressed consistently in antebellum slave narratives) Keckley as a slave does not name her white seducer, Minrose Gwin proposes that Keckley's purposeful but seemingly irrelevant comments in the next paragraph on the "current" whereabouts of the Reverend Mr. Burwell lead us to "infer that he was the father of her child" (50). Also, Joanne Braxton writes that Keckley's "master placed Elizabeth with another white man, by whom she bore a son" (40). Braxton, for some reason, does not note that Keckley writes of being placed with only one other white man in her narrative, the son of her owner—the good Reverend Burwell.[7] According to Keckley's text, her real master, Colonel A. Burwell, loaned her out when she was fourteen years old, sending her "to live with my master's eldest son, a Presbyterian minister" (31); she also notes that she became a mother during the years she was with the Reverend and his wife.

I agree with Gwin that the "white man" to whom both Braxton and Keckley refer, the white man who fathered Keckley's child, is indeed the Reverend Mr. Burwell. It would seem, then, that the breaking of Lizzie's pride is not the only or the primary reason that Mrs. Burwell needs to punish Lizzie. We must note that at the time of these beatings, Keckley has not yet had her baby (which suggests that Mrs. Burwell became aware of her husband's sexual pursuit before Lizzie became pregnant), that his pursuit continued after (and probably even during) the beatings, and that Mrs. Burwell continued to be tormented with the knowledge of that pursuit. Wilson, Jacobs, and Keckley each shows how factors—brutality in the slave system, belief in the racial inferiority of blacks, belief in the gender inferiority of black women, and jealousy—tainted many contacts between nineteenth-century black and white women, creating an adversarial situation that broke—or at least greatly strained—the bonds of sisterhood. Fortunately, these three autobiographers also found some white women with whom they could forge a bond.

While they often assume the roles of cruel, jealous, and sometimes vindictive mistresses in the personal narratives of African American women writers, European American women also emerge at times as supportive figures, joining African American women within a community of women. When Linda Brent first went into hiding in *Incidents*, the white mistress of a neighboring plantation defied the Southern laws by hiding her in an upstairs bedroom and later under the floorboards in her kitchen. In Wilson's *Our Nig*, both Aunt Abby and the invalid Jane Bellmont offered as much comfort and protection to Frado as they dared. These white women are rarely, however, the mistresses under whose authority the slave or servant lives; they are generally women who live within the extended community and have befriended the young black girls. African American women, in their battles to resist oppression, usually come to the conclusion that they have to trust someone outside of their own immediate cultural families, someone who can provide some degree of protection or some means by which they can improve their current conditions. In most cases, this someone is European American. In such relationships, European American and African American women shared information and kept confidences. The African American women made confessions regarding their loss of virtue and/or faith during their enslavement, and the European American women commiserated.

The confessional aspects of intimate exchanges of information create bonds that lead to a certain amount of empowerment for both parties. Michel Foucault's definition of the confession, though not written in a slave-to-mistress context, is nonetheless helpful here:

> For a long time, the individual was vouched for by the reference of others and the demonstration of his ties to the commonweal (family, allegiance, protection); then he was authenticated by the discourse of truth he was able or obliged to pronounce concerning himself. The truthful confession was inscribed at the heart of the procedures of individualization by power. . . . One does not confess without the presence (or virtual presence) of a partner who is not simply the interlocutor but the authority who requires the confession, prescribes and appreciates it, and intervenes in order to judge, punish, forgive, console, and reconcile; [confession is] a ritual in which the

truth is corroborated by the obstacles and resistances it has had to surmount in order to be formulated. . . . Spoken in time, to the proper party, and by the person who was both the bearer of it and the one responsible for it, the truth healed. (*Sexuality* 58–59, 61–62, 67)

As this theory applies to the woman-as-fellow-woman (-sister, -mother) relationships that developed in these nineteenth-century communities of women, African American women felt obliged to confess the sexual violations of their bodies and the spiritual questioning in their souls. By doing so, they sought understanding, sympathy, and, in some cases, forgiveness from European American women, women who had themselves been molded in the image of the true woman and who, therefore, would expect such confessions of lost virtue. The popularity of sentimental fiction was grounded in its familiarity, and its readers had certain expectations about scenarios and plots. These narratives supported cultural beliefs that their predominantly white women readers already held, and they functioned on a formula that, according to Jane Tompkins, "allowed them to operate as instruments of cultural self-definition" (xvii). The stories were improbable, but predictable, relying on the formulaic presence of stereotyped characters, trite expressions, and sensational plots, all tied together by a forceful, expressive literary style punctuated with "sudden burst[s] of feeling" (xviii). Even though the sentimental genre was predictable, it contained enough excitement and spiritual soothing to assure its continuing popularity through the mid-nineteenth century, with "the endlessly repeated rescue scenes, . . . the separation of families, . . . the Job-like trials of faith, . . . the benevolent rescuers, . . . and the sacrificial mothers" (xvii). These sentimental novels derive their power from their ability to do the cultural work they were designed to do (xv), and sentimental fiction was designed to reinforce the "cult of true womanhood."

Black women autobiographers, however, who made extensive use of the sentimental fiction model, and again I refer specifically to Wilson, Jacobs, and Keckley, were masterful in depicting the breakdown of sentimental values as they pertained to the plight of nineteenth-century black women. Although sentimental fiction was supposedly grounded in the desire for union/unity, Carla L. Peterson suggests that "Jacobs's autobiography . . . lays bare the limits of sentimental sympathy as an adequate corrective to the social ills besetting the nation" (*Doers* 160). How is union, and therefore healing, possible based on a sentimentality rife with "superficiality, hypocrisy, even danger"? Peterson highlights the performative and destructive essences of the sentimental in noting Mrs. Flint's reaction to the death of her slave and foster sister, Linda's Aunt Nancy: "The pure externality of her [Mrs. Flint's] sentimentality is made evident in her plan to provide a 'beautiful illustration of the attachment existing between slaveholder and slave' by having Nancy buried in the Flint family burial place. Such an illustration is not only hypocritical but disempowering to the slave community, for whom, as Albert Raboteau has shown, funeral rites are acts of resistance and the burial ground a sacred place" (160).

Carolyn Sorisio further notes that Jacobs deviates from the expected ending of a sentimental discourse, fooling a readership that "has been finessed into thinking that the mask we have been viewing is in fact Jacobs" ("'There is Might in Each'" 11). Rather than ending her narrative in the expected way—with the death or marriage of the heroine—Jacobs "suggests that the stories of slave women cannot fit into the genres she has used. . . . Jacobs revises the genre of sentimental fiction to challenge her audience's assumptions" (11).

Peterson then shows that Wilson uses the scenarios surrounding Mrs. Bellmont to challenge the stronghold of sentimental fiction: "Wilson offered [her 'colored brethren'] the portrait of a white woman that subverts the private sphere ideology, in particular the sentimental responses of sympathy and disciplinary intimacy as social correctives; . . . Mrs. Bellmont perverts the feminine values of the private sphere . . . by reconstructing it as a place organized according to a capitalist ethic of ownership and accumulation" (*Doers* 168). Mrs. Bellmont's position as a true woman in a sentimental narrative sense is thus confounded by her public business-like attitude in her treatment of Frado. The breakdown of the sentimental ideology in Wilson's *Our Nig* is also the subject of Elizabeth Ammons's "mother-savior" comparison between *Our Nig* and Harriet Beecher Stowe's *Uncle Tom's Cabin*, a purposeful distortion in Ammons's opinion. For instance, Ammons, along with Peterson, points out the absence of an effective positive force in *Our Nig* to balance the negative energies of Mrs. Bellmont: "[T]here is in this book no nurturant maternal world. . . . There is no balancing portrait of some gentle, sisterly, *effective* white female" (181; Ammons's emphasis). The result is that the maternal ideology offered in Stowe's sentimental epic is twisted and subverted to such a degree by Wilson that "*Our Nig* jeers at the myth of the mother-savior. . . . The most powerful person in *Our Nig* is a mother, and she is a 'she-devil'" (182).

Finally, in her article "Unmasking the Genteel Performer: Elizabeth Keckley's *Behind the Scenes* and the Politics of Public Wrath," Sorisio again addresses a black woman autobiographer's successful tactic of engaging the collapse of sentimental narrative characteristics when they are applied to a nineteenth-century black woman. What makes Keckley's treatment so interesting is that, without making direct statements, she implies that she is more genteel, that is, more of a true woman, than the white woman with whom she is most often associated, Mary Todd Lincoln. Sorisio states that "by veiling her private life and emotions, Keckley marks herself in mid-nineteenth-century terms as sincere and genteel" ("Unmasking" 28). While claiming that it is her desire to support Mary Todd Lincoln, Keckley offers a text that seems to belie that claim as *Behind the Scenes* presents, compared to herself, a very ungenteel Mrs. Lincoln: "Keckley's revelations about Mary Todd Lincoln are threatening because they unmask a white woman's genteel performance" (29). By unmasking the genteel performers (white true women) Keckley reveals the hypocrisy of sentimental fiction.[8]

White women affected by the sentimental novel tradition, while seeing themselves as true women in the sentimental narrative tradition, nevertheless felt shame and guilt about the wrongs that members of their own culture (and gender) were inflicting upon their black sisters, and, therefore, they assumed the role of confidante and protector. These women included Amy Post and both the first and second Mrs. Bruce in *Incidents* and Aunt Abby and Jane Bellmont in *Our Nig*. However, the white mistress who would attempt to support and protect individual African American women suffering under oppressive conditions, while doing little or nothing to destroy the system that oppressed them, fails to see the irony of her position. Deborah M. Garfield calls this syndrome "upright hypocrisy" and points to Mrs. Martha Hoskins, a character in Jacobs's *Incidents*, as an example of the "coexistence of savior and enslaver" within one white, female body (278). In another example from *Incidents*, Mrs. Blount, a slave owner herself, provides sanctuary for the runaway Linda Brent and thereby becomes "simultaneously a familiar helpmate and a domestic intruder in that cadre of figures who . . . risk their lives and reputations to inch Jacobs slowly toward 'freedom'" (278). Although the European American woman's presence in this African American community of women is conflicted, it is necessary, for it offers the possibility of escape to freedom for Linda and presents a small opening within which Jacobs, the writer, carves out a space for her own voice. By assuming the white woman's mode of literary expression, the sentimental novel, and then subverting it to fit the story of their black woman protagonists, Jacobs, Wilson, and Keckley not only control this white medium but also use it to criticize and expose those whites (women and men) who produced, read, and perpetuated this false genre of womanhood under the guise of feminine virtue and purity. By nurturing a woman-to-woman link through the sentimental novel format, black women autobiographers increased their literary powers. Their most formidable obstacle, however, was to be white men's dismissal of women's attempts to enter into the public sphere.

Twentieth-century feminist scholarship clearly documents the marginal position of nineteenth-century European American women, noting that "patriarchal notions of woman's inherent and consequent social role have denied or severely proscribed her access to the public space" (S. Smith, *Poetics* 7). For the most part, nineteenth-century European American women were figuratively locked into domestic areas such as the kitchen, the bedroom, the nursery, the sewing room, and other private spaces within the home. Women's early efforts to break free of these confines and to explore the public arenas of politics, social development, and advanced education were met with resistance from European American men; they challenged, or ridiculed, or ignored these attempted intrusions.[9] Because of this patriarchal resistance, women writing their personal narratives, seeking to procure a public platform from which to release their voices, found that platform patronizingly claimed and jealously guarded by European American men. Sidonie Smith writes,

> The woman [read white woman] who writes autobiography is doubly estranged when she enters the autobiographical contract. Precisely because she approaches her storytelling as one who speaks from the margins of autobiographical discourse, thus as one who is both of the prevailing culture and on the outskirts of it, she brings to her project a particularly troubled relationship to her reader. Since autobiography is a public expression, she speaks before and to "man." Attuned to the ways women [read white women] have been dressed up for public exposure, attuned also to the price women [read white women] pay for public self-disclosure, the autobiographer reveals in her speaking posture and narrative structure her understanding of the possible readings she will receive from a public that has the power of her reputation in its hands. (*Poetics* 49)

I note "white women" in this passage because they are obviously the women to whom Smith refers as she describes these women autobiographers as being "dressed up," suggestive of the decorative element of the cult of true womanhood. At any rate, this white woman autobiographer knew that her acceptance and her success relied on her ability to smudge, or at least camouflage, the sociopolitical lines that privileged manhood over womanhood, masculine behavior over feminine behavior.[10]

While their levels of oppression were different, both white and black women experienced similar problems when confronting the apparently impermeable wall of written discourse guarded by white male writers, editors, and publishers. When nineteenth-century women began to defy the assertion that they could not adequately function in the public realm, they wrote and also published personal narratives that demonstrated their resistance to such confinement. Their voices are recorded in various and sundry discourses, such as letters, diaries, journals, autobiographies, sermons, memoirs, and various public statements. And although most of these written documents were kept in what were still private areas of the home, they could not be contained there, given our contemporary demands for a more inclusive "canon"; consequently, they have steadily emerged into the public arenas as important social, historical, and literary records of an extraordinary period in American literary development. The stories that African American women soon began to tell and the manner in which they did the telling take on, in the words of Marlene Kadar, the characteristics of "life writing, . . . a genre of documents or fragments of documents written out of a life, or . . . out of a personal experience of the writer" (152). In other words, it is writing that addresses the bits and pieces, the "incidents" and "sketches," of one's life.

During the nineteenth century, black women autobiographers usually found themselves dealing with these bits and pieces of life and writing their lives in very personal, very intimate ways, not necessarily writing or speaking, states Kadar, "in a language or style that suited the judges of good taste" in literature (157). So how did these black women engaged in life-writing operate within the established genre of autobiography? The answer is, they did not; they moved in a different direction, establishing what was to become a new approach to autobiography. The "judges," however, summarily dismissed black women's narratives as being "obviously hysterical," "emotional," or "too personal" (157). In the eyes of the judges, these women were incapable of understanding and adhering to the conventions of autobiographical writing; the judges never considered the possibility that these women writers had dismissed the conventions in search of a form that better suited their stories. This "sincere, probing disregard for genre and its rules" led to women writing narratives that became "the site of new language and new grammars. . . . It is the site of the other" (152–53). Although Kadar is writing about women autobiographers in general, it is easy by extension to see that black women autobiographers experienced from these "judges" a rejection even more dehumanizing. They devised methods of life-writing that were necessarily more creative, subversive, original, and, overall, more reflective of their cultural traditions. I do not want to get into a spitting contest about who is most "other," who is most deeply smothered under white-male conventions, but the sites from which black women autobiographers write are so buried that it took the heteroglossia of an African American mother tongue to dig a way out.

African American autobiographers Wilson, Jacobs, Keckley, and Taylor tested the waters before plunging in, knowing that, being members of both the "weaker" sex and the "inferior" race, their entry into the world of literacy would be especially unwelcome. While they took the courageous steps necessary to force open the doors of American society, each found her passage difficult. In her attempt to produce a text that would appeal to her white nineteenth-century-American reading (and buying) audience, each had to deal with the duality that straddling two cultures necessarily created. It is common knowledge that W.E.B. DuBois was one of the first and is by far the most recognized interpreter of what he defined as "the problem of the Twentieth Century," that being "the problem of the color-line" (9). Of course, the use of skin color to separate and classify people was not invented in America. But the combination of black dehumanization, which was used to drive the American slavery system, and a racial hierarchy that placed blacks at the bottom of the social ladder led to the far-reaching and abhorrent act of establishing the worthiness (or rather, "un"-worthiness) of an entire culture. This "color-line" problem has been so intrusive that other factors demonstrating the character or contributions of individuals were placed in its shadow, even for those African Americans who were legally "free" blacks (Wilson) and for those who eventually gained their freedom through purchase (Jacobs and Keckley) or as a result of the Northern victory in the Civil War (Taylor). The overriding concern for nineteenth-century European Americans rested with whether the individual was "black" or "white"—a concern still holding sway in the United States in this twenty-first century.

While we can, and many of us do, see race merely as a construct put in place by the existing white power structures in order to establish and maintain their perceived positions of superiority, we cannot deny or ignore the reality that race continues to be a Western Anglo-Saxon ideological weapon that psychologically demeans and diminishes people of color. We need only look at some of the more powerful literary works that African American writers produce to see the problems that the concentration on race and the "color-line" in Western society has created. As with other weapons used against them, however, people of color found ways to reverse the effects of racial bias. Gradually, they adopted this construct of race and, writes Evelyn Brooks Higginbotham, "fashioned race into a cultural identity that resisted white hegemonic discourses" (107). At various times in history, African Americans took the idea of race and re-directed it, politicizing it to confound the idea of black being lesser— focusing on it being different and, in some cases, better: "Blacks constructed and valorized a self-representation essentially antithetical to that of whites" (109).[11]

African American autobiographers likewise challenge the minimization of their heritage, accentuating their efforts in the building of America. This attitude is particularly evident in the closing chapters of Taylor's postbellum *Reminiscences*, wherein she celebrates the sacrifices and contributions that African American men and women made during and following the Civil War. While Taylor makes no plea for herself in her autobiography, her closing chapters contain an impassioned plea on behalf of her race. Many scholars note the Bakhtinian double-voiced characteristics of the narratives written by Wilson and Jacobs, and Taylor exhibits this same characteristic in *Reminiscences*, a double-voice especially noticeable in her attack on American racism. Taylor is simultaneously the "official, courageous self-sacrificing woman . . . and the independent ex-slave woman who is a spokesperson for her race and for her sex" (Mason 340–41). On behalf of her race, Taylor concludes her narrative with the following plea to white America: "Justice we ask,—to be citizens of these United States, where so many of our people have shed their blood with their white comrades, that the stars and stripes should never be polluted" (75–76).

While DuBois describes the world seen through the eyes of the Negro as one "which yields him no true self-consciousness, but only lets him see himself through the revelation of the other world" (2), I must point out that the eyes he represents are specifically male. Still unrecognized was the fact that Negro women saw and experienced this same world of exclusion and minimization. However, the basis of DuBois's argument remains sound and is later echoed by Stephen Butterfield when he writes that "black writers . . . live in two worlds: American and Black, public mask and private face" (17). The obvious difference is that, unlike African American men, African American women encountered the additional negating distinction of gender, creating for them a third world.

Several contemporary American scholars have theorized about the ramifications of what Rose Brewer labels the "polyvocality of multiple social locations," which African American women and African American women writers negotiate in their attempts to secure a place in American culture and American literatures (13).[12] Most feminist theorists now acknowledge that one of the factors separating European American and African American feminists in the 1960s and 1970s was the failure on the part of early white feminist pioneers to recognize this polyvocality in their black sisters.[13]

Most African American women could not embrace the precepts of the white feminist approaches because these approaches too often appeared to force a choice between gender and race, a separation that was not acceptable to most African American women; this difference in perception and failure in communication created a divisive situation in the feminist movement as it pertained to the inclusion of black women.[14] While contemporary black feminist scholars champion the fight for gender equality that is at the heart of feminism, they continue to be leery about their own equal standing as black women within this movement. The conflict is summarized by bell hooks: "Every woman's movement in America from its earliest origin to the present day has been built on a racist foundation—a fact which in no way invalidates feminism as a political ideology. The racial apartheid social structure that characterized 19th and early 20th century American life was mirrored in the women's rights movement. The first white women's rights advocates were never seeking social equality for all women; they were seeking social equality for white women" (*Ain't I a Woman* 124).

At the same time that the 1970s feminist programs focused on white women, many of the black studies programs in American colleges, with their emphasis on the contributions of African American men, also appeared to suggest that African American women writers must choose between gender and race in order to enter the black literary curriculum. Because few of them did, few black women writers received much attention during the first two-thirds of the twentieth century. Brewer, however, in noting that the African American woman could not disregard some parts of herself for the sake of other parts, writes that "gender as a category of analysis cannot be understood decontextualized from race and class in Black feminist theorizing, [and] gender takes on meaning and is embedded institutionally in the context of the racial and class order" (17). The fluidity of these constructed relationships—race, gender, class—demonstrates how intertwined are their tissues, and it is within this construction that African American women writers must maneuver. Barbara Smith, one of the earliest of the black women critics to address the multifaceted world of black women writers, arrived at a similar conclusion, noting that "the politics of sex as well as the politics of race and class are crucially interlocking factors in the works of black women writers" (159). Because of these sociopolitical constructs, the voice of the nineteenth-century African American woman autobiographer often fell into a black hole of hegemonic dismissal and was seemingly swallowed up by this void.

According to Sidonie Smith, if the person attempting to write an autobiography is both working-class and a woman of color, "she faces even more complex imbroglios of male-female figures: here ideologies of race and class, sometimes even of nationality, intersect and confound those of gender" (*Poetics* 51). Such constructs, when they go unchallenged, succeed in shaping a perceived reality that limits the visibility of women, people of color, and those in lower economic or social positions. Higginbotham, in addressing contemporary oppressive conditions resulting from the existence of such constructs, writes that the "categorization of class and racial groups according to culturally constituted sexual identities facilitated blacks' subordination within a stratified society and rendered them powerless against the intrusion of the state into their innermost private lives" (105). While I challenge Higginbotham's conclusion that blacks were left "powerless," I support her statement that the categories of race, class, and "sexual identities" were used by white-male holders of power as weapons in an attempt to render blacks, especially black women, powerless. That these attempts were unsuccessful is borne out by the existence of nineteenth-century social discourses written by the black women autobiographers I discuss in this book.

Very little notice has been given to the influence of class as it affected African Americans prior to the twentieth century; the concept appears moot because of the reductive actions taken by members of the white ruling class to make blacks appear less than human and, as a result, "classless." While it is true that blacks did not participate in America's class system in traditional ways, awareness of class stratification did exist within the African American community. Some practices were adopted from the white model presented to them and some were retained from African traditions, which I will address more fully in chapter three as they pertain to the Yoruba traditions of Nigeria. However, the development of America's class system had a profound effect on race and gender positions within the society, especially in the North.

In the early decades of the nineteenth century, America was experiencing a major influx of immigrants, most of whom came from poor, working-class backgrounds. In addition, it saw growing segments of white women and free blacks entering the work force. One of the results was that the established American power force—white males born in this country—fought to hold onto their dominant positions, leading to more clear-cut delineations of class. Eric Lott claims, "The insecurity that attended class stratification produced a whole series of working-class fears about the status of whiteness; working-class men, Richard Slotkin points out, began to perceive 'the form of labor degradation in racial and sexual terms,' rejecting such degradation by affirming positions of white male superiority" (70–71). Between the years of 1825 and 1835, the Northeast witnessed the emergence of a bourgeoisie, a clear picture of a middle-class America (69). Lott further cites Karen Halttunen's thesis that antebellum sentimentalism was at the heart of the middle-class structure, a structure that then placed "the family at the center of middle-class formation—the child-rearing practices, familial values, and domestic ideologies that became . . . the 'cradle of the middle class'" (69). We can see how this emphasis would reinforce the concept of true womanhood in white American society, making the American woman—the *white* American woman—the keeper of the moral integrity of the society and, thereby, keeping her firmly situated within the domestic circle of the home and minimizing her presence in the public workplace.

In *Our Nig*, Wilson presents Mag, Frado's white mother, as a young innocent woman with aspirations of elevating herself within America's class structure: "As she merged into womanhood, unprotected, uncherished, uncared for, there fell on her ear the music of love. . . . It whispered of an elevation before unaspired to; of ease and plenty her simple heart had never dreamed of as hers. She knew the voice of her charmer, so ravishing, sounded far above her" (5–6). In her effort to "elevate" herself to a life of "ease and plenty," Mag falls, having yielded to the temptations offered by her seducer, a young white gentleman who is "above her." In this way, Wilson addresses the implication of class, showing it to be another weapon in the white-male arsenal for controlling and limiting "others." So, although Mag is white, her reduction by class is one of the elements used to make her "lesser." However, she establishes a model through which Frado soon aspires to elevate herself within the class hierarchy. For example, when Frado is first left with the Bellmonts, she is awed by the "things" she sees in the Bellmont home. At that point, she thinks that it will not be so bad benefiting from this experience. She envisions herself being elevated in class as a result of her contact with the Bellmonts.

Dr. Flint in Jacobs's *Incidents* wields added power within his community because he is a doctor, occupying a high rung in the American class structure. A similar level of power is also claimed by Mr. Sands, the white father of Linda's children, because of his positions of attorney and, later, United States congressman. Class, race, and gender protect these men, even from each other. For instance, even after Dr. Flint learns that Mr. Sands has fathered Linda's children, he cannot punish Mr. Sands as he could have retaliated against a lower-class white man or against any black man. Jacobs also demonstrates the recognition of a class structure within the black community. Aunt Marthy, for example, enjoys an elevated class status (in the eyes of both blacks and whites) because she owns her own home and because she operates within a somewhat professional public arena—as a baker and seller of her goods.

The question of class and the question of its relationship to race and gender are also addressed, although covertly, in Keckley's *Behind the Scenes*. While Keckley had established herself as an independent businesswoman, there are several instances within her personal narrative that show her behaving in a humble, even servile, manner reminiscent of the behavior of an oppressed slave. While crediting the hardships of slavery for making her a stronger person and for teaching her "youth's important lesson of self-reliance" (19–20), Keckley undermines and complicates this statement when she describes a number of incidents that, while she attempts to romanticize them, actually cast her in subservient, lower-class roles, as reflected in the following excerpts: "I never approved of ladies, attached to the Presidential household, coming to my rooms [her place of business as a dressmaker]" (152). These "ladies" commonly went to the "rooms" of white modistes; however, Keckley seems reluctant to place herself in a position that suggests that she has elevated herself above or even to the level of whites. Black women and other white women who

were, perhaps, not of the class of the "ladies" from the Presidential household came to Keckley at her "rooms," and were expected to do so. When
Andrew Johnson assumed the office of President, his daughters came to
Mrs. Keckley; she did not go to them because, in her opinion, they were
not of the same class as those in the Lincoln White House. For the
Lincolns, Keckley also was willing to perform the role of hairdresser and
servant:

> I had often combed his [Lincoln's] head. When almost ready to go to
> a reception, he would turn to me with a quizzical look: "Well,
> Madam Elizabeth, will you brush my bristles down to-night?"
>
> "Yes, Mr. Lincoln."
>
> Then he would take his seat in an easy-chair, and sit quietly while I
> arranged his hair. (202–3)

Although she was neither maid nor personal attendant to Lincoln, she was
not insulted by his familiarity and seemed pleased to perform this servile
task. While race, gender, and class are separate constructs, they are invari-
ably linked historically and socially.[15]

As America made its way closer to the Civil War, issues of class and race
took on prominence and became more closely aligned. Between 1850 and
1915, according to Joel Williamson, major shifts occurred within the three
major segments of Southern society, "the white elite, the black community, and the white masses," according to the following scenario: "At the
start of the period, the white elite had close links with the black population
through slavery, and connections that were at best tenuous and uncertain
with most whites. By the end, the white elite had abandoned blacks, destroying their voting power and rendering them 'invisible' through segregation, while bonding itself increasingly closely to lower class whites"
(512). Therefore, in the end, with Southern white men's perceived fear of
black domination, it was race, that is, whiteness, that was a defining factor
in class affiliation—whiteness superseded "class." Taylor, writing her
Reminiscences at the turn of the century, angrily addresses the lines
drawn according to race in postslavery America: "In this 'land of the free'
we are burned, tortured, and denied a fair trial, murdered for any imaginary wrong conceived in the brain of the negro-hating white man" (61).
Regardless of other considerations, it was whiteness that unified the so-

ciopolitical powers of America, and black women began to take notice from the marginalized place on which they had been situated.

Nineteenth-century African American women were faced with the formidable task of dismantling the negative connotations that the constructs of race, class, and gender placed on them. These women, as writers, squared off before such challenges and proceeded to re-shape autobiography, thereby denying the power of race, class, and gender.

Joanne Braxton places the black woman "at the center of critical discourse and her own literary experience," the current debate over centeredness and marginality notwithstanding; she accurately suggests that "the autobiography of the black American woman [is] an attempt to define a life work retrospectively and [is] a form of symbolic memory that evokes the black woman's deepest consciousness" (9–10). As a result, black women autobiographers reached beyond the oppressions of their most recent experiences—the oppressions of gender, race, and class—and called upon ancestral links in recording their life stories. Jacqueline Jones Royster cites Edmund Barry Gaither's "Heritage Reclaimed: An Historical Perspective and Chronology" in which he claims, "'Groups of slaves as well as free Africans brought to the Americas . . . possessed a framework—religious, mythical, political, historical, psychological, and ontological—from which they drew the meaning of their lives. This framework with its myriad components provided a profound sense of relationship to their ancestors, nature and the world as they knew it'" (85).

Ultimately, black women autobiographers' ability to assume a central position in claiming their voice required that they take possession of and remold the literary tools and linguistic techniques of the dominant white society. The autobiographical texts that nineteenth-century black women wrote encompassed the storytelling traditions of Africa, of the African American slave community, and of various European and European American literary genres. The results were curious and creative blendings of linguistic styles, word choices, and re-definitions. Personal narratives became creative outlets for the expression of black women's thoughts and emotions; they used limited resources to craft their works just as they used limited resources in other creative expressions—quilting, cooking, gardening, and even the act of sweeping patterns into the dirt of their yards.[16]

Displaying a subtle difference in linguistic styles and language use freed African American women autobiographers to infuse their narratives with hidden, veiled, masked meanings, meanings that they felt might represent a danger if displayed more overtly within a society that had powerful weapons for retaliation. Armed with this sense of linguistic freedom and writing a text within plain sight of white society, though apparently inchoate and in most cases indecipherable in the eyes of white readers, nineteenth-century African American women autobiographers triumphantly claimed agency for themselves and confounded the attempts of their oppressors to render them powerless. Most nineteenth-century African American autobiographers successfully encoded their texts with a private language into which other African Americans—free blacks, slaves, and former slaves—could tap. Thus, African American women's autobiographical texts represented the many ways in which the black woman, the person thought to have the least voice, managed to put forth powerful statements under the guise of an African American mother tongue, giving her, paradoxically, the greatest voice because it was a voice that white society dismissed as being inconsequential.

While the various forms of slavery and servitude had forced its intended victims to cloak themselves in secrecy, Wilson, Jacobs, Keckley, and Taylor—among others—discovered literary avenues that provided them with opportunities, although still limited, for presenting their stories. They need only reject the prevailing notions and beliefs that they—as women, as African Americans, and as poor, enslaved people—were mute and powerless.

A Patchwork of Cultures

Journeys of African American Women Autobiographers

> The tall, blond, blue-eyed, white-skinned man is shooting
> an elephant
> a native
> a wild animal
> a Black
> a woman
> a child
> somewhere
> **—Philip,** *She Tries Her Tongue*

Perhaps nothing more strongly conveys the power of African American literary tradition than tracing similarities in African American literature from the earliest days of American slavery to the present. Specifically, the American literary world has begun to look more closely at black women's slave narratives and at black women's autobiographies that emerged in the second half of the nineteenth century. Yet prior to Jean Fagan Yellin's exhaustive treatment of Harriet Jacobs's *Incidents in the Life of a Slave Girl* in the 1980s, literary critics had generally overlooked the possibility that these works might be substantial or groundbreaking. Fairly recent scholarship has led to the welcome re-discovery (and in some cases, discovery) of the primary personal narratives I treat here—Harriet Jacobs's *Incidents,* Harriet Wilson's *Our Nig,* Elizabeth Keckley's *Behind the Scenes,* and Susie King Taylor's *Reminiscences.* P. Gabrielle Foreman credits the "recognition of contemporary authors like Alice Walker, Toni Morrison, and Gloria Naylor" for a renewed interest in Jacobs and for the more recent interest in Wilson (313).

Although interest in post–Civil War black women's personal narratives—such as Keckley's and Taylor's—has been minimal, all four of these nineteenth-century African American women autobiographers are important links in a storytelling continuum that began before New World slavery. The seeds of the African American literary tradition are deeply rooted in the oral storytelling histories of the various cultures of West Africa.[1] Virtually all personal narratives written by African Americans in the nineteenth century reflect in some way both the characteristics of their spiritual and linguistic attachment to the mystic memories of Africa—the motherland—and a sense of displacement associated with the painful realities of American enslavement. Any discussion of African American women's autobiography must, therefore, take into account the historical times, places, and spaces of West African culture because, as Jacqueline Jones Royster proposes, "African American women . . . understand—whether by intuition or instinct, through the spirit or by storytelling, or by some other process—who we are, how we should see the world, how we should perceive ourselves in it, and also how we might assume the authority to speak and to act as thinkers, writers, and leaders, even in the face of contending forces within a new geographical and cultural context" (89) . I focus in this chapter on these African and Western interactions as they are seen in African American women's personal narratives in mid- to late-nineteenth-century America. I particularly explore the ways in which these intercultural echoes encourage the development of an African American mother tongue.

For African American writers, the concept of time is rooted in ancestral origins. Time in West African society is almost synonymous with timelessness because there is neither starting nor ending point.[2] Time in that tradition is recursive, cyclical, recurrent—a living thing. There is always the possibility of recovering the past because time is always turning back on itself, and this African concept of time as circular is seen also in African American narratives. Western time leads writers to see personal history as a straight line moving chronologically from the past, through the present, and on into the future; Western time is not jumbled, cluttered, or unpredictable, as time in the West African worldview tends to be. Western man tries to define time, to pin it down, and to control it, while the West African (as well as African American) approach to time is to recognize its fluid, free nature and to accept its uncontrollability. For nineteenth-century African American women autobiographers, beliefs and myths from West Africa still existed and still influenced the shaping of narratives as these writers acknowledge no temporal discontinuity between the two cultures. Karla Holloway notes that black women writers used their "texts as a vehicle for aligning real and imaginative events in both the present and the past, [thus] dissolving the temporal and spatial bridges between them" (25). Like the griots of West Africa, African American women writers have, according to John Hope Franklin and Alfred Moss, "kept in their memories the history, law, and traditions of their people" (23). These women then took traditional oral literatures, or "oratures," passed down to them through time and repetition and incorporated them into the written literary genres of their New World culture.

In Western time, most nineteenth-century African Americans were several generations removed from the cultures of West Africa. Yet memories of those cultures lived on through the beliefs and myths that were passed from one generation to the next. And memory always has a prominent place when recording one's life experiences. For nineteenth-century African Americans, this memory stretched back to West Africa through the survival of many customs, myths, and traditions. For example, one tradition that survived the Middle Passage was a respect for the elders of the community, a respect for seniority. In Yoruba tradition, hierarchy within clans was based on seniority, and seniority determined positions of power and respect. William Bascom discovered while studying the Yoruba of Southwestern Nigeria that one's biological sex was not important to status: "[C]ollateral relatives were referred to simply as 'elder sibling' or 'younger sibling,' depending on relative age" (49). In other words, the relationship between siblings, "collateral relatives," was noted in terms of seniority, not biological sexual differences; there were no words for "brother" or "sister."

When addressing the Western construct of gender, Oyèrónké Oyěwùmí reinforces the importance of seniority: "[G]ender was not an organizing principle in Yoruba society prior to colonization by the West. The social categories 'men' and 'women' were nonexistent, and hence no gender system was in place. Rather, the primary principle of social organization was seniority, defined by relative age" (31). Hierarchal power, then, was determined by factors such as one's age and one's position within the community. Jacqueline Jones writes that this respect for senior status "found new meaning among American slaves; for most women, old age brought increased influence within the slave community even as their economic value to the master declined" (40). Many of these women were descendants of the female planters and harvesters of their African motherland and in the New World took on the roles of healers, root doctors, spiritualists, and conjurers.[3] In these roles, they combined the spiritual with the material, the sacred with the profane, and as such, "these revered (and sometimes feared) women served as a tangible link" between the American present and the African past (40).

I want to address some specific customs and traditions that helped to define the Yoruba culture and which later resurfaced in the Pan-African cultures of the diaspora, customs and traditions pertaining to family, slavery, spirituality, and orality. The family was the central social, economic, and political structure of West African cultures, with the families and their respective heads forming the networks of communication and commerce within their respective villages. What is particularly relevant to my analysis, however, is the position of the married female as wife and/or mother within the family structure. In the Yoruba clan structure, "the immediate family, consisting of a man, his wives, and their children" in the polygamous family structure, is of less importance than the "sub-family, consisting of a wife and her children" (Bascom 46). This custom speaks to the powerful and protected position of the wife who bears a child, for in any dispute or disagreement, this mother is guaranteed the support of her children, who will take her side against the father's other wives and even against the father himself (46). The Yoruba subfamily is also known as "'origun,' or corner, a term which applies . . . to the lineal descendants of a grandmother or a great-grandmother" (46). The New World continuation of this matrilineal tradition is seen in black women's autobiography.

When Harriet Jacobs gives a brief history of Linda Brent's family, Linda says, "I had . . . a great treasure in my maternal grandmother"; she goes on to note that what she knows of her family history came from "the story my grandmother used to tell me" (5). Likewise, Susie King Taylor traces her lineage in *Reminiscences* through mother, grandmother, great-grandmother, and great-great-grandmother (1–2). In *Behind the Scenes,* Elizabeth Keckley, for reasons I will address later, distances herself from connections with her slave past, but she does state that she "was a child of slave parents" (17), speaks fondly of her mother, and shows remorse at not knowing the exact spot of her mother's grave. One of the more interesting and unusual echoes of West African clan structure comes from Harriet Wilson in *Our Nig.* While Frado's mother, Mag, is white, and while we are given little information regarding Mag's parentage, Wilson still privileges the matrilineal. We know much more about Mag than we know about Frado's black father, Jim. We know that Mag "*had* a loving, trusting heart," that she was "early deprived of parental guardianship," and that she was "far removed from relatives" (1*; Wilson's emphasis).

Even from this scanty background, Wilson still emphasizes the mother-child linkage, even though the mother is white.

Unlike the European American emphasis on the lineage of the husband, Franklin and Moss write that in Africa, "there was the widespread practice of tracing relationships through the mother.... [T]he woman did not legally belong to her husband, but to her own family" (16). It is my argument that this arrangement is key to the place that the African American woman eventually occupied in the slave community and, later, in European American literary society. The Western ritual of marriage during the nineteenth century defined the woman as the property of the man; she was given in marriage by one man (father, uncle, or brother) to another (husband). She was more accountable to her husband in the eyes of the law than to her own family, as she had been given away. She lost the sense of herself, of her familial continuity, and, unlike what was taking place in Yoruba tradition, the children were also the property, the charge, of the husband/father. The Yoruba wife/mother, on the other hand, retained a connectedness that was familial (not contractual). The blood relation, including that between mother and child, superseded the contract of marriage. Thus, while the Yoruba wife enjoyed a higher level of selfhood, of independence, than did her European counterpart, she also maintained a never-ending duty and responsibility to her blood relatives (that is, to her own family and to her children, not necessarily to her husband), a situation that fostered a need to maintain and support the family unit and lineage. This relationship was, thus, a result of biological connection, not societal mandate.

At the same time, however, when the Yoruba husband/father died, the wife/mother did not inherit from his personal property—there was no biological connection between them. His property was divided in approximately equal parts among his wives who had produced children, and "essentially it is the children ... who inherit, and the eldest child of each wife takes one share in the name of all the children of his [or her] mother" (Bascom 46). A childless wife "may" receive a token payment until she remarries. Interestingly enough, however, some Yoruba females who never had children could still be referred to as "mothers" if they "contributed in significant ways to their communities," for they were celebrated "as mothers of the greater society, matriarchs for the living" (Pemberton and Afolayan 45). This Yoruba tradition then establishes the important role of the mother as preserver of the community. When the African American woman wrote her personal narrative, she wrote both as an individual with a strong sense of self and as a representative of her family/community, representing a vital link in the familial network—the very network that the New World slavery system sought to obliterate. In order for New World slavery to work, the feelings of familial connections and selfhood had to be dulled, if not eliminated.

Slavery, of course, was not unique to the New World; it holds a prominent place in the histories of most, if not all, cultures, going back to biblical times and the Greek and Roman empires. However, as Franklin and Moss point out, these slaves were not merely economic investments, but personal servants for the ruling class (27). As such, "opportunities for education and cultural advancement" were often made available to them (27). The slavery systems that existed between the cultures on the continent of Africa operated in a similar manner, serving both economic and social functions. However, in African slave systems, "the children of slaves could not be sold" (18). Such was not the case, of course, with children born of African American slaves, who were viewed as valuable commodities by their owners. Franklin and Moss are among a number of historians who credit (or blame) the Renaissance (with its emphasis on new and unquestioned freedoms for the European man) and the Commercial Revolution (with its emphasis on the acquisition of wealth and power at any cost) for introducing modern slave trade and its culturally demeaning system of slavery that was to prove most destructive to West Africans. A combination of unbridled freedom and economic competition led to the "ruthless exploitation of any commodities that could be viewed as economic goods," including African slaves (28). The resultant increase in the slave trade received, in many cases, the formal support of sovereign European nations, including Portugal, Spain, and England. Even more remarkable than this governmental sanctioning of flesh-peddling was the blessing that the slave trade received from the European Christian churches.

Although spirituality was an integral part of all West African cultures, the concept of Western religion (spirits that hover outside of and over mankind and that are separate from the earth) was alien to them. For West Africans, the spirits were everywhere and in everything, whether animate or inanimate. The worship of these spirits was as never-ending as time itself and was reflected in all aspects of life—sacred and secular, historical and mythological. One of the New World myths that was derived from the Yoruba culture involves Esu, considered to be the original trickster figure from which the African American figure of the Signifying Monkey grew.[4] As Henry Louis Gates Jr. asserts, the Signifying Monkey and other

New World myths descend from Esu and "speak eloquently of the unbroken arc of metaphysical presupposition and patterns of figuration shared through space and time among black cultures in West Africa, South America, the Caribbean, and in the United States" (*Figures in Black* 237).[5] Franklin and Moss, addressing the concept of ancestor worship as the basis for early African spirituality, also stress the merging of the secular and the sacred—the merging of this world and the next: "It was devoutly believed that the spirit that dwelled in a relative was deified upon death and that it continued to live and take an active interest in the family. Not only were the spirits of deceased members of the family worshiped, but a similar high regard was held for the spirits that dwelt in the family land, the trees and the rocks in the community of the kinship group, and the sky above the community" (20).

A reference in Keckley's *Behind the Scenes* suggests an African ancestral link when she explains why she does not visit her mother's grave site: "My mother was buried in a public ground, and the marks of her grave . . . were so obscure that the spot could not be readily designated. To look upon a grave, and not feel certain whose ashes repose beneath the sod, is painful, and the doubt which mystifies you, weakens the force, if not the purity, of the love-offering from the heart" (240). Since the exact piece of earth in which her mother's body is resting cannot be identified, Keckley feels a break in the spiritual ancestral connection. Keckley's knowledge of this tradition had to have been passed on to her through her mother. This feeling recalls West African traditions and beliefs surrounding the sacredness of the burial places of family members. Keckley's reaction represents the continuation of this spiritual knowledge, a linkage of African American spirituality to that of those in the motherland and, thereby, a re-affirmation of the survival of a matriarchal heritage that encompasses the memory and storytelling passed down.

It was under the guise of spirituality—that is, religion—and Christian charity that the Portuguese and Spanish slave traders moved deep into Africa. Professing the slave trade to be a religious duty, these traders claimed that they were saving the African heathens by bringing them out of their darkness and into the healing light of Christianity: "If they were chaining Negroes together for the purpose of consigning them to a lifetime of enforced servitude, it was a 'holy cause' in which they had the blessing of both their king and their church" (Franklin and Moss 29). While Christianity was to be a major aspect of the changing culture of West Africans and the emerging culture of African Americans—in slavery and beyond—attempts to reconcile the words of Christianity with the religious practices of their European and European American oppressors would remain a problem for both Africans and African Americans, even after slavery.[6]

The system of slavery that developed in the American South is the epitome of human brutality: destruction of African and African American families; reduction of slaves to the status of animals, denying their humanity; subjection of slaves to the harshest physical, mental, and emotional traumas; and denial of slaves' ability to communicate with each other in their native tongues or through the use of drums. In the long run, the most devastating act may have been the attempt to deny slaves new skills by which they could grow and prosper as a culture within this alien Western society—access to reading and writing.

Reading and writing had not been the linguistic tools of the societies of West Africa as they were societies that relied on a complex system of oral transmission of information, history, and culture. Even when African Americans mastered and subverted the English language for their own use, they continued the practice of orally transmitting information, myths, histories, and customs, a practice that had been important in their homeland and that continued to be an important aspect of the development of African American mother tongue techniques. Holloway writes that the ties between West African sources and black writers in America allow for "an exploration of the intertextual shared images and patterns among writers with a common cultural history to emerge in the midst of the acknowledged differences between them" (20–21). West Africans who survived the Middle Passage brought the richness of their oral cultures with them, and, contrary to the beliefs and writings of some European American sociologists, specifically E. Franklin Frazier, these cultures did indeed survive and took root in the slave communities of the New World, continuing to flourish, albeit in forms varying from the West African originals.[7]

Neither the passage of time nor the displacement of West Africans erased the cultural history that arrived with them on the shores of the New World. Calling the belief that the Middle Passage created a "tabula rasa of consciousness" in the African "odd," Gates points out the obvious survival of West African cultures in customs that the captives, by will of force, refused to let die—cultural elements such as "their music, . . . their myths, their expressive institutional structures, their metaphysical systems of order, and their forms of performance" (*Signifying* 4).[8] Similarities between the animal or beast tales coming out of the slave quarters and those that have been recorded in West Africa point to Africa as being at least one site of origin for trickster tales.[9] Even more important, the existence of such tales and myths in the New World points to the survival of oral repetition in West African cultures, the basis for a sustained memory from one generation to another, from one continent to another.

As long as this transported African memory remained alive, active, and recursive, so did African myths, traditions, and customs. African American women autobiographers may not have been able to name the African origin of their storytelling traditions, but they were the beneficiaries of that sustained memory, a memory that then surfaced in the structures and linguistic techniques of their narratives. For centuries, these methods of transmission were oral and were limited to specific communities, villages, and cultures within Africa. Much of the history of early African Americans is also untraceable through formal records, for it survived as memory—not as written documents.[10] Contemporary theorists note the irony of having to use a written tradition to preserve a spoken one. But the voices of African American slaves have been salvaged because slaves and former slaves were determined to tell their own stories and because these stories were not left solely to the interpretations of other-culture anthropologists, sociologists, and historians. African American autobiographers and slave narrators, though utilizing the literary models put in place by white-male writers of "self" and by abolitionists, respectively, still managed to create a link between these Western written media and the oral legacy of their African ancestors.

There is a power in oral discourse, a linguistic power that nineteenth-century Western society minimizes and considers primitive (in the negative sense) because of the high value that European-based society places on the written word. Writing that "those in power control 'domains of knowledge,'" Freida High W. Tesfagiorgis cites the theories of Foucault to show how oral histories and oral linguistic traditions are judged as being "located low down on the hierarchy, beneath the required level of cognition or scientificity" (238). Toni Morrison notes that the cultures of Africa were further minimized by destructive comments from highly regarded scholars such as Georg Wilhelm Friedrich Hegel, who claimed in 1813 that "Africans had no 'history' and couldn't write in modern languages," implying again that such illiteracy was evidence of the Africans' cultural and intellectual inferiority (108). In this way, written history and literary discourse were aggrandized while the oral discourses of cultures like the

Yoruba, discourses stored in the memories of griots and mothers, were labeled inferior.

I specifically mention mothers here because of the role that the Yoruba mother played in sustaining many of the oral traditions. Holloway traces this tradition through African and African American histories, writing that in many West African societies, "[storytellers] were women and their stories and songs were the oral archives of their culture" (24). Jacqueline Jones Royster points to "traces, faint or strong, of the historical connections between the lives of African women . . . and the lives that African American women assumed in the United States" to explain the continuation of the role of black women as "storytellers, members of the community who taught the parables" (90, 101). This is not to suggest that men did not tell stories in the Yoruba culture, for they did. But as Holloway implies and as Ifi Amadiume states, it was generally the women in Yoruba society who "transmitted cultural ideas and their own comments on them through stories as well as songs" (84).[11] Amadiume notes that the stories told by men tended to deal with "wars, travel, adventures with spirits." The stories women told, whether they were told by biological mothers or community mothers, sustained the importance of culture, beliefs, traditions, and heritage.

According to Wole Soyinka, "Morality for the Yoruba is that which creates harmony in the cosmos" (156). Thus, Yoruba women, as the teachers of ethics and morality through their practice of storytelling, may also be seen to represent the cohesive element that ensures harmony, not only within the community but also throughout the "cosmos." The Yoruba oral tradition reinforces the idea of a woman's role in maintaining harmony and happiness through the analogy of the mother's maintenance of a safe, warm environment for her children. Amadiume points out that the majority of the stories told by both men and women glorified motherhood "by showing the suffering and loneliness of children who had no mother" (84). The disruption of the Yoruba mother/child unit, then, is analogous to the disruption of the community, an analogy repeated in the black familial disruptions brought about by New World slavery. We can see this pattern of disruption played out in the writings of nineteenth-century African American women autobiographers.

All four of the primary autobiographers I address are affected by and reflect in their personal narratives the results of such disruptions. Wilson's Frado, abandoned by her mother, never recovers from her feelings of loneliness and isolation. Jacobs's Linda suffers from being or-

phaned early in life and, because of the inhumanity of slavery, must isolate herself from her children in order to try to secure their freedom.
Young Lizzie lives in the shadow of the white master's children on whom
her mother dotes, and she later seems to neglect her own child while privileging the Lincoln children. And Susie King Taylor, who as a child lost
contact with her mother because of slavery and the unstable years of the
Civil War, is so consumed with her own survival after the war and so
lacking in maternal role models that she appears to pay little attention to
the child she bore. All four women, however, represent a continuation of
a Yoruba tradition—for all were mothers and, by virtue of producing a
personal narrative, storytellers as well. Unfortunately, because of the
breakdown of mother-child links caused by enslavement and other related
oppressive conditions, their roles as "community" storytellers were subverted. Wilson's son dies while he is still a child; Keckley's son dies in the
Civil War, leaving no heirs; and Taylor's son dies of yellow fever, with
Taylor making no mention of grandchildren. With the exception of Jacobs,
then, who was able to establish a continuing relationship with her daughter once they both reached the North, these other three black mothers
were unable to pass their stories directly to their children; however, the
continuum was not altogether broken, because through their personal
narratives, all four autobiographers made sure that their stories reached
us.

The memories of African women resurfaced in the memories and in
the oratures and literatures of their African American sisters. The combination of these shared memories and the verbal arts they embodied gave
nineteenth-century African American women writers the communicative
tools they needed to restructure the language of the oppressors. African
American women writers used the vehicle of the myth, according to
Holloway, to "vitalize language, giving it a presence outside of the inter-
pretative mode and forcing its significance to a level where the community's shared meanings are the basis of its understandings and interactions with both the spiritual and the physical worlds" (31).[12]

When nineteenth-century African American women autobiographers
altered the English language to characterize their ways of speaking, they
redefined the various places, spaces, and gaps they occupied in the world.
The ability to claim the written word gave them agency and fostered
their literary creativity. When African American women writers "imagina-
tively engage this English language in their text[s], the sociocultural history in these words requires the processes of revision. . . . Ownership of

the creative word means making these words work in cultural and gendered ways that undermine the hegemony of the West" (Holloway 27). African American women autobiographers re-define issues of race and gender in their subversion of negative terms and definitions that European American men have established to limit their humanity, to render them silent and voiceless. Those demeaning tactics did not work in the nineteenth century any better than they work today. As Oyĕwùmí has noted, the concept of gender (the elevation of the male ["okùnrin"] to a higher level in the sociopolitical structure over the female ["obìnrin"] simply because of his anatomical difference) did not even exist in Yoruba culture prior to European colonization: "[T]he colonizer differentiated between male and female bodies and acted accordingly. Men were the primary target of policy, and, as such, they were the natives and so were visible. . . . Thus, in the colonial situation, there was a hierarchy of four, not two, categories. Beginning at the top, these were: men (European), women (European), native (African men), and Other (African women)" (122).[13] Although historically there were female chiefs as well as male chiefs in the Yoruba tradition and with no lesser power, European men refused to recognize their leadership, simply because they were "women." As a result, many male chiefs assumed that their positions within the Yoruba society should be elevated, simply because they were "men," in accordance with the European ideology that had invaded Yoruba society.

The centuries-old social structures of West African cultures were strong enough, however, to avoid the total erasure of their traditions and mores. While the African woman's voice may have been shut out of the colonial public sphere and while the colonizers may have ignored her voice altogether, she was never silenced. For instance, citing from Henry Drewal, John Pemberton writes in "The Dreadful God and the Divine King" that in the traditional festival honoring the spirit "Ògún," while the crown placed on the king's head is symbolic of his power, the large bird perched at the top of the crown represents "the vital force possessed by females (living, ancestral, deified), collectively known as 'our mothers'" (123). Pemberton further points out that the crown is placed on the king's head by his senior wife, "who possesses the covert power of 'the mothers'" (138–39).

In the secular realm, there is also evidence and acknowledgment that the African woman successfully resisted silencing by males. Amadiume records that in modern Nnobi society, women are very vocal and respected: "The women have always monopolized singing and dancing during most ceremonies. Sometimes, their songs contained statements from dominant Nnobi models which they shared with the men. At others they contained ideas generated by the women as commentaries on dominant ideas or as statements of facts from the woman's point of view. Nnobi women were not, and are still not, tongue-tied" (69).[14] Amadiume further illustrates colonization's failure to render the African woman mute by noting that the Nnobi woman's involvement and "prominence in public rituals and ceremonies" gives her "access to the medium of communication" and, thereby, to the "ideology-making processes and the management of meaning" (70). The refusal on the part of black women in America to be silenced has its roots buried deeply in the paradigm of resistance established hundreds of years ago and thousands of miles away by their African foremothers. This resistance was embraced by nineteenth-century African American women autobiographers who also were not "tongue-tied."

The journey of African American women autobiographers was as much figurative as literal. Figuratively, they combined the memories of West African verbal arts with African American folktales, slave narratives, and European American sentimental, seduction, and adventure narratives. Literally, their travels extended from their African motherland, through the Southern slave plantation, to the Northern free states (Wilson's literal journey, of course, did not follow this same route, but it did entail a physical journey as she moved from the locus of her indentureship to other Northern locations that represented her freedom). The figurative and literal journeys are also characterized by intricate intermediary movements. Figuratively, these women commandeered bits and pieces of existing literary and communicative techniques, patiently altering and restructuring them to create the unique literary gaps from which black women writers' voices would speak. Literally, enslaved African American women moved to a number of intermediary locations within each primary site that they occupied. For instance, within the major site of plantation slavery, slave women (Jacobs, Keckley, and Taylor in this case) moved from the fields, to the slave quarters, to the "big house," to the nearby towns, to other plantations, and so forth. Wilson's intermediary physical movements were similar: from the "white house" (and her garretlike room within it), to the fields, to the barn, to school, to church, et cetera. As a result, black women were always and at once occupying new places and the spaces that these shifts created. At the same time, these constant transitions allowed them a unique view of the operations of the power-holders from the various geographical sites they occupied, just as their use of different genres brought them into contact with the various literary forms that flourished during their time.

What emerges from these figurative and literal journeys is a singular blending of oral and written literary genres and rhetorical techniques that allows African American women writers to speak in voices unique to their experiences. The merging of African orality with European written genres occupies an important place in American literature. Bernard Bell writes that "residual elements of the oral tradition of Africa, each fulfilling a psychological and social need in the lives of the slaves, fused with white American culture and created a new system of shared symbols that, even though complementary, was different in pattern and emphases from both its European and African antecedents" (17).[15] Therefore, the double-consciousness of African Americans proposed by W.E.B. DuBois is both created by and is a result of this merging of cultures. The place occupied by the African American woman, however, constantly shifts within this dominant European American culture—a shifting more far-reaching than those affecting the places occupied by white men (with their privilege of whiteness and maleness), or white women (with their privilege of whiteness), or black men (with their privilege of maleness).

Like the tectonic plates of the ocean's floor—those large, shifting land masses that cause the earth to quake and re-align itself—American society is made up of shifting cultures and ideologies. We witness throughout the nineteenth century the shifting of various racial and gender attitudes, class structures, sociopolitical positions, and economic theories and practices in America, causing the footing of African American women to be slippery and unsure. As a result, DuBois's double-consciousness, for them, increases manyfold. In addition to the multiple positioning created by the European/African merger of customs, traditions, and histories, they must also contend with their place in society as women, as African American women, in many cases as poor African American women, and sometimes as poor African American women who are also mothers. When these women enter the public sphere as writers, they must make a space for themselves in a world that largely excludes them. Their multiconsciousness creates what Gwendolyn Etter-Lewis calls a "multilayered reality" that exists within African American women: "On one level is an overwhelming silence, a complete systemic envelopment that renders African American women all but invisible. Yet they have been present all the while, whispering and shouting in their own resonant voices" ("Work Place" 156).[16]

Being situated on the margins of American society gave African American women autobiographers an advantage in that they were able to observe much of what was happening within a society from which they were virtually excluded; they were not invisible to members of the dominant society, but because they were not deemed worthy of much concern, members of the dominant society took little notice of them or of the discourses they were producing. They found ways, therefore, to maneuver. For the creator of a personal narrative, write Sidonie Smith and Julia Watson, "The autobiographical occasion . . . became a site on which cultural ideologies intersect and dissect one another, in contradiction, consonance, and adjacency. Thus the site is rife with diverse potentials" (xix). If we picture society as a sphere wherein white men have situated themselves at the center, leaving women and people of color to circle the perimeter, occasionally passing through the core to reach the other side of the circle, we can see the potential for these "others" to appropriate spaces outside the notice of centered white men. And as these "others" interact with each other, they are able to form connections (of varying degrees of strength and longevity) and ideologies that transform, and sometimes mutate, the basic core of white-male-generated ideologies and linguistic meanings. Smith and Watson suggest that "to enter into language is to press back against total inscription in dominating structures" and that by using autobiographical practices to "go against the grain" of the traditional white-male autobiography, women autobiographers "may constitute an 'I' that becomes a place of creative and, by implication, political intervention" (xix). Women writers who write themselves into their texts are then no longer merely female objects to be directed by male subjects.

The nineteenth-century white-male denial or minimization of women's personal narratives was instrumental in perpetuating their marginalization and in belittling their contributions to literature and to society. There has been much recent debate about the implications of using such loaded terms as "margin" and "center" in discussing relationships between the oppressed and the oppressors. Is it possible to discuss the differences between margin and center without inadvertently privileging the primacy of the center? Analouise Keating addresses this question in her essay, "(De)Centering the Margins? Identity Politics and Tactical (Re)Naming," noting that the very language used by theorists in contemporary U.S. literary and ethnic studies "reinforces a problematic binary structure, thus undermining the goals they seek to achieve" (23). Some years earlier, Gates considered this margin/center binary, concluding that because the center in effect defines the margin, the dominant hegemony, that is, the center, determines the margin's "privileged site of cultural critique" ("Ethnic and Minority" 298). He too concluded that as long as the "others" (another contested term) along the margin continue to measure themselves by privileging the center (the white man) as the point of comparison, the power will remain with the center while the various "others" continue "breeding new margins within margins" that will not only emphasize differences but also possibly lead to fragmentation (298).

While Keating concurs that such binaries suggest that the "marginal becomes a reified oppositional . . . position, defined (and thus controlled) by the invisible center," she also asks a very important question: "What happens when the self-identified other neither dissolves nor maintains all inside/outside oppositions?" (24). Keating's question raises two points. First, the term "self-identified other" suggests a willing, purposeful move on the part of the "other" to name and to embrace the characteristics by which she/he has determined to be identified. In other words, this "other," this victim of oppression, assumes a position of empowerment because of, rather than in spite of, this otherness. Second, while Gates sees the possible fragmentation of "others" as a negative, Keating notes the very real possibilities that these "others" will *not* "dissolve," that is, disappear, and also that the line between inside and outside is not impenetrable. As a matter of fact, if I read Keating correctly, not only will there be more "others" to attack the integrity of the center because of continuing fragmentation but also there will be a constant movement of "others" from margin to center, and back again, movements from different points along the margin and from different categories of "other." The assaults upon the center will eventually become so numerous and indefensible as to confound, and possibly destroy, the whole idea of a "center."

When members of disempowered groups pick up pens and write themselves into existence, they are attacking the center. Women writing in nineteenth-century America challenged the gendered center by asserting that they were important subjects. As Renae Moore Bredin writes, these women, both black and white, used their pens as "tools of resistance" to break the silence imposed upon them by white men (228). Black women, however, were attacking a racialized as well as a gendered center. Theirs was a "surprise attack across the borders of racial demarcation/categorization" (229). I noted earlier Keating's reference to an "invisible center." What makes the center invisible is its whiteness. Bredin writes, "Whiteness, according to 'white' folks such as Richard Dyer . . . is scripted as 'everything and nothing, [which] is the source of its representational power.' It is 'invisible because it is *natural*,' 'colourless multi-colouredness,' and is read as the positive pole in the binaries of modernity/backwardness, reason/irrationality, order/chaos, stability/violence, and most specifically for Dyer, masculine, not feminine" (229; Bredin's emphasis).[17] Most scholars, critics, and writers who challenge the central or positive pole position occupied by white men rally around the need to deconstruct the notion of whiteness and maleness as the norms by which "others" are measured (and measure themselves). Should that ever happen, what would then become the new measuring stick, or will we be able to dispense with the need for one? Would we be satisfied with not establishing ways to exclude—points of comparison? Would we benignly agree not to notice or discuss differences, or if we do, not in a qualitative manner? Would we, individually and collectively, resist the temptations to compare our various characteristics with those of others in an attempt to justify our own worthiness? Would those of us labeled "other," in the end, be able to resist trying to build our own towers of Babel after toppling that of white men?

There are, of course, no definitive answers to these questions, and there is not enough space here for the full philosophical, philological, and psychological discussion they warrant. But it is clear that as long as one group is considered normal, worthy, and in control of determining meaning while any others are considered abnormal, unworthy, and incapable of original thought, we will have the task of trying to equalize the situation. For now, that task involves demystifying whiteness. According to Bredin, we need to make whiteness the "focus of study" so that we can "denaturalize" it. She cites from Marilyn Frye's *The Politics of Reality: Essays in Feminist Theory*, adopting Frye's term, "whiteliness," and pointing out that "'whiteliness' [is] not a matter of skin color but of a 'deeply ingrained way of being in the world,' . . . of being 'judge . . . peacemaker . . . preacher . . . martyr' by virtue of the superiority or privilege accruing to whiteliness" (Bredin 230). Once we denaturalize whiteness so that we do not expect our political leaders and our "saviors" to be white, we can move beyond at least that one set of oppositional points.

At this juncture, those points still exist, just as they existed in nineteenth-century America—although marginality has now become problematic for the center. While marginality continues to evoke debates about reification, in nineteenth-century America, those who were considered (or who considered themselves) marginal refused to be locked into fixed locations. As Carla L. Peterson sees it, positions along the periphery tended to "move and slide along the circumference [and] black women . . . repeatedly shifted approaches, strategies, and venues as they sought to achieve their goals of racial uplift" ("Doers" 185). They began to re-write history in order to uncover and to credit the woman's story and role in the literary development of personal narratives. Smith and Watson write that "in order to unstick both . . . man and his meanings, we need to adjust, to reframe, our understanding of both traditional and countertraditional autobiographical practices" (xviii). If autobiographical discourses, personal narratives, and other discourses of identity are "heterogeneous even in their seeming hegemony, then we make a space in autobiographical practices for the agency of the autobiographical subject" (xx), be that subject the European American woman, the African American man, or the often-disregarded African American woman. Once black women autobiographers see themselves as subjects and assume authority over their literary as well as their oral texts, they are better able to look inward for their creative inspiration and present it in a form that celebrates both literacy and orality. Their autobiographies, then, become more than just literary exercises; they take on the power and responsibility of being social discourses, too, which challenge the existing assumptions about what is normal, worthy, and meaningful in assessing "personhood."

The so-called silence of nineteenth-century African American women actually spoke volumes. Using their forced placement on the periphery of American white-male-dominated society to observe the shifting of societal attitudes, they eventually merged the knowledge they obtained with the mythical memories passed on to them by their foremothers. African American women autobiographers then told their stories, stories hidden under a complex linguistic re-structuring of oral storytelling techniques and masked behind a veil of silence. The more we explore the writing of women, the more we see that much of woman's so-called silence was labeled as such by a male society that refused to hear her voice, a matter addressed by Abena P. A. Busia in "Silencing Sycorax":

> The systematic refusal to hear our speech is not the same thing as our silence. That we have hitherto been spoken of as absent or silenced does not mean we have been so. . . . The systematic refusal to

hear our speech which colonial literature mirrors, though it has historically removed us from the nexus of certain kinds of power, does not and never actually could render us silent. In unmasking the dispossessions of the silences of fiction and the fictions of silence, we (re)construct self-understanding. Furthermore, for women, "Narrative" is not always and only, or even necessarily, a speech act. We women signify: we have many modes of (re)dress. (103–4)

Of course, to be silenced and to use silence are two vastly different matters. The former implies objectification; the latter suggests the assumption of agency, making one's self an active subject. Silence was and remains an important communicative tool for women. However, socially constructed men and women interpret silence differently. While man has taken the concept of silence, characterized it as being negative and powerless, and then (calling it "feminine") used it to justify the subjugation and oppression of women, woman has taken possession of this attempt to repress her, empowered it with her secret voice, and made it a central weapon in her battle to claim and establish her presence. She made it a tool of the mother tongue. As I've noted before, all nineteenth-century American women, black and white, used silence both defensively and offensively. Women who were not silent, who spoke too much, who spoke about inappropriate "public" topics, who evidenced dissatisfaction with domestic roles, were often labeled hysterical or diagnosed as having some type of illness requiring the attentions of a doctor (male) to prescribe a healing potion. Charlotte Perkins Gilman cites in her autobiographical work, *Living*, the following advice from her doctor: "'Live as domestic a life as possible. Have your child with you all the time. . . . Lie down an hour after each meal. Have but two hours' intellectual life a day. And never touch pen, brush or pencil as long as you live'" (96). Embodied in this statement is more than white men's reductive action against women; there is a fear here—a fear of the power that women might assume if white men were not vigilant in keeping them silent and in denying them access to the written word.

African American women appropriated the English language in the same way that all women have appropriated silence, claiming it and then using it to their advantage. They molded and reshaped it. They turned parts of it upside down, or backwards, or eliminated parts altogether. They took the product created by this operation and encoded it with messages and suggestions, making the word (as they had made silence) "both a tool and a weapon to correct, to create, and to confirm [their] visions of life as it was and as it could become" (Foster, *Written* 2). These messages, like the concept of sacred time that exists in black women's West African culture, simultaneously stretched backwards and reached forward, repeating and revising along the way. And the codes that alter or reverse apparent meanings have survived and perhaps were strengthened by the oppressivity of the American slave system. The secrecy that was necessarily a defensive mechanism in the slave community manifested itself in the codes employed by nineteenth-century African American women autobiographers. In order to get to the core of meaning, a reader needed to know and understand the various codes and signs—which ones contained additional or different meanings and which ones did not. These "multilevels of meanings in African American speech," according to Gwendolyn Etter-Lewis, "indicate that surface structures must not be regarded as direct and complete representations of a speaker's intended message. Words alone and in isolation of context are not as informative as words immersed in the richness of personal experience" ("Work Place" 158). The stated message (or written message) and the intended message are not necessarily synonymous. As will become evident in the next chapter and in my close readings of Wilson, Jacobs, Keckley, and Taylor, coded silences and secrecy join a host of other communicative devices as significant tools of the mother tongue.

Until the middle of the nineteenth century, most autobiography celebrated the superiority of white men's contributions to life and society. Making no apparent contributions to that society, women were not deemed worthy of celebration. Autobiography is "the space into which the writing subject disappears," but it honors the passing man while the "woman autobiographer, . . . caught in the act of self-representation, disappears without a trace" (Gilmore 90–91). Many white women autobiographers suffered anxieties over this exclusion and minimization. But black women autobiographers, already excluded from the sociopolitical workings of a European American society, continued to operate from the periphery, escaping, because of their multileveled invisibility, the anxiety experienced by their white sisters.[18] Removed from white men's observing and judgmental eye, they re-created autobiography, and in doing so, re-created themselves, denying the stereotypes that denied their humanity. Their texts, in turn, also denied the minstrel stereotypes that portrayed them either as licentious harlots or as fat, breeding mammy figures. In "Images, Ideology, and Women of Color," Leith Mullings writes that the European American vision of African American women cast them as "(1) 'Jezebel,' the sexually aggressive, provocative woman governed entirely by libido; and (2) 'Mammy,' the religious, loyal, motherly slave devoted to the care of the slaveowner's family" (267).[19] African American women were not, and never could be, "true" women. Unlike European American women, black women received no social privileges for being women and none for being mothers. And unlike the practices of the Yoruba tradition, the children of nineteenth-century slave women could not protect them as their mothers.

Left to fend for themselves in most cases, African American women were forced to develop their own mechanisms to protect their families, their communities, their culture, and themselves. They devised ways to resist sexual, physical, and emotional oppressions. Although not always successful, they were at times able to launch their own attacks with positive results. Oppression inevitably leads to resistance, as noted by Foucault in *The History of Sexuality:* "Where there is power, there is resistance. . . . These points of resistance are present everywhere in the power network. . . . [T]he swarm of points of resistance traverses social stratifications and individual unities. . . . [T]he strategic codification of these points of resistance makes a revolution possible" (95–96). Nineteenth-century African American women autobiographers traversed such "points of resistance." They began to write, but not just about being victims of brutality and rape, because they saw themselves as more than victims. They were often victorious in claiming power over their bodies and over their voices, and they celebrated their victories by writing about the "strength with which [African American women] met [the] force" of European American oppression and withstood it (Foster, *Witnessing* xxxiv).

Nineteenth-century African American women were able to foster the continuation of African-linked social structures through their command of the word, that is, the oral traditions that they knew and continued to develop within and between African American communities. Etter-Lewis writes that African American women autobiographers "situate themselves and/or their generation within the context of the family's past" ("Inside Out" 176). These black women are links who remind the members of their families and communities of the recursive, sacred nature of life and time: "Words and phrases of family stories were embedded in the bonds of kinship and in the spirit of survival. African American oral family histories are significant not only because of their sociohistorical content, but also because of their function as means of establishing group solidarity" (171). The oral traditions within African American communities made it possible for blacks to resist slavery's effort to erase their cultures.

In writing their personal narratives, nineteenth-century African American women describe the devastating effects of the peculiar institution of slavery and racism on their communities. Their battles involved overcoming the barriers that denied them the political avenues and economic resources to publish their stories. The freedom to write was firmly connected with power politics, so African American women autobiographers had to become political, had to find ways to fool the system, or at least manipulate it to their advantage. If the power inherent in freedom of speech can be denied to a particular segment of a society, people within that segment can be effectively silenced. Foucault writes, "In appearance, speech may well be of little account, but the prohibitions surrounding it soon reveal its link with desire and power. . . . Speech is not merely the medium which manifests—or dissembles—desire; it is also the object of desire. . . . Historians have constantly impressed upon us that speech is no mere verbalization of conflicts and systems of domination, but that it is the very object of man's conflicts" (*Archaeology* 216). Foucault presupposes that these conflicts are between men (white men) and are highly political. When women enter the conflict, and when those women are African American, men (white men) are at once surprised, amused, uninterested, and (ultimately) resistant. However, when these women write down their speech, it becomes impossible for white men to ignore or deny this speech indefinitely, and black women writers become forces to be suppressed if the white power structure is to be maintained.

Black women writing autobiography in the nineteenth century wrote out of anger, frustration, desperation, and defiance. While African American men who escaped slavery and wrote narratives about their lives and their ordeals were characterized as "articulate heroes," Joanne Braxton suggests that "we consider as a counterpart to the articulate hero the archetype of the outraged mother. She is mother because motherhood was virtually unavoidable under slavery; she is outraged because of the intimacy of her oppression" (19).[20] African Americans, both men and women, went through rites of passage in their respective journeys to freedom and/or adulthood. Yet many black women (or more accurately, black girls) were forced to move from the sexual innocence of childhood to the sexual awareness of adulthood at the onset of puberty through intrusive violations of their bodies. While these young black girls usually lost the battle and were raped at the hands of slave owners, masters, overseers, or other white men, the battle made them aware of the realities and dangers of the Southern slave system and of racism, an awareness that usually strengthened their ties with their black communities. The rites of passage that involved the physical journey to freedom was generally a movement from the South to the North, from rural (or small town) to urban. Such a journey was more difficult for slave women traveling alone than for slave men, yet many of these women, displaying as much heroic stamina as found in the black male "articulate heroes," were able to complete it. These slave women were more than just individuals who could strike out alone with no ties to detain them; they were mothers, sisters, and daughters. Yet despite the strength of these ties to family in the Southern slave communities, many of these women could not deny the hunger for freedom.

Having survived various delays and impediments in their quests for freedom, many slaves who successfully completed their physical journeys and reached Pennsylvania, New York, Massachusetts, or some other Northern state that held the promise of peace and equality, found the land of Canaan to be a disappointment, for they encountered the racism and color prejudice with which Northern-born Harriet Wilson was all too familiar. Slave narratives published between the years of 1850 and 1865 show that these literate, educated former slaves were increasingly frustrated by the limited freedom and equality that the North actually afforded them. In her slave-narrative-like autobiography, Wilson refers specifically to the hypocrisy of Northern abolitionists and antislavery activists "who did n't want slaves at the South, nor niggers in their own houses, North" (129). Jacobs's Linda Brent experiences the disappointment of discovering a racially biased North soon after arriving in the land of the free. When she attempts to secure first-class passage on a Philadelphia train, she finds that no amount of money can purchase her equal treatment: "This was the first chill to my enthusiasm about the Free states. Colored people were allowed to ride in a filthy box, behind white people, at the south, but there they were not required to pay for the privilege. It made me sad to find how the north aped the customs of slavery" (162–63).

Perhaps attitudes and laws in the North provided a more welcoming climate for blacks after the Civil War, for in their postbellum narratives, neither Keckley nor Taylor overtly suggest encountering much unjust treatment in the North as a result of their being black. Although Taylor is very angry when recounting incidents of racism she experiences in the postwar South, the few instances of color prejudice mentioned in relation to the North by both Keckley and Taylor are simply stated, with no apparent tone of bitterness. For instance, on the occasion of President Lincoln's second inauguration, Keckley notes that "orders were issued not to admit [colored people]" to the official ball (158). This statement is followed by no angry comment or expression of outrage. On the contrary, Keckley proceeds to describe how a white congressman, seeing Frederick Douglass in the crowd of blacks outside the White House, appealed to the President and gained entrance for Mr. Douglass to the gala, an incident that, Keckley writes, gave "great pleasure to myself and others" (160). Taylor goes so far as to suggest that she rode unsegregated public transportation in the North after the Civil War, experiencing "Jim Crow" treatment only when, traveling to Louisiana to visit her dying son, she was about to board a train out of Cincinnati that was going into the Southern states:

> [O]n the sixth of February I left Boston to go to him. I reached Cincinnati on the eighth.... I asked a white man standing near ... what car I should take. "Take that one," he said.... "But that is a smoking car!" "Well," he replied, "that is the car for colored people." (69)

After the death of her son, Taylor observes on her return trip from Louisiana to Boston:

> [When] we reached the Ohio River, ... the door was opened and the porter passed through, saying, "The Ohio River! change to the other car." I thought, "... We have been riding all this distance in separate cars, and now we are all to sit together." Why not let the negroes, if their appearance and respectability warrant it, be allowed to ride as they do in the North, East, or West? (74)

But again, these apparently loosened restrictions being attributed to the North occur after the Civil War. Prior to 1865, blacks living in or arriving in most areas in the North found their liberties limited. They were free from the chains of slavery (providing they were not betrayed and returned to their former owners), but they were still shackled by the stigma of racial inferiority that Northern whites, including many abolitionists, used to bind them. As a result, the slave narratives published in the 1850s and through the Civil War reflect a "deepening sense of frustration and injustice," according to William L. Andrews. He writes, "It is not surprising to discover black autobiographers increasingly depicting their fugitive careers as a lingering limbo of dreams deferred, not as a linear quest lead-ing to a new world" (*Free Story* 179). Black equality, the expected pot of gold at the end of the rainbow, was nonexistent.

The North, this place that was supposed to represent a return, literally and figuratively, to freedom, proved to be an intermediary site on that journey, somewhere between freedom and slavery. And while "black women have been recording and influencing American history since their earliest arrival upon these shores," these late-nineteenth-century black women autobiographers initiated an even more direct entry into the so-ciopolitical arenas of European American society (Foster, *Written* 1). Afri-can American women autobiographers expressed sometimes veiled, sometimes direct, challenges to their predominantly white readerships on this score. Gates asserts that "the black English vernacular, as early as [1828], was a sign of black difference, blackness of tongue" (*Signifying* 92), and Braxton reinforces this concept when she cites the words of Temma Kaplan: "'The mother tongue is not just the words or even the array of cultural symbols available to a people to resist its tormentors. The mother tongue *is* the oral tradition'" (quoted in Braxton 5; Kaplan's em-phasis). Fortified by the mystical and mythical forces of sacred time, the figurative and literal assumption of places within the literary network of European American society, and the occupation—and sometimes cre-ation—of spaces and gaps within this network, nineteenth-century Afri-can American women autobiographers gradually developed, defined, and forced the emergence of an African American mother tongue. Its screams and its silences, its fluidity and its stillness, its clarity and its opaqueness at once offer and refuse entry into a system of communication that was uniquely a part of the accumulated cultures of African American women.

4

The Emergence of an African American Mother Tongue

English is
my father tongue.
A father tongue is
a foreign language,
therefore English is
a foreign language
not a mother tongue.

—Philip, *She Tries Her Tongue*

The autobiographical form, despite its inherent conflict between the individual self and the collective voices of the community, remained the primary vehicle of literary expression for many mid-nineteenth-century African American women. Each of the four primary black women autobiographers I treat in this study had some specific sociopolitical goals in mind as she set pen to paper. Through *Our Nig*, Wilson wanted to show that racial abuse was just as prominent in the North as it was in the South. Jacobs used *Incidents* to expose the sexual exploitation of slave women and the destruction of black slave families; her hope was that her Northern white sisters would become involved and actively denounce slavery. The two postbellum narratives, Keckley's *Behind the Scenes* and Taylor's *Reminiscences,* focused more on self-reliance and on the contributions of African Americans in the making of "America." And while Keckley's autobiography also addresses the first thirty years of her life in slavery, her emphasis is clearly placed on the life she made for herself after gaining her freedom. Taylor's narrative, published thirty-six years after the conclusion of the Civil War, establishes the chronology of her former slave status more as a historical reference point than as an issue to engage her readers. Like Keckley, she emphasizes the contributions that African Americans had made and were continuing to make in the building and healing of the United States of America. Each of these four women, in varying degrees, saw herself situated within her African American community as well as within the broader scope of an American community that, thus far, had been defined by a dominant European American culture. As she sought to find a way to tell her story, each African American woman autobiographer had to create new ways of expression—each had to develop an African American mother tongue.

One would expect a narrative written by a former female slave to highlight the brutalities associated with the slavery system of the American Southern states. To find such brutalities documented in an autobiographical text written by a free black woman of the American North was less expected. But such was the case when Wilson published *Our Nig; or, Sketches from the Life of a Free Black, in a Two-Story White House, North. Showing that Slavery's Shadows Fall Even There*, by "Our Nig" in 1859. Published two years earlier than Jacobs's more widely known *Incidents in the Life of a Slave Girl, Written by Herself, Our Nig* is a forceful and at times cunning attack on the hypocrisy of nineteenth-century Northern whites, especially those purporting to be Christian and sympathetic to the abolitionist cause. Among narratives written by former slaves, Jacobs's *Incidents* is also unique. Commonly regarded as the only extant slave narrative written by a runaway slave woman of antebellum America, *Incidents*, in addition to addressing the brutalities of slavery in general, also concerns itself with the intimate details of the special sexual horrors to which the slave woman was subjected. Also, along with Wilson's *Our Nig, Incidents* represents one of the more prominent examples of a black woman writer's merger of various literary styles to create a new American literary form and, in doing so, take on the role of social critic as well as author. Both of these antebellum women borrowed from the genres of the slave narrative, the sentimental novel, and the autobiography, with Jacobs occasionally drawing from the adventure narrative and Wilson from the gothic novel and captivity narrative.

In their rejection of the linguistic limitations characteristic of the established literary genres of their time, Wilson and Jacobs show that no one literary style was broad enough, flexible enough, or complex enough to contain the sadness, rage, frustration, pain, and joy of their lives in pre–Civil War America. Within none of those genres alone could either of these pre-emancipation African American women autobiographers adequately express her existence. Elizabeth Breau has suggested that in his introduction to *Our Nig*, Henry Louis Gates Jr. minimizes Wilson's creative abilities: "The picture drawn of Wilson in Gates' Introduction is . . . not that of a creative writer comfortably in control of her material, but instead that of a nearly illiterate woman who stumbled onto originality because her life story—the only story she was equipped to tell—did not conform entirely to contemporary literary convention" (455). However, I suggest that Gates's point is not that Wilson lacked the ability to follow an established literary style, but that she purposefully *chose* not to do so, that the presentation of her own narrative style is indicative of the inadequacy of "contemporary literary convention" and indicative of her need to create a tongue rich enough to address the breadth of her experiences and her emotions. Rather than disparaging Wilson's literary abilities, Gates acknowledges that much of what Wilson does with the subversion of plots and techniques is a creative and conscious act: "These significant discrepancies of plot development suggest that the author of *Our Nig* created a novel that partakes of the received structure of American women's fiction, but often inverts that same structure, ironically enough, precisely at its most crucial points. Harriet E. Wilson used the plot structure of her contemporary white female novelists, yet abandoned that structure when it failed to satisfy the needs of her well-crafted tale" (xlvi).

Our Nig, so long regarded as a work of fiction instead of the autobiographical narrative that it has been proven to be, is deeply steeped in the language and linguistic patterns of the sentimental novel. But its highly critical attacks on the cultural politics of the North also take it into the realm of the haunting and haunted voices of the gothic novel. Julia Stern writes that while the sentimental frame of *Our Nig* "attempts to function as a structure of containment, it cannot quite suppress, and indeed underscores, the gothic protest seething beneath the narrative's surface" (439). Briefly defined, the gothic novel is a nineteenth-century genre characterized by a gloomy setting, grotesque, mysterious, or violent events, and an atmosphere of degeneration and decay. This gothic presence speaks to the isolation that Frado experiences, to the violence that is so much a part of her young life, and to the degenerative death and destruction that beset the Bellmont family. The prominent gothic elements that surface in *Our Nig* include the distraught heroine (Frado), the forbidding mansion with a prisonlike upper room (the "two-story white house" and Frado's little L-shaped room), and the powerfully repressive antagonist (Mrs. Bellmont).[1]

In using aspects of the slave narrative in her text, Wilson, the author and indentured servant, demonstrates that her treatment in the North is not definably different from the treatment her enslaved colored brethren and sisters of the South receive. Slave narrative characteristics include beatings at the hands of the master (or mistress), denial of the slave's humanity by the dominant culture, and attempts on the part of the slave to gain a sense of self as well as physical, mental, and spiritual freedom from oppression.

Finally, *Our Nig* demonstrates some characteristics of the captivity narrative, a genre that intersects with both the sentimental novel and the slave narrative as they each act out the victimization of oppressed members of American society—women and blacks (Stern 441).[2] The traditional captivity narrative obscures the clear determination of who is the dominant, oppressing culture; in the traditional scenario we have a situation wherein oppressed peoples of color (the American Indians) in turn oppress the female member of the culture that oppresses them (white Americans). Interestingly enough, the idea of woman's oppression remains constant.

When Jacobs began writing *Incidents* in the mid-1850s, she likewise used a combination of genres in her search for a literary voice that would speak to her specific situation and concerns. As Wilson had done two years earlier and as Keckley would do seven years later, Jacobs adopts the style of the sentimental novel as her mainstay. In addressing the "happy, free women" of her reading audience, Jacobs appears to take pains not to alienate them. She uses sentimental terminology to cajole the members of her audience into reading her story; at the same time, she maintains her own integrity by expressing within her text her dissatisfaction with the social, cultural, political, and economic injustices of America. Foster notes that because Jacobs "anticipated a hostile and incredulous reception to her narrative," the writer purposefully "created a transcultural text that begged, borrowed, stole, and devised the techniques that would allow her maximum freedom to tell her story in her own way and to her own ends" ("Resisting" 72). Jacobs encodes her autobiography in such a way that the careful reader, looking beyond the veneer of the sentimental novel format, becomes aware of her delicate irony and sarcasm. She employs these mother tongue tools for two specific reasons: first, to chastise her seemingly complacent white female readers for their failure to confront the abominations committed against their sisters in slavery; and second, to attack the institution of American slavery and the attendant social phenomenon of racism by challenging and minimizing the supposed good character and sense of honor claimed by those who take part in or silently support these aberrations.

Both Elizabeth Keckley, author of the 1868 *Behind the Scenes,* and Susie King Taylor, author of the 1902 *Reminiscences,* following the black women's literary models that had appeared before them, blur the boundaries that defined the genre of autobiography by nipping and tucking, stretching and expanding, molding and reshaping traditional autobiographical styles to accommodate their stories. In most cases, however, these techniques differ from those used in the antebellum African American women's autobiographies written by Wilson and Jacobs because both the sociopolitical climate and the personal goals are different for these postbellum women autobiographers. There are still some similarities, however, between Wilson's and Jacobs's antebellum and Keckley's and Taylor's postbellum personal narratives as they interface and dialogue with each other. Subsequently, these later texts learn from and build on those previously written. And the content of the narratives continues to inform the shaping—the structure—of the text.

With the oppressions of slavery no longer a major factor, African American autobiographers during the post-Civil War era attempted to locate their personal narratives within the American history of which they had been a part. Those who had been enslaved were intent on celebrating their newly won status as free Americans by embracing their country and by showing European Americans the value—past, present, and future—of their contributions to this country's greatness. As African American women writers appropriating the genre of autobiography moved beyond slavery and into Reconstruction, their narratives began taking on a decidedly activist tone, challenging through the directness of their rhetoric and through their statements of self-worth the political and social power structures that were in place. Susanna Egan writes that the African American autobiography that develops during the Reconstruction years "determines not just the objective, historical identity or political purpose of the autobiographer but also, increasingly, the manner in which the autobiographer is seen to exist" (85). In view of the dramatic decrease in the amount of attention given to the plight of American blacks during Reconstruction, it was not surprising to see black autobiographers both "defin[ing] their human worth in white terms" and fighting against such limitations at the same time (85). Whereas the securing of freedom from slavery was the primary topic of antebellum autobiographies, Benjamin Franklin's principles of self-reliance became the watchwords for many postbellum black narratives. Securing freedom from enslavement was no longer an issue for postbellum African American women autobiographers; they soon discovered, however, that the underlying cancer of racism and color prejudice did not dissipate with the abolition of slavery.

Although both Taylor and Keckley wrote in the postwar period, Keckley's proximity to the war—both in time and in location—made her position as an African American woman autobiographer less stable than the more distant position enjoyed by Taylor when she decided to publish her 1902 personal narrative. Keckley's residence in Washington, D.C., and the publication of *Behind the Scenes* only two years after the end of the Civil War are two factors that had an adverse effect on her perception of literary freedom. Taylor's *Reminiscences,* on the other hand, was published over thirty years after the conclusion of the war (a time when many war sentiments had perhaps calmed) and was published in Boston—a city not located on the crossroads between North and South, as was Washington. As a result, Taylor exhibits a greater freedom in thought and expression than does Keckley. However, both women produced personal narratives that demonstrate the nineteenth-century black woman autobiographer's continued resistance to oppressive ideologies, and both embrace the African American mother tongue as the medium for autobiographical writing.

Keckley merges aspects of the slave narrative and the sentimental novel within the overall frame of a historical memoir in her 1868 autobiography. James Olney calls Keckley's narrative a "mixed middle ground between history and fiction, . . . a mixed production of historical narrative that displays many of the conventions of sentimental fiction" (introduction xxvii). The slave narrative focus, which represents Keckley's thirty years as a slave, takes up, for some, a surprisingly minor portion of her text—only the first three chapters. The remaining twelve chapters highlight her movement into and her actions as a part of the Washington, D.C., social, political, and economic scene. Keckley makes a conscious decision to take the offensive by minimizing the details of her life in slavery and maximizing what she determines are her successes as a free woman; the structuring of her text reflects this decision.

Although William L. Andrews refers to Keckley's autobiography as the "key transitional text" between antebellum and postbellum narratives, he goes on to disparage the lasting value of her narrative: "*Behind the Scenes* might well be regarded as more a book of gossip about whites than a key contribution to black women's first-person writing" ("Changing Moral Discourse" 227). Andrews fails to acknowledge the important underlying themes that emerge from Keckley's narrative, themes that speak to the relationship between postbellum professional and/or lettered freemen and freewomen, African American entrepreneurship, the continuing relationships between former slaves and their former owners, and many other historical and sociological situations upon which she comments. Far from being merely "gossip," *Behind the Scenes* captures Keckley's attempt to situate herself and to find her voice. Her mixture of so many different literary genres is indicative of the whirlwind in which she lived:

> *Behind the Scenes* is . . . not altogether a slave narrative and not exactly an autobiography, although it partakes in part of both of these, nor is it a romance or sentimental novel, even though it reads at times as if it could be so classified. After the first three chapters, the book could best be described as "memoirs"—i.e., the sort of narrative that is grown out of personal experience but that does not focus on the personal element and describes instead external events and figures who occupy some important place in the affairs of the world. (Olney, introduction xxxiii)

Keckley's narrative, like Wilson's and Jacobs's, is another example of the countergenre position that African American women's autobiography assumed. And Andrews was not alone in questioning the value of the somewhat convoluted *Behind the Scenes*. As a matter of fact, Keckley's text was the butt of a parodic publication entitled *Behind the Seams*.[3]

When we look at the literary style of Taylor's postbellum *Reminiscences*, we observe the same approach to memoir-writing apparent in Keckley's text. Taylor's period of slavery was not only much shorter than that of Keckley but also, if we can make an assumption based on what she omits from her text, she may not have suffered the physical and sexual abuses that Keckley did. Her 1902 autobiography primarily echoes the form of the slave narrative, historical memoir, and adventure narrative. Although she traces her family connections through her mother and grandmother early in the text, and she indicates her various movements up to the outbreak of the Civil War, Susie King Taylor is not the real subject of this autobiography. The majority of her narrative "supplants a community of black military men and women in place of the author as its focal point" (Moody 53). *Reminiscences* is written in the first person; however, the tone is oddly third person, with Taylor describing, sometimes in minute detail, "the experiences and opinions of others, while ostensibly suppressing [her] own" (53). Perhaps Taylor's narrative has received so little critical attention because it gives virtually no insight, in the traditional ways, into much of the author's personal life. Also, she exhibits little of the emotion characteristic of other black women autobiographers. Taylor indicates in her preface that friends had to talk her into writing her story, and it still appears that much of her story remains unwritten. Moody suggests that Taylor was still being influenced by the postbellum training in the codes of the "cult of true womanhood," noting her rather submissive approach to the writing of her text and the modest way she refers to her husband as "Sergeant King" within her narrative (53, 54).

As noted before, African American women were not considered worthy of membership in the "cult" prior to the Civil War; at its conclusion, however, Northern whites expended a great deal of effort in training newly freed black women in the art of true womanhood. These efforts, for the most part, were spearheaded by white male representatives of the Freedmen's Bureau charged with expediting the assimilation of blacks into European American society. Dorothy Sterling offers the following as an example of the instruction that white America used to train former slave women in the art of becoming acceptable wives: "'Do not think of getting married until you know how to knit and sew, to mend clothes and bake good bread, to keep a nice clean house and cultivate a garden, and to read and write. A wife should take good care of her person, be clean, neat, tidy, and look as pretty as possible'" (320).[4] This "recipe" had apparently worked in keeping nineteenth-century white women in check, so white men assumed that it would also work to silence and control black women, especially if they were trying to become true American women. This is not to suggest that white men felt that black women could ever achieve the status of true women. The creation of this recipe served, however, to reinforce the controlling hand of the white man by allowing him to assume the position of teacher to the black woman, even regarding issues of domesticity and hygiene. He, therefore, establishes his unshakeable position as representative of the superior race and of the superior gender.

The need to establish themselves as "American women" is an obvious driving force behind both Keckley's and Taylor's narratives, but it was also important for both that they establish their origins, perhaps to better impress upon their readership how far they had come from the oppressions of the past. In typical slave narrative form, Keckley and Taylor each begins by establishing who she is—where she was born, who her family was, and who her owners were. Keckley writes: "I was born a slave. . . . My birthplace was Dinwiddie Court-house, in Virginia. . . . My master, Col. A. Burwell, was somewhat unsettled in his business affairs, and while I was yet an infant he made several removals" (17, 19).

Taylor, likewise, introduces herself systematically, establishing the facts of her origin without subjective comment. As Jacobs does in *Incidents*, Taylor noticeably highlights her matriarchal line of descent, titling her opening chapter "A Brief Sketch of My Ancestors":

> My great-great-grandmother was 120 years old when she died. . . .
> My great-grandmother, one of her daughters, named Susanna, was
> married to Peter Simons, and was one hundred years old when she
> died. . . . In 1820 my grandmother was born, . . . and in 1833 she
> married Fortune Lambert Reed. . . . My mother was born in 1834.
> She married Raymond Baker in 1847. Nine children were born to
> them. . . . I was the first born. I was born on the Grest Farm, . . .
> Liberty County, about thirty-five miles from Savannah, Ga., on
> August 6, 1848, my mother being waitress for the Grest family.
> (1–2)[5]

Since most children of slavery did not have such minute details of their ancestry, especially information on who was married to whom and when, the thoroughness of this passage is particularly striking and sets the stage for the very specific historical detailing in the context of Taylor's narrative and for the objective, journalistic structuring that characterizes the text itself. Keckley also sprinkles her text with specific historical notations; however, a clear difference between these two narratives is Keckley's sentimental-novel slant to her presentation and the limited use of this approach in Taylor's *Reminiscences*. Even Keckley's view of the Civil War—unlike Taylor's realistic, straightforward narrative with its specific dates, locations, and skirmishes—dwells on her romanticized vision of the conflict:

> The war was now in progress, and every day brought stirring news
> from the front—the front, where the Gray opposed the Blue, where
> flashed the bright sabre in the sunshine, where were heard the angry
> notes of battle, the deep roar of cannon, and the fearful rattle of
> musketry; where new graves were being made every day, where
> brother forgot a mother's early blessing and sought the life-blood of
> brother, and friend raised the deadly knife against friend. Oh, the

front, with its stirring battle-scenes! Oh, the front, with its ghastly heaps of dead! (91–2)

Behind the Scenes relied on the sentimental literary genre that was most appealing to Keckley's predominantly white female readership; Taylor, however, opted for an approach that, at times, echoed the narrative genre usually affiliated with the European American man—the adventure novel. This genre was traditionally a masculine tale of adventures and camaraderie that was "noteworthy not merely for its distancing from the domestic zone but also for its immersion in the details and lexicon of work" (Elliott 51). The adventure novel, then, further defined a gender-based literary division between the private woman's sphere of the home and the public man's sphere of the world by specifically aligning itself with the work of man and separating itself from the domesticity of woman. But just as the "woman's" sentimental novel was predictable because of its formulaic approach to the genre, so was the "man's" adventure novel—its plots always situated in a primitive arena with heroes, enemies, battles, victories, and defeats. This is the formula that best suited Taylor's story.

Taylor adopts this man's genre and fills *Reminiscences* with descriptions of actual battles, told in such an on-the-scene manner and with such colorful detail as to draw the reader into the adventure of the actual conflict. Taylor seemed to know that much of her story required a certain degree of authorial detachment so that the reader could focus on the material of her narrative—its context—rather than on the writer of it. She describes one adventure-novel-like incident in which members of her company, Company C, are involved in skirmishes with enemy rebels hiding on St. Simon's Island off the coast of Georgia: "On Wednesday, John Baker, the man shot on Monday, was found in a terrible condition by Henry Batchlott, who carried him to the Beach, where he was attended by the surgeon. He told us how, after being shot, he lay quiet for a day. On the second day he managed to reach some wild grapes growing near him. These he ate, to satisfy his hunger and intense thirst, then he crawled slowly, every movement causing agony, until he got to the side of the road. He lived only three months after they found him" (13).[6]

Since Taylor is presuming to write an autobiography, however, she is clever enough and creative enough to provide some bits of information about the adventures she experienced without dwelling too much on herself. She presents this information in the same objective tone as she uses in most of her narrative. For instance, during one period of the war, she describes being a passenger, along with two other women and a child, on a yacht that was attacked and sunk sailing from Hilton Head to Beaufort, South Carolina: "I remember going down twice. As I rose the second time, I caught hold of the sail and managed to hold fast. Mrs. Walker held onto her child with one hand, while with the other she managed to hold fast to some part of the boat, and we drifted and shouted as loud as we could. . . . They found us at last, nearly dead from exposure. In fact, the poor little baby was dead, although her mother still held her by her clothing, with her teeth" (37–38). Taylor continues to use aspects of a linear adventure narrative in recording her independent life even after the war, describing how she opened schools for blacks in various locations and detailing her travels in the North during her later employment as a maid and companion. Taylor's approach to her autobiography, combining elements of the adventure narrative with those of the slave narrative and historical memoir, gives her work a literary uniqueness; also, she was adept in the use of innovative mother tongue techniques found in the autobiographies of the nineteenth-century black women preceding her. Using autobiography as a countergenre, she reshapes her material to represent her life experiences.

I want to take a moment to delve a bit deeper into Keckley's heavy use of the sentimental style in reshaping the autobiographical form of her narrative, especially as she addresses her thirty years in slavery. Since she devotes only the first three chapters of her fifteen-chapter text to her life as a slave while devoting the remaining twelve chapters to her four-year affiliation with the White House, it is safe to say that Keckley is determined to minimize her years of oppression and maximize her years of freedom and self-reliance. She chooses to use language and certain characteristics of existing literary genres to assume control over her life and her narrative, skewing both toward their most positive and complimentary angles. This literary and sociopolitical approach differed from that of the antebellum autobiographers, who relied on their readers' reactions to the oppressions and horrors described in their narratives to evoke a demand for change.

Although some scholars raise questions concerning the honesty of such a skewed version of the experiences recorded in Keckley's autobiography, most recognize and accept a certain amount of creative enhancement that all writers of "self" incorporate into their narratives: throughout history, all autobiographers have taken liberties, in varying degrees, when determining the focus of their narratives. In this act of re-creating one's life, Keckley is no different from St. Augustine selectively relating his "confessions," Wilson determining which "sketches" she would include, or Jacobs picking the most relevant and influential "incidents" in her life. Just as Keckley chooses her language and her literary genres, she also chooses what occurrences in her life to include, in what form to present them, and where to locate them within her story: "[A]s I gaze upon the panorama of the past, I realize how crowded with incidents my life has been. Every day seems like a romance within itself, and the years grow into ponderous volumes. As I cannot condense, I must omit many strange passages in my history. . . . I will confine my story to the most important incidents which I believe influenced the moulding of my character" (18).

Taking Keckley's introductory comments into account and then looking at her final product, it is apparent that she felt that most of the incidents in her years of servitude, though they taught her valuable lessons, were not as important to the "moulding" of her character as were her experiences at the White House. In tune with the "romance" she felt her life to be, she paints a sentimental picture of her need to write her story, not only to justify her later relationship with Mary Todd Lincoln but also to satisfy the romantic needs of her readers, to titillate them, and to elicit their sympathies: "The labor of a lifetime has brought me nothing in a pecuniary way. I have worked hard, but fortune, fickle dame, has not smiled upon me. If poverty did not weigh me down as it does, I would not now be toiling by day with my needle, and writing by night, in the plain little room on the fourth floor of No. 14 Carroll Place. And yet I have learned to love the *garret*-like room" (330; my emphasis). That Keckley would choose to use the term "garret" suggests the possibility that she is purposely communicating with (dialoguing with) Jacobs's narrative. While Jacobs's "garret" was an oppressive cell into which she was driven for almost seven years of her life, Keckley seems to present hers as a place of domestic security.

Keckley's purpose for writing her narrative very much determines the narrative style she adopts. Her style suggests a need to pacify her white readership, as she is dependent upon their patronage because of her financial situation; therefore, most of the linguistic techniques she chooses are softer than those we later find in Taylor. Also, publishing her text only a couple of years after the end of the Civil War, Keckley displays a certain amount of sincerity in her romantic notions about America; she is still optimistic about the promises of freedom for all, having already enjoyed, from her point of view, relative freedom and acceptance within the dominant white society.

Taylor, unlike Wilson, Jacobs, and Keckley, was neither looking for sympathy from her readers, nor aiming her text at European American women readers of sentimental narratives. Additionally, she appeared not to depend upon the sales of her autobiography to pull her out of poverty, as was the case with Wilson and Keckley. Taylor had a different perspective on what her narrative might accomplish and for whom.

Having been active in the public arena during the war (as laundress, teacher, nurse), Taylor aims her voice primarily at the white-male leaders of the country and speaks words that are not veiled behind a sentimental curtain.[7] Discouraged by continuing racism against African Americans, she follows urgings from her colleagues in the Women's Relief Corp and documents the contributions that members of her race made in the cause of freedom, especially emphasizing the role that black women played during the war: "[T]here were 'loyal women,' as well as men, in those days, who did not fear shell or shot, who cared for the sick and dying; women who camped and fared as the boys did, and who are still caring for the comrades in their declining years" (vi).

Although she stresses the contributions of black women in the slaves' struggle for freedom, Taylor noticeably does not address the issue of bonding between black and white women within her autobiography, and she makes no effort to build a textual linkage between white women readers and herself. Friendship relationships between black and white women do develop, however, within the contexts of Wilson's, Jacobs's, and Keckley's more sentimental personal narratives; these contextual relationships subsequently project the textual relationships that these African American women autobiographers needed in order to engage their predominantly European American women readers. This linkage emerged from a society that relied on woman-to-woman secrecy in nineteenth-century America. "This covert women's community," writes Andrews about *Incidents*, "did not document itself through private written sources; it was knit together by oral means . . . through the most private and personal of all communications—secrets. Jacobs approaches her woman-identified reader with a personal history of secrets whose revelation, she hopes, will initiate that reader into the community of confidence and support that nineteenth-century women needed in order to speak out above a whisper against their oppression" (*Free Story* 254).

Although Taylor does not indicate in *Reminiscences* that she is veiling or withholding any information in the telling of her story or engaging in a secretive liaison with white women, Wilson, Jacobs, and Keckley all do. These tactics of secrecy and concealment are relevant to the discussion of the difficulties that many nineteenth-century African American women faced in compiling and writing their autobiographies; also, we do not find in *Reminiscences* the confessions that Jacobs and Keckley make to their female audiences, or statements about incident selectivity that Wilson, Jacobs, and Keckley all make in their respective texts when admitting that they do not reveal everything to the reader. Toni Morrison suggests, and I agree, that many African American slave narrators (and for the sake of argument, I will include Wilson in this grouping) withheld information to soften the more violent aspects of certain incidents that might ring false to their readers because of the severity of the violence: "Over and over, the writers pull the narrative up short with a phrase such as, 'But let us drop a veil over these proceedings too terrible to relate.' In shaping the experience to make it palatable to those who were in a position to alleviate it, they were silent about many things, and they 'forgot' many other things" (109).

Wilson writes in her preface to *Our Nig:* "I do not pretend to divulge every transaction in my own life, which the unprejudiced would declare unfavorable in comparison with treatment of legal bondmen; I have purposely omitted what would most provoke shame in our good anti-slavery friends at home" (3). In her preface to *Incidents,* Jacobs makes the following statement to her readers: "I have not exaggerated the wrongs inflicted by Slavery; on the contrary, my descriptions fall far short of the facts. I have concealed the names of places, and given the persons fictitious names. I have no motive for secrecy on my own account, but I deemed it kind and considerate towards others to pursue this course" (1). Finally, Keckley indicates in her preface that she is writing her narrative at the urgings of her friends because her life has been so "eventful": "I have acceded to the importunities of my friends, and have hastily sketched some of the striking incidents that go to make up my history. My life, so full of romance, may sound like a dream to the matter-of-fact reader, nevertheless everything I have written is strictly true; much has been omitted, but nothing has been exaggerated" (xi). Clearly, Wilson, Jacobs, and Keckley each wants to send a message to her readers—in most cases, European American women of the North—that she has a story to tell, and that this story, though selective in its recounting of personal incidents, is aimed at them.

Taylor undoubtedly might have offered powerful, violent accounts of her experiences, but not only does she choose to omit such incidents, she offers no excuses for their omission. She addresses the topics she feels are relevant to her purpose without attempting to establish a confessional or secretive bond with her readers. Taylor focuses on presenting a historical record of her involvement with the 33rd United States Colored Troops. As a result, she writes a text whose audience is neither gender- nor race-specific, a text which at one point or another is aimed at all Americans. She writes in her preface that she wants to "show how much service and good we can do to each other, and what sacrifices we can make for our liberty and our rights" (vi). Regardless of their methods and specific literary approaches, by situating blacks within the society that was America, Wilson, Jacobs, Keckley, and Taylor all make it clear that they are claiming ownership of their social, political, and literary voices and assuming a role in the defining of American society, often relying on ancestral or other-mother oral traditions to strengthen their resolve.

Contemporary European feminists and their European American counterparts theorize about the need for women writers to think back through their mothers and, as Sidonie Smith cites from Sandra Gilbert and Susan Gubar, to "discover 'woman's command of language as against language's command of woman'" (*Poetics* 57).[8] This theoretical position rejects the patriarchal tongue that, as these theorists suggest, has whipped women into silence, and it proposes a return to the language of the mother. Smith states that a woman writer, in locating a language with which to write her story, "may, as Margaret Homans suggests, *remember* and then reinvest with her own meaning a maternal language through which to probe a legitimate gynocentric self-representation" (*Poetics* 58; my emphasis). I emphasize "remember" in this passage because its use addresses the differences in a basic aspect of a European American woman's mother tongue compared to an African American woman's mother tongue. Like the characteristics of the construct of "woman," these mother tongue differences are not biological, but are the result of differences in cultural development. For African American women autobiographers whose spirits have passed from Africa, through the Middle Passage, through New World slavery, through Reconstruction, and on up to the present, there is no need to "remember" a connection to their mothers. This connection was never forgotten, and its existence and perpetuation define the African American literary tradition, especially for the black mother.

African American women writers could not forget the mother or her language because, as the embodiment of the next generation of women, they represent the preservation of a culture that took on added relevance because of the efforts of slavery and racism to eradicate it. And while theories of a woman's language introduced by European feminists offer important proposals for feminism, their suggestion that the woman auto-biographer must "return to her origins in the mother" (S. Smith, *Poetics* 58)[9] does not apply to African American women writers who were never removed from those origins in spirit. African American women writers were always aware of the collective voices of women empowering their texts. When black poet Marlene NourbeSe Philip was asked, "How does one really speak," she responded that one speaks "'through the anatomi-cal organs of speech, through the cultural histories embedded in a "mother tongue," through an oppressive force; through all of these in their collectivity and multiplicity'" (quoted in Davies 161). Just as African American women appropriated and subverted the language of their op-pressors, re-molding its shapes, distorting its meanings, and imbuing it with their own cultural specificity, African American women autobiogra-phers then took this resultant mother tongue and placed it on the pages of their texts, recording that "black woman's voice" identified by Barbara Smith. Carol Boyce Davies writes, "The repositioning of women in lan-guage occurs when we reverse, interrupt or dismantle the cultural my-thologies which position women in language in negative ways. . . . [T]he multiple ways of voicing that reside in Black women's textualities . . . range from the presymbolic 'baby talk' of the mother tongue in African and Native American contexts, to the politically challenging critical speech which 'talks back' . . . and all of the other modes in which gestures, expressions, language are voiced" (163, 164).

There are a number of contemporary black women scholars, however, who do not necessarily subscribe to the concept of a black woman's speech, Deborah McDowell and Hazel Carby to name two. McDowell was one of the early and by far the most critical of those voices challenging Barbara Smith's 1977 assertions of a black woman's way of speech and the need for a critical approach to black women's writing that lent an eye (and ear) to the sociopolitical circumstances that shaped it. McDowell's initial response in 1980 questioned Smith's apparently essentialist statement that black women writers expressed themselves using a "specifically black female language," further stating that Smith "failed to describe or to pro-vide examples of this unique language" (8). Although McDowell revisited and even altered some of her criticism of Smith in a follow-up essay ten years later, I must agree in principle with her challenge of Smith's earlier use of the term "female" language, because I too note biological essentialism embedded in the word "female" (as opposed to bonding characteristics associated with the sociopolitically constructed "woman"). Hazel Carby, likewise, writes that "there are major problems with Smith's essay as a critical manifesto, particularly in its assertion of the existence of an essential black female experience and an exclusive black female language in which this experience is embodied" (9). I must qualify my agreement with these two scholars by noting, on Smith's behalf, that at the time she wrote her essay, society made little distinction between the biologically descriptive term "female" and the socially constructed term "woman." Although Smith does state "female language" in her text, it is obvious from her description of this "language" that she was attempting to address the socially and politically informed language of the black "woman" when she wrote that "the politics of sex as well as the politics of race and class are crucially interlocking factors in the works of Black women writers" (159).[10]

Just as I would replace "female" with "woman" in Smith's statement, I would also replace "sex" with "gender" as an updated clarification of Smith's assertion. Both changes reflect the current terminology that more accurately establishes the differences between anatomy and agency. While McDowell was right to challenge Smith's apparently biological basis for naming a woman's way of speaking, she later admits that her fervor in denouncing this biologically essentialistic characteristic sent her to "the other extreme" where she attempted "to formulate a definition so inclusive in its scope that it nearly gutted black feminist thinking of any distinctiveness and explanatory power as a critical category" (17). That Smith did not initially provide descriptions or examples to support her thesis of the existence of a sociopolitically driven black woman's language and the consequent existence of commonalities in black women's texts does not necessarily belie the veracity of her statement. However, until statements are proven, they are merely hypotheses. Smith's statements required proof, and I believe that the necessary proof has been provided in the ensuing twenty-year period of black feminist scholarship. And my four autobiographers in this study also bear out her argument.

While McDowell avows that she has abandoned the "linear models of literary history" that have driven the literary "tradition" of Western thought, she still expresses an uneasiness about supporting ideological concepts of black women's writing that go against mainstream critical and theoretical models. Again critiquing statements made by Smith, McDowell writes, "[T]he assumption that . . . there is an organic line of descent and connection from black women writers to black women critics to literary characters and that 'black women writers . . . constitute an identifiable literary tradition' evident in the 'innumerable commonalities' of language and theme that structure their work, would all be challenged as epistemologically suspect by the most salient claims of postmodernist thought" (21, 22). At the risk of being thought naive, I must respond, "So what?" So what if these black-woman-specific ideas of language- and theme-driven commonalities work counter to current theories of language and literary ideology? Black women writers have always, out of necessity, had to maneuver outside of the dominant literary system. Why, then, is it a surprise that neither the literary nor critical traditions of black women writers fit mainstream paradigms? Or, to whom is this a surprise?

Their exclusion from the mainstream literary traditions of nineteenth-century America led early African American women writers to find alternative means of communicating, drawing upon their own experiences of oppression and resistance to shape their texts and to represent the characters and situations within them. The resultant African American mother tongue became black women's subversive communicative system, containing tools and weapons specific to their sociopolitical position in society. It does not embody, as McDowell suggests, an "organic" line of descent, but a line of descent born out of shared experiences of oppression. Black women developed these survival techniques and honed them from their shared spaces on the margins of society. In a statement that appears to be contradictory to her earlier criticism of Smith, Carby writes the following about black women's slave narratives: "[T]he issue involved in the establishment of a public voice [is] related to the necessity for black women, as writers, to develop their own discourse of black womanhood" (39). I'm gratified to see that the "line of descent" that Smith proposes and that McDowell questions receives the support of Carby:

> Black women writers would continue to adopt and adapt dominant literary conventions and to challenge racist sexual ideologies. Like Jacobs, they would explore a variety of narrative forms in the attempt to establish a public presence and continue to find ways to invent black heroines who could transcend their negative comparison to the figure of the white heroine. The consequences of being a

slave woman did not end with the abolition of slavery as an institution but haunted the texts of black women throughout the nineteenth century and into the twentieth. (61)

The line of descent that connects generations of black women, black women writers, and the black women characters in their texts supports the existence of a specifically black woman's way of communicating. An African American vernacular has always been recognized as a black way of speaking, and like all vernaculars, it grew out of a need to speak subversively, to speak in a "language" that was shared by other members of the "community" but that confounded those outside of it. What these nineteenth-century African American women writers spoke and wrote was not really a new language, but a re-shaping of the existing language of the dominant culture.

As the black vernacular grew and strengthened in the midst of the European American hegemony, members of the dominant white society noticed the existence of this different way of speaking. For some, it was an amusing example of black mimicry and creativity; for others, it represented an exciting and innovative art form that they appropriated and then distorted to create what was to become known as American minstrelsy; for yet others, it was a threat because this different way of speaking contained encoded messages that many members of the dominant white society (most specifically white men) recognized as indecipherable. European American reactions varied from increased efforts to silence this veiled discourse to attempts to reproduce and then minimize it as well as the culture that had produced it.

One of the more visible attempts to ridicule the black vernacular, aside from the minstrel shows, came in the form of broadside parodies. Gates writes that one such publication parodied letters supposedly written by early African American poet, Phillis Wheatley: "The broadside is a salient example of Signifyin(g) and suggests that as early as 1828 what we might think of as the signifying black difference—Afro-American spoken vernacular discourse—could be the object and the mechanism of parody" (*Signifying* 92). For the dominant society to take notice of and then try to squash, through ridicule, the subverted language forms being used by blacks indicates the degree of the threat. The specific broadside to which Gates refers was published in London in 1846 and was titled "A Black Lecture on Language." It pictures a caricature of an African American woman, dressed in academic cap and gown, delivering a lecture from behind a podium that prominently displays a variety of labeled "tongues": "Foreign Tongue," "Mother Tongue," "Vulgar Tongue," "Pickled Tongue," "Double Tongue," "Woman's Tongue," and the largest specimen, which is held aloft by the speaker, "Unknown Tongue" (*Signifying* 93). For those promoting this broadside, the placement of the "unknown tongue" in the hand of the speaker indicates white men's belief in the ignorance of nineteenth-century African American women. However, even more telling, it also unwittingly suggests white men's suspicion (and fear) that the black woman is concealing her communicative techniques, thereby making her real knowledge unknown to them. After all, the "unknown tongue" is in *her* hand, under *her* power.

African American women employed various communicative tools that characterized their mother tongue. Considered individually, most of these tools are not specifically African American or specific to "women"; when viewed collectively, however, they take on sociopolitical significance and signify to the European American man, to the European American woman, and to the African American man that the black woman's tongue is unique. Many would argue that irony is irony, whether employed by white men, black men, white women, or black women. To a degree, that is true. However, irony is an important linguistic tool for those writing from positions of marginality because it is inherently disruptive and is usually not recognized as such by many who experience it. Therefore, women and people of color who write can experience a great deal of communicative freedom under the protecting cloak of irony. That same protection can be enjoyed through the use of whispers, allusions, and metaphors. None are race- or gender-inflected taken in isolation. They gain their distinction in an African American mother tongue because of the ways in which they interact with other techniques that *are* race- and gender-inflected and because of the social forces that drive black women autobiographers' need to speak. Following is a list of some of the tools of the African American mother tongue (although this list is far from being complete, new techniques being added as the need arises): "back talk," biblical allegory, body language, concealment, deception, dissembling, guile, hesitations, humor, impertinence, impudence, innuendo, insolence, invective, irony, ironic humor, laughter, lying, masking, metaphor, misdirection, mumbling, rage, sarcasm, sass, satire, secrecy, shifts in point of view, signals, silence, song, understatement, whispering.

When I invoke the term "mother tongue," I use it loosely to reflect communicative actions in general, verbal (linguistic) as well as nonverbal (nonlinguistic). Nonverbal communicative techniques used by the personae within the narrative are established by the autobiographer in her use of syntactical structures (such as dashes and ellipses to represent hesitations or silences) or verbal descriptions to note a particular look, movement, or attitude that carries characteristics of a mother tongue resistive technique. Such structures force readers to pause and consider possible subversive or masked authorial intents embodied in such usage.[11] Keckley uses such mother tongue structural devices within her text to show the hesitation and embarrassment that she, young Lizzie, experienced as a target of slavery's sexual abuse: "I do not care to dwell upon the subject, for it is one that is fraught with pain. Suffice it to say, that [a white man] persecuted me for four years, and I—I—became a mother" (39). The hesitation represented by the dashes is indicative of the sorrow felt by the persona at her loss of virtue and of the disdain felt by the writer at having to recall and reveal this period of oppression in her life.

The techniques listed above were used in a variety of ways as nineteenth-century African American women applied them in their dealings with those who attempted to suppress or minimize them, whether the oppressors be black men, white men, white women, or, at times, other black women. These tools were used to mislead, to confuse, to trick, or to make a fool of the oppressor; they were used to lull the oppressor into a false sense of confidence; and they were used to build and reinforce a sense of self for the African American woman. Their ultimate purpose was to provide means by which black women could resist oppression by keeping the oppressor off balance. I have loosely divided the mother tongue techniques listed above into three categories. Some of the techniques as they are used by various writers might fall into more than one category, according to the tone the autobiographer chooses to assume; however, I am assigning each technique to only one category to avoid confusion. The communicative techniques in category 1 represent tools of subtle resistance, which are especially effective in making a resistive statement to the oppressor, but softening its meaning at the same time: concealment, guile, hesitations, mumbling, secrecy, shifts in point of view (including the use of rhetorical questions), silence, and whispering. Techniques that fall into category 2 represent masking—tools that suggest or say one thing, but mean something else: biblical allegory, body language, dissembling, innuendo, ironic humor, laughter, metaphor, misdirection, sarcasm, satire, signals, song, and understatement. I characterize the techniques in category

3 as tools of flagrant resistance: "back talk," impertinence, impudence, insolence, invective, irony, lying, rage, and sass.

In *Talking Back* bell hooks writes that women (and children—both seemed to be placed in the same category in the eyes of men) have always been discouraged from talking. Calling the act of speaking as an equal to an authority figure or stating one's opinion "talking back" or "back talk," she writes, "To speak . . . when one was not spoken to was a courageous act—an act of risk and daring" (5). Many nineteenth-century African American women dared to take these risks, and some of them recorded their actions, even continuing to use the deceptive tools of the African American mother tongue in the actual shaping of their stories. The use of these tools took on far-reaching implications in the world of letters. As hooks explains: "For us [black women], true speaking is not solely an expression of creative power; it is an act of resistance, a political gesture that challenges politics of domination that would render us nameless and voiceless. . . . Moving from silence into speech is for the oppressed, the colonized, the exploited. . . . It is that act of speech, of 'talking back,' that is no mere gesture of empty words, that is the expression of our movement from object to subject—the liberated voice" (8, 9).

Because nineteenth-century African American women autobiographers' ways of communicating were informed by the level of and changes in their social, political, and economic status within American society (as America experienced slavery, racism, the Civil War, and Reconstruction), their literary styles, both oral and written, changed along with them. Their ways of communicating developed characteristics that were based on their antebellum and/or postbellum experiences, characteristics that were unique and specific to the places, spaces, and gaps they either chose to or were forced to occupy within American society.

Black women's antebellum and postbellum personal narratives have much in common, but the uniqueness of each text brought on by the individual writer's perceptions of "freedom" within her own sociopolitical arena is also apparent. I present in my next three chapters a detailed account of the African American mother tongue techniques I have proposed, by category, and apply those category-specific techniques to the texts and contexts of Wilson's *Our Nig*, Jacobs's *Incidents*, Keckley's *Behind the Scenes*, and Taylor's *Reminiscences*, noting how the tools changed, grew, or mutated in direct proportion to the amount and types of resistance required for each African American woman to speak as an American.

Subtle Resistance in *Our Nig, Incidents, Behind the Scenes,* and *Reminiscences*

oath   moan   mutter   chant
time grieves the dimension of other
babble   curse   chortle   sing
turns on its axis of silence
—**Philip,** *She Tries Her Tongue*

Black women communicating in nineteenth-century America, whether or not they were writing personal narratives, were always conscious of the need to protect themselves and those about whom they cared—family, community, helpmates. This consciousness came into play in their daily struggles to overcome race, gender, and class oppression. Often, subtlety was called for in the manner in which they chose to resist much of this oppression. In particular situations, they wanted their oppressors to note a certain amount of resistance on their parts, but at the same time, they usually stopped short of arousing such ire as to elicit undue punishment. Punishment in such cases was generally a verbal chastisement or perhaps merely a moment of awkward silence, a nervous laugh, or an attempt on the part of the dominant figure to ignore the offense. As a result, black women's use of indirect tools of resistive communication in the nineteenth century gave them a certain amount of power over the dominant society—an African American mother tongue as a tool of resistance.

Subtle communication, being indirect, can be difficult to perceive or understand; it can be cunning and crafty; or it can be skillful, clever, or ingenious. When nineteenth-century African American women used subtle communication as a tool of resistance in the recording and shaping of their personal narratives, its use encompassed all of these definitions. At the same time, many members of the dominant society attempting to maintain their power positions—masters, mistresses, overseers—also used subtle or indirect means to render blacks powerless, often turning black tools of resistance into white weapons of oppression. This reversal, however, did not provide the same degree of power as that engendered in black women's subtleties; these women were too adept at recognizing such ruses. The subtle resistance of black women was an effective weapon because the recipient of their communication was usually caught off-guard and had no immediate response—and then the moment was gone. This indecipherability created room within which black women and black women writers maneuvered. It allowed them to move outside traditional communication.

Of the subtle resistance techniques that nineteenth-century black women autobiographers present in their narratives and use to shape its structure, I will concentrate on those techniques that Wilson, Jacobs, Keckley, and Taylor most often put into service: concealment, silence, whispering, secrecy, guile, shifts in point of view, and hesitations.

The antebellum autobiographers, Wilson and Jacobs, highlight the importance of the body as a site of oppression in their respective narratives, specifically those parts of the body that are relevant to the acts of oral communication: ear, mouth, tongue, and throat. These are the body parts that the oppressors target, and the control of these areas of communication, if successful, allows the oppressors to manipulate, silence, and dominate their victims; it is this control that the oppressed must resist.

Many of the incidents of stealth and concealment in Jacobs's *Incidents* suggest the very real problem of slaves betraying other slaves in order to win favor or special material considerations from the master. The fear of such betrayal made a habit of whispering prevalent in slave communities. However, while whispering was a powerful means of protective subtle resistance for the oppressed, the oppressors too used whispering in their efforts to weaken and silence slaves; slaves then counteracted this invasion with a stoic silence. In *Incidents,* whispering is an aggressive weapon for Dr. Flint as he tries to gain power over the slave girl, Linda, through whispered sexual proposals. Linda describes the advent of Dr. Flint's attempts at seduction: "I now entered on my fifteenth year—a sad epoch in the life of a slave girl. My master began to whisper foul words in my ear. Young as I was, I could not remain ignorant of their import. I tried to treat them with indifference or contempt" (27).[1] Linda, as property within the Southern slavocracy, does not have the option of removing herself from this offensive situation. However, because of Dr. Flint's fear of damage to his reputation in a community that holds Linda's grandmother in such high regard, she is able to resist his early whispered overtures merely by not responding to them. During the course of her narrative, Jacobs revisits this type of manipulative whispering a number of times.

One incident illustrates Jacobs's skillful linking of text and context. During the time that the runaway Linda is living in New York, she is regularly able to visit her daughter Ellen, who works for her white father's cousin, Mrs. Hobbs. At one point in Jacobs's story, Linda mentions that Mrs. Hobbs's Southern brother, Mr. Thorne, is in town visiting his sister. What Linda does not know at that time, however, is that Mr. Thorne has attempted to seduce Ellen, whispering to Ellen in the same manner that Dr. Flint attempted to seduce her: "Though he professed too much gratitude to my grandmother to injure any of her descendants, [Mr. Thorne] had *poured foul language into the ears* of her innocent great-grandchild" (179; my emphasis). This discovery is particularly disturbing to Linda because it shows that being "free" and living in the North does not protect a young black girl from attacks upon her virtue. It saddens and angers her that the same "ear" violation she had suffered as a slave should also plague her daughter. Jacobs purposely uses almost the same terminology to describe the two situations, reinforcing her chastisement of those living in the North who feel no complicity with the practices of a slave system that they, nevertheless, continue to tolerate.

At the same time that the oppressors are making use of whispering to torment the oppressed in *Incidents*, would-be victims reverse this communicative tool to find solace in their shared experiences. The controlling nature of slavery usually made direct communications between slaves almost impossible; their clandestine whisperings represent the mother tongue's way of indirectly resisting oppression, making it a resistance that defies detection by the ruling white powers. Such whisperings offer comfort and counsel for Linda when she has no other way of expressing her thoughts and feelings. An early example of this empowerment through whispering occurs at the grave site of her mother, as Linda prepares for the first time to go into hiding: "I had received my mother's blessing when she died; and in many an hour of tribulation I had seemed to hear her voice, sometimes chiding me, sometimes whispering loving words into my wounded heart" (90).

After Linda has secluded herself in the garret space over her grandmother's attic, Jacobs inscribes several instances where whispers pass between Linda and her loved ones, helping her to maintain her strength and helping her to claim the power to orchestrate certain aspects of her own life. For instance, in order to throw Dr. Flint off her trail, Linda, making use of guile, writes letters to this tormentor and contrives to have them mailed from the North by a helpmate; this secret she shares with some members of her family: "I . . . told my plan to aunt Nancy, in order that she might report to us what was said at Dr. Flint's house. I whispered it to her through a crack, and she whispered back, 'I hope it will succeed'" (129). For as long as she lived, Aunt Nancy continued to support and encourage Linda through her whisperings: "After I was shut up in my dark cell, [Aunt Nancy] stole away, whenever she could, to bring me the news and say something cheering. How often did I kneel down to listen to her words of consolation, whispered through a crack!" (144).

The final example I offer of the power of whispering from the vantage point of the oppressed in *Incidents* involves the bond that Jacobs describes between mother and daughter—between Linda and Ellen—as Ellen is about to be taken North. For fear that they might inadvertently give away their mother's whereabouts, Linda's two young children have never been told of her hiding place. Insisting on letting her daughter know where she has been all of these years, Linda convinces her family to let Ellen spend this final night with her. Before parting from her mother the next morning, Ellen "gave her last kiss, and whispered in my ear, 'Mother, I will never tell.' And she never did" (141).

Whispering as a form of resistance is not a major factor in Wilson's *Our Nig,* aside from the private conversations Frado has with her dog, Fido. Frado early learns the important lesson of suffering in silence around Mrs. Bellmont and is afforded little opportunity to seek comfort in whispered confidence with others suffering as she is, because there are none available to her. Thus, while whispering does not play as significant a role in Wilson's narrative as it does in Jacobs's *Incidents,* references to the mouth and tongue abound in both. Often when these references appear, each autobiographer uses metaphors of the blockage or welding of the mouth or tongue as a means of describing the silencing and dehumanization of the oppressed. Beginning with Mag's experiences, Wilson writes that "some foul tongue," in an effort to minimize Mag, has passed on information about her fall from virtue. Wilson's primary focus in the application of silencing tools by the oppressor, however—and probably the most powerful image in her text—revolves around the punishments suffered by Frado whereby Mrs. Bellmont or Mary literally stifle Frado's mouth and tongue to silence her voice. Ironically, these punishments are not the results of lies, but occur when Frado attempts to tell the truth.

Wilson presents three incidents that lead to the stuffing of Frado's mouth. The first incident occurs after Mary Bellmont has accused Frado of pushing her into the stream. Although Mr. Bellmont indicates that he believes Frado's version of the story, he departs, leaving Frado at the mercy of the angry Mrs. Bellmont and her vengeful daughter: "No sooner was he out of sight than Mrs. B. and Mary commenced beating [Frado] inhumanly; then propping her mouth open with a piece of wood, shut her up in a dark room, without any supper" (34–35). Not only do Mrs. Bellmont and Mary "shut" Frado up by locking her in a dark room and by blocking her mouth, the additional irony here is that while one normally opens the mouth to speak, in this case, Mrs. Bellmont forces Frado's mouth open before denying her speech by stuffing that open mouth.

Frado unwittingly provokes the second incident when, having been chastised by Mrs. Bellmont and ordered back to work, she informs her mistress that she is not feeling well: "Angry that [Frado] should venture a reply to her command, [Mrs. Bellmont] suddenly inflicted a blow which lay the tottering girl prostrate on the floor. Excited by so much indulgence of a dangerous passion, [Mrs. Bellmont] seemed left to unrestrained malice; and snatching a towel, stuffed the mouth of the sufferer, and beat her cruelly" (82). The final assault to Frado's mouth occurs when she truthfully answers the ailing James Bellmont about the reason his Aunt Abby no longer visits his room. Although fear of Mrs. Bellmont has kept James's wife, Susan, from revealing that Mrs. Bellmont has lied to Aunt Abby (informing her that James no longer wants to see her), Frado reports the incident honestly when James asks her. Angered by what she sees as impertinence, Mrs. Bellmont takes the next available opportunity to silence Frado: "Seizing Frado, [Mrs. Bellmont] said that she would 'cure her of tale-bearing,' and, placing the wedge of wood between her teeth, she beat her cruelly with the raw-hide" (93). Use of the towel, but especially use of the blocks of wood, to immobilize Frado's mouth is reminiscent of the slavery practice of putting a wooden bit in the mouths of trouble-making slaves to silence their voices and reduce them to the level of mute animals. Wilson, by drawing on this analogy, uses her text to demonstrate the similarities between the free state of the North and the slave state of the South.

Mrs. Bellmont's attempts to silence Frado by stuffing her mouth and blocking her tongue do not have long-lasting success, as Frado continues to resist her oppressive situation in one way or another, many times with amusing consequences. Because of James's influence, Frado is eventually permitted to eat the same food as the members of the Bellmont family and is even allowed to sit at the table. Mrs. Bellmont, bristling at such impropriety, demands that Frado not get a clean dish, but that she eat her meal from Mrs. Bellmont's soiled one: "Quickly looking about, [Frado] took the plate, called Fido [her dog] to wash it, which he did to the best of his ability; then, wiping her knife and fork on the cloth, she proceeded to eat her dinner" (71). Although this pantomime amuses other Bellmont family members, Mrs. Bellmont is enraged. Later, she thoroughly beat Frado "and threatened, if she ever exposed her to James, she would 'cut her tongue out'" (72). Paradoxically, in relating this episode, Wilson presents the tongue as being simultaneously the site of oppression and the site of resistance to that oppression. Mrs. Bellmont's social, legal, and political controls over Frado give her the psychological power to limit Frado's freedoms, including the freedom of speech; however, Frado's acts of using Fido to lick Mrs. Bellmont's plate clean and then wordlessly wiping off the used silverware indicate that she will continue, victim though she may appear, to communicate her feelings.

While I have noted that punishment to subtle resistance was generally mild, Mrs. Bellmont's reactions obviously are exceptions. Much of this has to do with Mrs. Bellmont's almost unquestioned position of power within the household. She feels that she can act, and react, with a certain degree of impunity in punishing Frado because, for the most part, she goes unchallenged by members of her family and members of the community. Frado's physical antics, however, allow her a degree of power in a seemingly hopeless situation, even though punishment for these antics may follow. Wilson is resisting in the same way through the act of writing and publishing her narrative—she subsumes much of what she could write about the extent of her suffering, but even such silence amidst this act of "speaking" demonstrates her resistance to the suppression of her voice.

In *Incidents,* the tongue is synonymous with speech, which in turn is synonymous with empowerment; Jacobs, like Wilson, stresses how this instrument can be a threat to those who maintain their dominant place in society by suppressing the tongues of "others." When suggesting that women should keep quiet, men often tell them to hold their tongues. In such cases, men fear the truth of the words that women might utter, knowing this truth to be a threat to their positions of power. In the early pages of her narrative, Jacobs writes of an incident in which the looseness of a slave woman's tongue presents such a threat for her master that it results in her being sold away from her family. As was common on many plantations, this slave woman has given birth to a child as the result of forced sex with her master, Dr. Flint: "When the mother was delivered into the trader's hands, she said, 'You *promised* to treat me well.' To which [Dr. Flint] replied, 'You have let your tongue run too far; damn you!' She had forgotten that it was a crime for a slave to tell who was the father of her child" (13; Jacobs's emphasis).

Linda, like all slaves, knows how precious is the freedom to unleash the tongue. When she falls in love with a free black man who is in a position to enjoy such freedom, she insists that he pursue it. Knowing that her lover will never have true freedom in the South, where Dr. Flint has determined to torment this rival for Linda's body, Linda is willing to end their relationship for the sake of his freedom: "He was going to Savannah to see about a little property left him by an uncle; and hard as it was to bring my feelings to it, I earnestly entreated him not to come back. I advised him to go to the Free States, where his tongue would not be tied" (42). Later, relating a period during which she has a temporary loss of speech because of the severity of the second winter spent in her hidden garret, Linda focuses on how the cold has diminished her ability to communicate: "I had a very painful sensation of coldness in my head; even my face and tongue stiffened, and I lost the power of speech" (122).

The final communicative body part that Jacobs addresses in her narrative, one that is implied in Wilson's narrative but of which she does not speak directly, is the throat. The throat is the site of the larynx—the voice box. By stuffing it, the oppressor again attacks the site of speech and agency—and words cannot get past the throat to be heard in a public place. Stuffing the throat also serves to reinforce the characterization that the black, made dumb in this way, is more animal than human. One incident described by Jacobs illustrates Dr. Flint's cruelty to those who serve him as he punishes a slave woman by forcing her into wordless obedience: "Dr. Flint was an epicure. The cook never sent a dinner to his table without fear and trembling; for if there happened to be a dish not to his liking, he would either order her to be whipped, or compel her to eat every mouthful of it in his presence. The poor, hungry creature might not have objected to eating it; but she did object to having her master cram it down her throat till she choked" (12).

While oppressors like Mrs. Bellmont and Dr. Flint use silencing to control the enslaved, Wilson and Jacobs continue to show that their apparent victims also use silence as a mother tongue technique of subtle resistance to their oppression; they use it to withhold information as well as to communicate among themselves when words are not necessary. Silence allows them to conceal from those who might harm them what they really think, feel, see, and hear. Again, because of the abusive nature of American slavery, acts like silence and concealment are more prevalent in *Incidents* than in *Our Nig,* although there are an amazing number of silence instances in Wilson's text as well.

Some of the incidents in *Our Nig* represent periods of chosen silence on the part of Bellmont family members seeking to avoid a confrontation with Mrs. Bellmont. But again, most of the uses of this tool revolve around Frado's attempts to maintain silence to avoid punishment at the hands of this woman. Yet silence as a tool is not limited to the action within the body of the narrative. It often helps to shape the narrative by calling attention to what the autobiographer (in this case, Wilson) omits. Earlier, I noted how these autobiographers pointedly tell their readers that they will not be divulging everything in their narratives. But my point here is different, for it involves the autobiographer's (specifically Wilson's) purposeful misleading of the reader to avoid having to address topics that must, in the end, offend or embarrass those readers. While Frado, the persona, uses the mother tongue element of silence within the context of the autobiography, Wilson, the writer, uses the technique of silence to avoid making some direct statements that might antagonize her readership.

One important area of silence might relate to possible sexual abuse suffered by Frado at the hands of the Bellmont men. Wilson makes no direct reference to any sexual incidents in her text; however, her description of a very attractive Frado, her comparison of Frado's indentureship with the slave system of the South, and her intimation of Mrs. Bellmont's jealousy all suggest a purposeful silencing on Wilson's part. While Jacobs breaks the silence that was attached to the sexual abuse of slave women at the hands of their masters, Wilson holds her tongue in this earlier text. Her silence on the subject may speak for itself, however. Ronna Johnson proposes that "white male sexual abuse is a powerful if unspoken threat to the protagonist, Frado, though a threat suggested only indirectly, by means of the author's and the narrator's interventions and narrative elisions" (96). For Wilson to paint Frado in such a physically attractive light and then skirt any suggestion of sexual impropriety on the part of the Bellmont men is an inconsistency—a use of silence—that Wilson intentionally employs in shaping her text.

Within Wilson's narrative, silence under the control of Mrs. Bellmont is a weapon that she wields not only against Frado but also against the weaker white members of the Bellmont household. What is particularly interesting in Wilson's depiction of the Bellmont family is her apparent reversal of gender constructs as they pertain to Mr. and Mrs. Bellmont. One would expect the white-male head of the family to be strong, vocal, and decisive. Wilson, however, portrays Mr. Bellmont ambiguously. Although he refuses to punish Frado just because Mrs. Bellmont demands it, he usually does nothing to stop the punishment, silently allowing Mrs. Bellmont to do as she will. A case in point occurs when he refuses to believe that Frado has lied about pushing Mary into the stream: "'How do we know but she [Frado] has told the truth? I shall not punish her,' he replied, and left the house, as he usually did when a tempest threatened to envelop him" (34). So, although Mr. Bellmont is not totally silent in this instance, his refusal to punish Frado does not in itself save her. As a matter of fact, his failure to speak up and forbid his wife and daughter to punish Frado, and then his leaving her at the mercy of their anger, are indications of his weakness of character. This argument is further supported by Wilson's inclusion of other evidence of apparent gender role reversal in her first characterizations of Mr. and Mrs. Bellmont, wherein the white man, not the white woman, is silent and submissive.

When, early in the narrative, it becomes obvious to Mr. Bellmont that Frado's mother has abandoned her, Wilson writes that the situation "appealed to his sym[p]athy, and he felt inclined to succor her" (24). Nineteenth-century social codes that determined what was masculine or feminine behavior would have dictated that Mrs. Bellmont demonstrate this inclination to nurture an abandoned child, not Mr. Bellmont. As Wilson continues this passage wherein the family members debate what is to be done with the abandoned Frado, she builds on this gender role reversal by showing Mr. Bellmont fearful of his wife. To protect Frado "in opposition to Mrs. Bellmont's wishes, would be like encountering a whirlwind charged with fire, daggers and spikes. . . . [Mrs. Bellmont] was self-willed, haughty, undisciplined, arbitrary and severe. . . . Mr. B. remained silent during the consultation which follows, engaged in by mother, Mary and John" (24–25). With this description, Wilson establishes the pattern that Mrs. Bellmont will be the active aggressor and Mr. Bellmont will passively retreat, as will other members of the family who find that they are unable to protect themselves, let alone protect Frado, from Mrs. Bellmont's wrath. In situations of confrontation with Mrs. Bellmont regarding Frado, they retreat into their various pockets of self-protective silence. When the noise of a particularly vicious beating draws Mr. Bellmont and his sister, Aunt Abby, to the kitchen, they arrive in time to witness the last few blows being inflicted on Frado. Their reaction, however, is to withdraw: "Aunt Abby returned to her apartment, followed by John [Mr. Bellmont], who was muttering to himself" (44). Wilson later writes that Mr. Bellmont then "sauntered out to the barn to await the quieting of the storm" (45).

With the exception of Jack and James, the other Bellmonts prefer to withdraw into silence rather than face retaliation from this "she-devil," as Mag has named Mrs. Bellmont. Wilson writes that Jane, an invalid Bellmont daughter, "would gladly have concealed her [Frado] in her own chamber, and ministered to her wants, but she was dependent on Mary and her mother for care, and any displeasure caused by attention to Nig, was seriously felt" (46). And when Susan discovers that Aunt Abby has ceased to visit her dying husband, James, because of Mrs. Bellmont's lie that James no longer wants to see his aunt, Mrs. Bellmont stops interference on Susan's part with a veiled threat: "'You need make no stir about it; remember:' she added, with one of her fiery glances. Susan kept silence" (92–93). "Remember" what? The implication seems to be that Susan should remember that Mrs. Bellmont is the power under that roof, and a vengeful power she is.

Throughout *Our Nig,* Frado attempts to withdraw into silence so that her feelings of sorrow or unhappiness are not detected by Mrs. Bellmont, knowing that such detection will lead to chastisement for her ungratefulness, followed by brutal punishment: "She was often greatly wearied, and silently wept over her sad fate. At first she wept aloud, which Mrs. Bellmont noticed by applying a rawhide, always at hand in the kitchen. It was a symptom of discontent and complaining which must be 'Nipped in the bud,' she said" (30). And later, as James's condition worsens, she finds it difficult to conceal her tears: "Mrs. Bellmont found her weeping on his account, shut her up, and whipped her with the rawhide, adding an injunction never to be seen sniveling again because she had a little work to do. She was very careful never to shed tears on his account, in her presence, afterwards" (77).

In addition to concealing her tears, Frado often finds it necessary to conceal herself physically because of the abuses inflicted upon her. Her primary locus of seclusion is, of course, her little L-shaped room, "an unfinished chamber over the kitchen, the roof slanting nearly to the floor, so that the bed could stand only in the middle of the room. A small half window furnished light and air" (27). As stark and cheerless as it was, this "was one little spot seldom penetrated by her mistress' watchful eye: this was her room, uninviting and comfortless; but to herself a safe retreat" (87). Other hiding places that Frado uses are more consistent with the retreats used by runaway slaves. After particularly vicious beatings, she seeks protection in the woods, in the "swampy" lands, and in outbuildings, as would slaves in the South.

Concealment, as a mother tongue tool of resistance for Jacobs in her autobiography, combines with the related techniques of hiding, secrecy, and silence. To demonstrate the importance of the techniques of concealment, Jacobs uses variations of the terms concealment, hiding, secrecy, disguise, shield, veil, and screen ninety-six times in her narrative. She also uses concealment as a technique of linguistic subversion to disguise certain social criticisms within her text.

Disguise serves as an effective misdirection technique in *Incidents*, whereby slaves resist the chains of slavery, escape from those chains, and block the oppressor's gaze as they pursue their quests for freedom. Jacobs writes of six specific incidents in her narrative where Linda dons some type of disguise to deceive or divert the eyes of those who might recognize her. After running away from the plantation run by Dr. Flint's son, Linda cannot be moved from one hiding place to another except in disguise because of the reward offered for her capture: "Betty brought me a suit of sailor's clothes,—jacket, trowsers, and tarpaulin hat. . . . 'Put your hands in your pockets, and walk ricketty, like de sailors.' . . . I passed several people whom I knew, but they did not recognize me in my disguise" (111–12). A few days later, her secret garret being ready, Linda is brought out of the swamp by the black cook to be ensconced in her attic room, eerily reminiscent of Frado's little retreat, although less luxurious: "We were rowed ashore, and went boldly through the streets, to my grandmother's. I wore my sailor's clothes, and had blackened my face with charcoal. . . . The father of my children came so near that I brushed against his arm; but he had no idea who it was" (113). Even after arriving in the North, Linda knows that, as a runaway slave, it will be necessary for her to periodically assume disguises to avoid detection. In Philadelphia, she locates a shop "and bought some double veils and gloves" (159).

Much later in the narrative, Linda, with the help of her Northern employer, Mrs. Bruce, goes into hiding to escape from the family of the late

Dr. Flint, who have arrived in New York to claim their "property": "I had never seen the husband of my young mistress, and therefore I could not distinguish him from any other stranger. A carriage was hastily ordered; and, closely veiled, I followed Mrs. Bruce, taking the baby again with me into exile" (196–97).

Jacobs twice makes reference in her autobiography to the act of disguising the hand while writing letters—once by the oppressed and once by the oppressor. In the first incident, Linda, still confined in her garret, disguises her hand so that she can write a note to her brother, William, without being detected (133). The other incident involves trickery on the part of Dr. Flint in his crusade to persuade Linda to return to her owners. Not long after establishing herself up North, Linda writes to Miss Emily Flint, the niece of Dr. Flint and her true owner, asking that she be sold. Instead of receiving an answer from Miss Flint, she receives a letter supposedly written by Emily's younger brother: "This letter was signed by Emily's brother, who was as yet a mere lad. I knew, by the style, that it was not written by a person of his age, and though the writing was disguised, I had been made too unhappy by it, in former years, not to recognize at once the hand of Dr. Flint. O, the hypocrisy of slaveholders!" (172).

Jacobs's final reference to a disguise ironically celebrates the fact that one is no longer needed, as Linda's freedom has been purchased by Mrs. Bruce: "I had objected to having my freedom bought, yet I must confess that when it was done I felt as if a heavy load had been lifted from my weary shoulders. When I rode home in the cars I was no longer afraid to unveil my face and look at people as they passed" (200).

An excellent and often-cited example of the oppressed Linda using concealment to empower herself is her seven-year confinement in the "little cell" above her grandmother's attic, the last place Dr. Flint would expect her to be: "I thanked the heavenly Father for the safe retreat. Opposite my window was a pile of feather beds. On the top of these I could lie perfectly concealed, and command a view of the street through which Dr. Flint passed to his office" (100).

Aside from Linda's need for concealment, Jacobs notes several instances involving other members of her African American community in which hiding was an important tool for the enslaved black. This emphasis on hiding is both a use of the mother tongue and a means to certify Jacobs's veracity as an autobiographer. For instance, she tells the story of a free black man married to a slave woman hiding his children in the woods in an effort to prevent the mistress's new husband from claiming them as his own slaves (50). Later in her narrative, Jacobs writes that because marauding groups of poor whites are seizing the opportunity to terrorize black women at will during the Nat Turner uprising, "many women hid themselves in woods and swamps, to keep out of their way" (64). Twice in the narrative, Linda finds it necessary to hide behind a barrel. The first time occurs when she comes out of her garret and hides in her grandmother's storeroom to speak with Mr. Sands, the father of her children, before he leaves the state to assume a congressional seat in Washington. She is desperate to make sure that he has not forgotten his promise to free their son and daughter: "I crawled on my hands and knees to the window, and, screened behind a barrel, I waited for his coming" (125–26). The second incident occurs when the "mischievous housemaid," Jenny, surprises Linda and Aunt Marthy by entering the storeroom unannounced while the two are having one of their secret meetings: "I had slunk down behind a barrel, which entirely screened me" (152).

Secrecy was imperative within the slave community, since one did not know whom to trust. Slaves were careful not to speak directly about certain situations, using misdirection in case their words should be overheard by someone, or passed on to someone who could cause them harm. They were also secretive about their movements, and Jacobs emphasizes their need for stealth by using variations of the term "steal away" on a number of occasions. As children, Linda and her brother William "stole to ... grandmother's house" after hearing that their Uncle Benjamin had fought with his master; after Dr. Flint sends Linda to his son's plantation to separate her from her family, and especially from her children, she makes plans to visit them by night: "I was to go with a young man, who, I knew, often stole to town to see his mother" (87). When Linda determines to go into hiding, Jacobs writes that she "stole softly down stairs" to escape from the younger Flint's plantation (95); while Linda is in her seven-year confinement, her Aunt Nancy often "stole away" to visit her; and her grandmother frequently "stole up" the stairs to whisper words of encouragement to her (144, 151). Such stealth and secrecy were necessary ways of life for the enslaved in antebellum America.

Elizabeth Keckley's and Susie King Taylor's postwar autobiographies also show evidence of subtle resistance conveyed by concealment, silence, and secrecy, but in different ways and for different reasons. For instance, the signs of racism and discontent found in these two narratives tends to be presented in more subtle ways, as the emphasis shifts from the battle to obtain physical freedom to the struggle for self-reliance and sociopolitical equality.

Keckley's indirect approach in shaping *Behind the Scenes* is typical of the African American mother tongue strategies found in other nineteenth-century autobiographies written by black women. Keckley not only describes a number of incidents involving concealment, silence, and secrets but she herself also appears to be caught up in the most complete concealment of all—that of creating, retroactively, a sentimental, romanticized memory of the place of honor and respect she had held within the bosom of her former enslavers. It is a picture that many Southerners found appealing, as it supported their propaganda extolling the warm relationship that existed between master and slave. Despite the few early references in her text to the brutalities of her enslavement, Keckley wants to believe that this reciprocal warmth and affection does exist. For example, she speaks the following words in defense of her attachment to her former owners by telling white Northerners, "'You do not know the Southern people as well as I do—how warm is the attachment between master and slave'" (242). And when recording portions of a letter she has received from the daughter of her former owner, Keckley writes: "I give only a few extracts from the pleasant letter from Miss Maggie Garland. The reader will observe that she signs herself, 'Your child, Mag' an expression of love warmly appreciated by me" (264).

Keckley also presents, however, a number of incidents where silence is an important technique of subtle resistance allowing the enslaved to conceal real feelings or thoughts. When Keckley's mother is told by her mistress to stop crying about losing her husband, who has been taken out of state, and to pick out another mate, "[Keckley's mother] turned away in stoical silence, with a curl of that loathing scorn upon her lips which swelled in her heart" (25). Although she suggests in other areas of her narrative that her mother was happy under the protection of the Burwells, Keckley makes it clear in this passage that her mother was also adept at pulling down the veil when necessary.

Keckley inherited some of this stoicism from her mother, and she displays it in her narrative when the young Mrs. Burwell instructs the schoolmaster to flog Keckley because of her "stubborn pride"; it is Keckley's pride, however, that allows her to suffer her pain in silence and prevents her from crying out during these beatings: "I did not scream; I was too proud to let my tormentor know what I was suffering. I closed my lips firmly, that not even a groan might escape from them, and I stood like a statue while the keen lash cut deep into my flesh" (34). Keckley is eventually successful in her silent resistance to such brutality, as the school-teacher later refuses to continue lashing this proud, stoic black woman.

She later uses silence to shield herself and her dead husband from the eyes of the curious. Although her husband has deceived her by lying about being a free black, and although she later discovers him to be "dissipated," she writes, "With the simple explanation that I lived with him eight years, let charity draw around him the mantle of silence" (50). She further writes of Mr. Keckley: "Poor man; he had his faults, but over these faults death has drawn a veil. My husband is now sleeping in his grave, and in the silent grave I would bury all unpleasant memories of him" (64). Keckley has, apparently, decided to draw a veil of silence over most of her personal life. She tells the reader little about her husband, virtually nothing about any friends except for Mrs. Lincoln, and, after purchasing his freedom, only briefly mentions her son George's attendance at Wilberforce University and his later death fighting during the Civil War.[2] These omissions are symptomatic of her memoir approach: the major "Four Years in the White House" segment of her text focuses on the activities of celebrated personages around her and avoids paying attention to her private life.

A final instance of Keckley's use of silence is funereal and involves Mary Todd Lincoln's departure from the White House, a place that now is to be occupied by the Andrew Johnsons: "She passed down the public stairway, entered her carriage, and quietly drove to the depot where we took the cars. The silence was almost painful" (208).

In *Reminiscences,* Taylor describes various acts of concealment that members of both black and white communities use prior to and during the war, including some actions of her own. She describes how, as a child, she was helped by her grandmother to steal her education, much as Frederick Douglass had done two decades earlier,[3] defying the laws that forbade slaves to learn how to read and write: "My brother and I . . . were sent to a friend of my grandmother, Mrs. Woodhouse, . . . to learn to read and write. She was a free woman. . . . We went every day about nine o'clock, with our books wrapped in paper to prevent the police or white persons from seeing them. . . . After school we left the same way we entered, one by one" (5). Other incidents of concealment include the following: Taylor using the stolen writing skills she acquired as a child to forge "passes for my grand-mother" (7); her description of having to keep out of sight on a Yankee boat at the outbreak of the Civil War, as the captain "ordered all passengers between decks, so we could not be seen" by another approaching boat (10); and several incidents of reversal whereby Southern rebels, themselves now the targets of oppression, are obliged to conceal themselves— some "in the woods, hidden behind a large log" (12) and others saved by a former slave who "hid them up in the loft" of his house (14), this last description linking us to Frado's little L-shaped room and to Linda's garret above her grandmother's attic. As Linda had blackened her face in an action of disguise and concealment, Taylor writes of rebels, that "their faces [were] blackened to disguise themselves as negroes," getting close enough to slaughter several black troops (22–23). She further notes that other rebels were called "bushwhackers" because they "hid in the bushes and would shoot the Union boys every chance they got" (43).

Regarding Taylor's use of silence, there is one especially significant example in *Reminiscences;* it is significant because Taylor shows it being used dishonorably by a rebel officer, Lieutenant Scott, in a wartime truce situation. Scott uses his silence as a weapon to demean a Southern black captain of the Union army, another example that shows these writers were aware that such technique could oppress as well as resist oppression: "Major Jones was very cordial to our captain, but Lieutenant Scott would not extend his hand, and stood aside, in sullen silence, looking as if he would like to take revenge then and there" (41). Of course, when slaves used these tactics, the object of the disdain would not have been able to read such intentions upon their faces. They had learned to combine their silence with concealment so that their thoughts and feelings remained secret.

The last tool of subtle resistance I want to address appears almost exclusively in the two antebellum narratives, so I will concentrate on Wilson's *Our Nig* and Jacobs's *Incidents,* with only brief references to Keckley's *Behind the Scenes* and Taylor's *Reminiscences.* This final tool is the act of shifting point of view, that is, sprinkling the narrative with instances where the autobiographer speaks out from her text by making remarks directly to the reader in the form of general comments or rhetorical questions. In such instances, the author, narrator, and protagonist merge into one being and each author attacks or is critical of the members of her audience or of specific people and situations within her story. This stepping away from the narrative to insert a comment or criticism is a powerful mother tongue weapon for an African American woman writer, as she plays with the performance aspect of the oral storytelling tradition to decrease the distance between herself and her listeners. It also speaks to her insistence on disclosing what is on her mind in the face of society's efforts to silence her—many times she has her say either as an aside addressed to someone else or as a pronouncement just mumbled into the air.

Although I will deal more specifically with irony in a later chapter, in *Our Nig,* as well as in *Incidents,* there is an ironic edge associated with the subtle use of the term "gentle reader" as both Wilson and Jacobs use it to speak directly to their white-women readers and to chastise these inactive "true women" whose status as lady and mother is protected by European American law and custom. When Frado's dishonored white mother becomes destitute and agrees to marry black Jim, Wilson, speaking as the author, cautions her readers not to be so quick to judge something that they cannot possibly understand: "You can philosophize, gentle reader, upon the impropriety of such unions, and preach dozens of sermons on the evils of amalgamation. Want is a more powerful philosopher and preacher" (13). Similarly, Jacobs cautions her "gentle readers" not to judge Linda too harshly when she confesses to the sexual liaison she felt compelled to form with Mr. Sands: "But, O, ye happy women, whose purity has been sheltered from childhood, who have been free to choose the objects of your affection, whose homes are protected by law, do not judge the poor desolate slave girl too severely!" (54). And then, linking the textual with the contextual, Jacobs writes in Linda's voice: "Pity me, and pardon me, O virtuous reader! You never knew what it is to be a slave; to be entirely unprotected by law or custom; to have the laws reduce you to the condition of a chattel. . . . I know I did wrong. No one can feel it more sensibly than I do. . . . Still, in looking back, calmly, on the events of my life, I feel that the slave woman ought not to be judged by the same standard as others" (55–56).

Within Linda's plea for understanding is a statement of resistance to any criticism that Jacobs's white women readers might be tempted to impose. Jacobs wants to create a sisterly bond with her readers, but at the same time she denies them the opportunity to feel superior, pointing out that they have been allowed privileges that have been denied to the slave woman. Jacobs's tactic of speaking directly to white women from the pages of her text allows her to plead for their understanding regarding her own sexual conduct, asking that they not judge her based on the social standards that rule them. But even in her plea, she does not maintain this apparently passive stance, but makes the subject of sexual abuse against slave women a public and political issue. Jean Fagan Yellin writes that with women's issues as its impetus, *Incidents* is "an attempt to move women to political action" (*Women and Sisters* 92). She further states in her introduction to *Incidents* that "Jacobs moves her book out of the world of conventional nineteenth-century polite discourse" (xiv). Jacobs challenges the complacent position that free white women had assumed, and this challenge effectively allows her to form a feminist partnership with them. By implying that they are cut from the same cloth, Jacobs is able to propose an equalized relationship between herself and her readership, between black women and white women.

An interesting aspect of rhetorical questioning is that answers are neither expected nor wanted. Used as a technique by these African American autobiographers, rhetorical questioning becomes an outlet for members of a society whose voices were denied; the technique allows them to make their opinion heard without appearing to be making a declaratory statement. Nineteenth-century African American women, and women in general for that matter, were encouraged (or forced, if they were still in bondage) through a number of methods to hold their tongues in the company of European American men. As a result, many comments or questions that might have existed in the minds of women generally went unspoken. That is, these words were unspoken as direct discourse in the presence of European American men or in the presence of whomever the oppressors happened to be. A logical development, then, was the habit of speaking to one's self, even to the point of asking "rhetorical" questions that implied answers in themselves.

When Wilson and Jacobs address rhetorical questions to their readers, the questions are worded in such a way that the answers are obvious to all; however, to emphasize a point more strongly, both autobiographers, especially Jacobs, sometimes provide answers to the questions they pose to their readers. The rhetorical questions that we find in *Incidents* are more critical in tone than those we find in *Our Nig*. Jacobs wonders how her readers can sit idly by while slave women and slave girls continue to suffer: "[W]hy are ye silent, ye free men and women of the north? Why do your tongues falter in maintenance of the right?" (29–30). In the latter stages of her narrative, Wilson suggests that the reader should not be surprised when the now-independent Frado succumbs to the courting rituals of a "professed fugitive from slavery": "Such a one appeared in the new home of Frado; and as people of color were rare there, was it strange she should attract her dark brother; that he should inquire her out; succeed in seeing her; feel a strange sensation in his heart towards her; that he should toy with her shining curls, feel proud to provoke her to smile and expose the ivory concealed by thin, ruby lips; that her sparkling eyes should fascinate; that he should propose; that they should marry?" (126). Wilson suggests through her questions that, given the brutal treatment Frado has suffered in her life, the reader should not be surprised that she should gravitate toward the romantic hero promised to those who follow the sentimental edicts of the "cult of true womanhood." The sentimental model that dictates these questions is the only one she has to emulate in her search for earthly happiness.

Keckley's sentimental phrasing in speaking out from her text as the author is reminiscent of Jacobs's chastisement of her "gentle readers." She includes rhetorical questions, questions also tinged with a bit of irony, only once in her narrative. After being raped by a white man and giving birth to a son, she challenges on his behalf the stigma of race under which white society will have him live: "Why should my son be held in slavery? . . . The Anglo-Saxon blood as well as the African flowed in his veins; the two currents commingled—one singing of freedom, the other silent and sullen with generations of despair. . . . Must the life-current of one race bind the other race in chains as strong and enduring as if there had been no Anglo-Saxon taint?" (47). Keckley's specific use of the word "taint" in reference to her son's white blood reverses the common line of thought that it was the black blood, not the white, that was tainted. By creating this paradox within a question, Keckley emphasizes—without an obvious criticism of her current readers—the racist idea wherein one "blood" is put at odds with the other within one "warring body."[4] Keckley also succeeds here in demonstrating the absurdity of the construct of race and the illogical thought that would presume to assign superiority based on the supposed absence of "African" blood, a slippery slope that a number of scholars of race have addressed.[5]

Finally, near the end of *Reminiscences,* Taylor veers away from her more objective and historically focused text and aims a number of comments and rhetorical questions directly at the reader. As with Jacobs—the autobiographer who makes the most extensive use of this technique—Taylor's rhetorical questions do not seem to solicit an answer from her readers. Like Jacobs, she sometimes provides an answer herself just to emphasize her point: "My dear friends! Do we understand the meaning of war? Do we know or think of that war of '61? No, we do not[;] only those brave soldiers, and those who had occasion to be in it, can realize what it was" (50). These words also call to mind Jacobs's statements that those who do not experience or witness the brutalities of slavery cannot truly understand or truthfully represent its horrors.

At the time Wilson, Jacobs, Keckley, and Taylor shaped their respective narratives, each knew that her text would not enter the public sphere unless she was restrained and reticent in her use of language. But each also knew that language was not neutral ground and could be manipulated by her just as it was by members of the dominant society. For each, the power to write (however covertly) gave rise to the possibility that she might successfully manipulate society's preconceptions and even its prejudices to her own advantage in her role as cultural link for survivors of the African diaspora.

Allusion as Hidden Discourse in Black Women's Autobiography

double-imaged
double-imagined
dubbed dumb
can't-get-the-focus-right reality
of mulatto dougla niggerancoolie
that escaped the so-called truth of the shutter . . .
—**Philip,** *She Tries Her Tongue*

Much of what nineteenth-century black women autobiographers accomplished through their narratives came about through a specific type of concealment. Not only were actual meanings hidden but also they were hidden behind actions that suggested more benign meanings and intents. This very specific type of concealment is masking. The degree and recognizability of the masking technique varies from writer to writer. Perhaps the most successful texts are those in which the masking is most difficult to detect, and I am thinking particularly about Keckley's *Behind the Scenes.* How sincere is she in her statements of caring about her former owners and in her presentation of the bond between slaves and their masters? Is it possible that Keckley's pleasant, romanticized rhetoric is a mask? Perhaps answers to these questions will be forthcoming through the identification of the various tools of masking. In this chapter, I address those tools that Wilson, Jacobs, Keckley, and Taylor use most frequently in their narratives: biblical allusion/allegory, metaphor, song, laughter, signals, physical actions/antics, dissembling, misdirection, ironic humor, satire, and sarcasm.

Biblical allusion was for two reasons a powerful tool in nineteenth-century enslavement narratives. First of all, the Bible was used by both the oppressor and the oppressed to justify the position that each assumed. Second, the Bible provided easily recognizable points of reference both for the writer using it and for the reader. As a key text in women's sentimental discourse, the Bible then was itself a link between the text and the context of the black woman's autobiographical narrative, helping to shape its structure and its content because of its recognizable references.

Wilson's description of a young Mag's fall from virtue in *Our Nig* contains pointed biblical allusions. Specifically, I refer to Wilson's allusion to Genesis in her depiction of deception through violations of the "ear," through "whispering," and through the actions of a "charmer." For the reader, Mag's fall from grace under the charms of her young lover mirrors Eve's seduction under the spell of the serpent in the biblical Garden of Eden. Therefore, even before the reader knows that Mag will not recover from the social fall she suffers in this nineteenth-century American society, Wilson, through her use of a snake in an edenic setting, has prepared the reader for Mag's downfall. That the words of seduction are whispered so that others may not hear emphasizes the "charmer's" attempt to control his victim: "It seemed like an angel's, alluring her upward and onward. . . . She surrendered to him a priceless gem, which he proudly garnered as a trophy, with those of other victims, and left her to her fate" (6). Wilson need not go into great detail about Mag's fate, for her use of biblical allusion makes it unnecessary for her to search for other appropriate literary language to explain that Mag's road will take her into a world of pain and despair.

Jacobs uses even more snake imagery in *Incidents* than Wilson uses in *Our Nig:* the Northern abolitionists adopted the snake as a symbol of the evils of slavery.[1] While Wilson's snake reference was explicitly sexual, Jacobs's references, applied specifically to the enslavement of blacks, usually take on a racial tone; the atmosphere of evil and deception that surrounds the snake image is, however, just as specific. Jacobs's description of slavery as "that pit of abominations" in her preface is suggestive of a snake pit (2). She also applies this metaphor when she writes, "O, the serpent of Slavery has many and poisonous fangs!" (62). Likewise, the owners of slaves could not escape condemnation through Jacobs's use of biblical allusion: she depicts them as reptiles falsely bearing the banner of moral righteousness. When taking young Mary Bruce out for exercise during her summer months in New York, the fugitive Linda remarks, "[T]he city was swarming with Southerners, some of whom might recognize me. Hot weather brings out snakes and slaveholders, and I like one class of the venomous creatures as little as I do the other" (174).

When the Bruce family removes itself to Saratoga for relief from the city heat, Linda hopes to be away from slavery's threat, but she notes that even in that quiet country, she is "in the midst of a swarm of Southerners" (175). Earlier in the narrative, Jacobs explains how Mrs. Flint, convinced that Linda is having a sexual relationship with her husband, tries to trick Linda into talking in her sleep: "If she startled me, on such occasions, she would glide stealthily away," reminiscent of the surreptitious movement of a snake (34). Then, while describing Dr. Flint's anger that Linda has dared to declare her love for a free black man, Jacobs writes that the doctor speaks to the slave girl "in a hissing tone" (59). Jacobs further presents Dr. Flint as the personification of the horrors of slavery and a symbol of the satanic serpent when she recounts how he attempts to demean and ridicule Linda because of her fallen state: "He labored, most unnecessarily, to convince me that I had lowered myself. The venomous old reprobate had no need of descanting on that theme" (76).

Both Wilson and Jacobs use other allusions that are biblical in origin. Both refer to Judas Iscariot and his thirty pieces of silver, and in both instances, the Judas character is another woman who would betray her "sister" for monetary gain. Wilson's Judas is Mrs. Bellmont, who attempts to force her innocent, infirm, daughter, Jane, into a financially promising, though loveless, marriage: "Her mother wished her to encourage his [Henry Reed's] attentions. She [Mrs. Bellmont] had counted the acres which were to be transmitted to an only son; she knew there was silver in the purse; she would not have Jane too sentimental" (56). The allusion here is to the pieces of silver that was supposedly the payment given to Judas for betraying Jesus. In Jacobs's *Incidents*, the would-be betrayer is a young house slave named Jenny, whom the runaway Linda fears has spied her hiding in Aunt Marthy's storeroom and will betray her to Dr. Flint for the reward: "I afterwards believed that she did not see me; for nothing ever came of it, and she was one of those base characters that would have jumped to betray a suffering fellow being for the sake of thirty pieces of silver" (154).

There are four other biblical references of note in *Our Nig*, three having to do with water or rivers and one based on the story of Joseph. All illustrate Wilson's creative use of biblical allegory as a literary masking tool to create a framework within which to relate her tale of Frado's unchristian treatment by this Northern white family. The first incident occurs as the result of Mary Bellmont's jealousy of Frado's popularity with the other students at their school. While walking home one day, Mary decides to demonstrate her superior standing: "There was, on their way home, a field intersected by a stream over which a single plank was placed for a crossing. It occurred to Mary that it would be a punishment to Nig to compel her to cross over; so she dragged her to the edge, and told her authoritatively to go over. Nig hesitated, resisted. Mary placed herself behind the child, and, in the struggle to force her over, lost her footing and plunged into the stream" (33). The inclusion of this story not only illustrates Wilson's use of biblical references but also her use of ironic humor. First, Mary's attempt to put Nig in her place by putting her in a position to fall into the stream takes on the connotations of an attempt to baptize Nig with water, thereby suggesting Frado's need for cleansing in the presence of her master, Mary. Unfortunately for Mary, she fails to take into account that Frado may resist allowing herself to be put into such a dangerous position. The resultant ironic conclusion is that, in full view of the other students, it is Mary who takes the plunge. Perhaps it is Mary who is actually in need of the spiritual cleansing.

Another baptism and another indication of Frado's determination not to be a victim of oppression occurs in one of Wilson's "side stories" in the narrative, where Wilson uses the allegorical approach of making a direct point by indirect means. In this particular story, Frado decides to teach a lesson to one of the Bellmont sheep who tended to be mean and disruptive: "Among the sheep was a willful leader, who always persisted in being first served, and many times in his fury he had thrown down Nig, till, provoked, she resolved to punish him. . . . The first spare moments at her command, she ran to the pasture with a dish in her hand, and mounting the highest point of land nearest the stream, called the flock to her mock repast. . . . The willful sheep came furiously leaping and bounding far in advance of the flock. Just as he leaped for the dish, Frado suddenly jumped to one side, when he rolled into the river, and swimming across, remained alone till night" (54–55). Since both Mrs. Bellmont and Mary have on occasion "thrown down Nig," the willful sheep could represent either of them. Given Frado's earlier encounter with Mary and the stream, however, it is more likely that Wilson has modeled the sheep who learns his lesson here after the selfish and "willful" Mary Bellmont.

In the third biblical incident involving water, Frado gleefully celebrates Mary's recent death: "'She got into the *river* again, Aunt Abby, did n't she; the Jordan is a big one to tumble into, any how'" (107; Wilson's emphasis). This third allusion involving Mary's encounter with water is to the biblical River Jordan, but it also expresses connotations of freedom for Frado. For Hebrews enslaved in Egypt and for African Americans enslaved in the

South, the crossing of the River Jordan meant freedom. This figurative meaning for black slaves also took on a literal meaning as the River Jordan came to represent the Mississippi River. Again using the technique of ironic humor, Wilson shows that the death of her oppressor, Mary, leads to Frado's thoughts of freedom from the hardships of this world. A symbol of resistance and freedom, the River Jordan overcomes and destroys the symbol of oppression, Mary Bellmont.

Wilson's final biblical reference occurs at the close of her autobiographical saga. She suggests to her readers that the Bellmonts, a family Frado has served from the age of six to the age of eighteen, no longer give her another thought: "Frado has passed from their memories, as Joseph from the butler's" (131). Frado had faithfully served the Bellmonts, just as Joseph had aided the Pharaoh's butler while both men were confined in an Egyptian prison. And as the butler, once set free, forgot about the service Joseph had done for him, so the Bellmonts have forgotten the now-lame and impoverished Frado.

An analysis of Keckley's and Taylor's postbellum narratives shows that these two women also make use of biblical allusion and allegory, although not to as great an extent as we find in Wilson's and Jacobs's antebellum texts. While Keckley utilizes biblical references as a masking tool in her narrative, these references, like so many of her other strategies, are generally used to reinforce the romantic spin she places on her life story. Of the four biblical allusions appearing in *Behind the Scenes*, Keckley applies three to Abraham Lincoln and his presidency, and each use emphasizes the high regard she has for him. At one point, when Lincoln exhibits weariness from the pressures of the war, Keckley writes that he finds solace in the Bible: "I discovered that Mr. Lincoln was reading that divine comforter, Job. He read with Christian eagerness, and the courage and hope that he derived from the inspired pages made him a new man" (119). In a later biblical reference, Keckley regards Lincoln as the protector of the black race: "'He has been a Jehovah to my people—has lifted them out of bondage'" (154). Finally, after his death, she again presents him as the one who led her people to freedom—"No common mortal had died. The Moses of my people had fallen in the hour of his triumph" (190).

In contrast, when one of Andrew Johnson's daughters comes to Keckley's shop to have a dress made, Keckley uses a fourth biblical allusion to note that the girls she employs sarcastically refer to this young woman as "the daughter of our good Moses": "'I fear that Johnson will prove a poor Moses, and I would not work for any of the family,' remarked one of the girls. None of them appeared to like Mr. Lincoln's successor" (224–25). By attributing this statement to one of her employees, Keckley is able to avoid noting her own feelings about Andrew Johnson. Her inclusion of this passage in her narrative does more than indicate her workers' dislike of Johnson. She is making a political statement, under the guise of biblical allusion and employee gossip, that blacks in general do not trust Johnson to represent their interests. This guise allows her to express her negative feelings about Johnson without appearing to do so. Misdirection in this case becomes an effective technique of her mother tongue.

At times stepping outside her journalistic/memoir approach in *Reminiscences,* Taylor attempts to engage her readers with language that is more metaphorical, taking on a literary tone through biblical allusion that a strictly journalistic rendering would not allow. For Taylor, these moments are few, as she appears to be more concerned with making a political statement than with writing a personal narrative. Even her use of biblical allusions and metaphors as narrative tools brings the reader back to her concerns about the injustices perpetrated against the African American community. She notes the Southerners' attempt to dissuade slaves in their enthusiasm about the Yankee invasion by scaring them with printed notices comparing Yankees with rattlesnakes and wild animals. One of these notices reads, "'I am a rattlesnake; if you touch me I will strike!'" (8). It is ironic that these Southerners adopt the same serpent symbol that Northern abolitionists had long used to represent the evils of Southern slavery; certainly the notices also rely on biblical allusion that calls to mind the serpent in Genesis's Garden of Eden, whereby the Southerners suggest that the Yankees will cause the slaves to be cast out of paradise.

Taylor's other biblical references conjoin the concepts of spiritual freedom and Christian revenge. Two of these appear in the powerful chapter 13 ("Thoughts on the Present Conditions"), and a third is included in the final chapter as a beacon of hope. As so many other nineteenth-century black autobiographers do, Taylor looks to balance her chastisement of the dominant society with a suggestion of conciliation. In describing the limited freedoms and the suffering experienced by African Americans, she writes a passage that focuses on chastising those who brutalize blacks, warning them of the payment they will have to make: "Let us remember God says, 'He that sheds blood, his blood shall be required again.' I may not live to see it, but the time is approaching when the South will again have cause to repent for the blood it has shed of innocent black men, for their blood cries out for vengeance" (62). The next reference is a simple statement of equality and freedom and is similar to Keckley's statement that blacks were born with free minds and that man put them in chains ("I came upon the earth free in God-like thought, but fettered in action" [17]). Taylor writes, "God is just; when he created man he made him in his image, and never intended one should misuse the other" (67). It is also interesting to note that Keckley, in her apparent attempt to win Southern sentiment with her narrative, seemingly absolves Southerners of responsibility for her enslavement, blaming instead "the God of nature and the fathers who framed the Constitution for the United States" (xii), intimating that the slave owners should not be castigated.

While Taylor's third and final reference is meant to be conciliatory, she also uses it to emphasize her belief in the spiritual and human survival of her culture: "We are similar to the children of Israel, who, after many weary years in bondage, were led into that land of promise, there to thrive and be forever free from persecution; and I don't despair, for the Book which is our guide through life declares, 'Ethiopia shall stretch forth her hand'" (75).[2] Of course, Ethiopia "stretching forth" her hand has the possibility of dual meaning: one being the offer of a hand in brotherhood and friendship; the other suggesting vengeance against those who enslaved the sons and daughters of Ethiopia, as implied by the following lines from Frances E. W. Harper's 1853 poem, "Ethiopia":

> Yes! Ethiopia yet shall stretch
>   Her bleeding hands abroad;
> Her cry of agony shall reach
>   The burning throne of God.
> [. . . . .]
> Then, Ethiopia! stretch, oh! stretch
>   Thy bleeding hands abroad;
> Thy cry of agony shall reach
>   And find redress from God. (412)

Many of the biblical allusions used by all of these autobiographers rely heavily on metaphorical language, as does much African American literature, because metaphor lends itself to the creation of pictures.[3] Keckley especially uses metaphors to enhance her romanticized recollection of her life. She gives us an example of this visual, sentimental rhetoric when she describes her mother's relationship to the Burwell family. Keckley refuses to use this description to demonstrate the pain that she, little Lizzie, probably experienced at losing her own nurturing relationship with her mother to the demands of slavery's "mammy" system, a system wherein the black female slave nurses the white children of her master more often than she nurses her own. Instead, she presents the Burwell family as the stable nurturer of this black woman and her mother as the devoted servant who is dependent upon this nurturing: "She had been raised in the family, had watched the growth of each child from infancy to maturity; they had been the objects of her kindest care, and she was wound round about them as the vine winds itself about the rugged oak" (44). While this picture suggests on the surface the black's need for the support of the slaveholding family, very little in nineteenth-century black women's writing is what it appears to be. I suggest that behind this celebration of Southern nurturing is a masked bitterness on Keckley's part at the reduction of her mother to such apparent dependency. The passage continues: "They had been the central figures in her dream of life—a dream beautiful to her, since she had basked in the sunshine of no other" (44). I read in this passage a masterful example of dissembling by Keckley; in effect, she writes that one feels bound to a specific type of existence if that is the only type of life one has ever known. She intimates, however, that there is a "sunshine" for the heart and soul outside of slavery that most slaves, including her mother, will never experience, thus leaving them satisfied (and seemingly grateful) if their enslavement is not one of the more brutal types.

African American women and African American women autobiographers learned that many thoughts, ideas, and feelings could be exchanged with other members of their communities without the traditional use of the spoken word—either because the word was not strong enough to convey the emotion or because the word would betray the intentions of the speaker. Wilson, Jacobs, Keckley, and Taylor all use a certain amount of unspoken communication that effectively masks other meanings, techniques that include song, signals, physical antics or actions, and laughter. I include song in this nonlinguistic grouping because the meaning in the song is wordlessly enhanced, even changed, by the rhythm of the music that surrounds it, by the metaphorical meaning infused into it, and by the depth of the emotion reflected by it. Thereby, songs as tools of resistance to oppression represented variable, masked meanings for society's oppressed people as they lifted their voices in celebration and despair.

In two special instances in Wilson's *Our Nig,* Frado finds reason to sing, using song once as an emotional, spiritual release, and on another occasion to express relief and joy. The first incident is a result of her attendance at evening prayer meetings with Mr. Bellmont's sister, Aunt Abby, where Frado is exposed to the singing of Christian hymns: "Such perfect contrast in the melody and prayers of these good people to the harsh tones which fell on her ears during the day. Soon she had all their sacred songs at command, and enlivened her toil by accompanying it with this melody" (69). The second instance occurs on the occasion of Mary's departure to spend some time in Baltimore with her brother, Lewis. Frado expresses so much joy at being rid of Mary that Aunt Abby has to caution her not to celebrate so much as to forget her work and thereby bring punishment to herself: "Nig went as she was told, and her clear voice was heard as she went, singing in joyous notes the relief she felt at the removal of one of her tormentors" (81).

It is well documented that slaves were adept at using song to release their feelings of suffering, to send veiled messages to each other, and to rejoice in God. Jacobs recalls a number of incidents in her narrative wherein song represented both defiance and celebration. After Linda's Uncle Benjamin has been in jail for three months for attempting to escape slavery, he is heard singing and laughing in his cell. His master recognizes this as a sign of defiance, "and the overseer was ordered to re-chain him" (23). But William refuses to be broken, later sending his vermin-infested clothes to his master to show who indeed was the more inhumane/inhuman.

Spirituals are probably the quintessential site of the combining of joy and defiance. Jacobs notes that on one particular evening, "the slaves . . . went to enjoy a Methodist shout. They never *seem* so happy as when shouting and singing at religious meetings" (69; my emphasis). Jacobs does not fail to point out, however, that "seeming" is not the same as being, and that their songs represent more than the celebration of Christ. She states to her readers, "If you were to hear them at such times, you might think they were happy" (71). The defiance in the words of some of the spirituals belies the appearance of happiness, as in the following spiritual wherein "Ole Satan" is a metaphor for the slaveholder:

Ole Satan thought he had a mighty aim;
He missed my soul, and caught my sins.
Cry Amen, cry Amen, cry Amen to God!

He took my sins upon his back;

Went muttering and grumbling down to hell.
Cry Amen, cry Amen, cry Amen to God!

Ole Satan's church is here below.
Up to God's free church I hope to go.
Cry Amen, cry Amen, cry Amen to God! (71)

Contained within such songs are criticisms of Christian slave owners who, in the eyes of these slaves, live their lives in violation of the commandments that they espouse.

Taylor uses song and laughter to present some light moments in her military-like narrative so as not to be too distant from or impersonal to her readers. In such instances, she expresses the African American celebration of life, even in the face of oppression and death. The mother tongue techniques of song and laughter are normal relievers of tension during the war, and she strategically places incidents of laughter and celebration within her text to break the monotony of her war litany. For instance, the occasion of the reading of the Emancipation Proclamation to the troops on January 1, 1863, prompts a barbecue and celebration for Taylor's Company E: "The soldiers had a good time. They sang or shouted 'Hurrah!' all through the camp, and seemed overflowing with fun and frolic until taps were sounded, when many, no doubt, dreamt of this memorable day" (18). While it was an event to be celebrated, we cannot overlook Taylor's use of the word "seemed" in describing their "fun and frolic," reminiscent of Jacobs's choice of the same term when describing the seeming joy of slaves at the Methodist "shout." Again, even though the laughter is there, Taylor, like the other black women autobiographers, hints that other emotions are veiled by this laughter. In this case, I suspect it is the realization that, being at war, some may not live to enjoy the freedom that the Emancipation Proclamation appears to guarantee them, especially since the outcome of the war and their future state of freedom remain in doubt.

Another incident, a bit lighter in mood, is an example of contextual humor and shows no indication of masking. It centers around the regiment's adoption of a pig that a departing soldier leaves with the men of Company E and demonstrates the regiment's grasping at opportunities to ease the tensions of the war. Taylor writes that the "drummer boys" teach it tricks and that "every day at practice and dress parade, his pigship would march out with them, keeping perfect time with their music. . . . I shall never forget the fun we had in camp with 'Piggie'" (36). Again,

Taylor's selection and placement of this humorous aside is another attempt to add narrative variety to her autobiography and to personalize her "reminiscences" without becoming personal.

Although Taylor focuses much more attention on those fighting and working around her than she places on herself, characteristic of the memoir influence on her narrative, she does offer other attempts at personalizing her autobiography to show that she is able to poke fun at herself. She and a friend, Mary Shaw, ride in the camp's supply wagon to Beaufort, South Carolina, to collect some personal articles Taylor has left with an acquaintance, but they miss connecting with the supply wagon for the return trip to camp. Rather than spend the night in Beaufort, they decide to walk back to camp, underestimating the number of miles that lies between them and the camp, and also underestimating how quickly darkness will descend upon them. Scared and foot-weary, they finally reach their camp around eleven P.M., surprising the guard, who has assumed that they have chosen not to return until the following day: "He approached and saw who it was, reported, and we were admitted into the lines. They had the joke on us that night, and for a long time after would tease us; and sometimes some of the men who were on guard that night would call us deserters. They used to laugh at us, but we joined with them too" (20).

A bittersweet incident involving the singing of spirituals is not such a positive experience and occurs prior to the outbreak of the war. Taylor's grandmother and other black worshipers are removed from a church outside Savannah and placed in jail because of the hymn they are singing. By this point in history, Southern whites know that many hymns created by slaves are often encoded with messages about escaping and freedom. Because of the tension generated by the possibility of imminent attack from the Yankees, Southern whites are even more sensitive about possible black coding and masking in song. Taylor describes the incident:

> I remember, one night, my grandmother went out into the suburbs of the city to a church meeting, and they were fervently singing this old hymn,—

> "Yes, we all shall be free,
> Yes, we all shall be free,
> Yes, we all shall be free,
> When the Lord shall appear,"—

> when the police came in and arrested all who were there, saying they
> were planning freedom, and sang "the Lord," in place of "Yankee," to
> blind any one who might be listening. (8)

Southern whites, hearing the words of the song and not knowing what the
singers *really* meant, automatically assumed that the song was subversive, masking a plot by the Yankees and blacks to join in an uprising
against them. Taylor suggests that there is a double threat here for white
Southerners: the threat of collective action within the black community
and fear of black collusion with the Yankees. The irony is that the fear was
justified.

Because of Keckley's resistance to the degradations of enslavement and
because of her commitment to self-motivation and self-reliance, it is not
surprising that her *Behind the Scenes* memoir contains virtually no incidents of African Americans engaged in song or laughter to mask their
despair. However, this omission raises the question of whether Keckley is
silencing herself (in the negative sense) or whether she is using silence—
in the form of this very obvious omission—in a subversive condemnation
of white society's attempts to silence her. The techniques of song and
laughter in the African American community quite possibly represent the
most subversive of the masked African American tools of resistance to
European American hegemonic oppression. They shielded the slaves from
the gaze of the white oppressors, but because song and laughter most represented covert defiance, their defiance was seldom detectable by the slave
owners at the time. That is why these techniques were so powerful. Denial
of the existence, the necessity, and the importance of these acts of resistance is a denial of the oppression that led to their birth. One might then
wonder if Keckley, in order to maintain a romantic sense of her own accomplishments in the eyes of her sentimental readers, felt compelled to
downplay her oppression in this postwar era, or whether she is emphasizing it by highlighting the superficiality of the sentimental through her
omission of the subversive acts of song and laughter, thereby maintaining
silence in areas that would shatter the illusion she is creating for her readers.

Those outside the oppressed class assumed that, like the singing of the
slaves, the laughter of blacks was an indication of their happiness and con-
tentment and nothing more. Black laughter has always been a means of
resistance. Used often to mask the enslaved's real feelings, it said that regardless of how wretched one's life may be, the oppressed black woman or

black man would not surrender by denying herself or himself as much joy as could be found in life. Laughter was and is the African American's way of saying that she or he will survive the oppressions of enslavement and racial prejudice in order to pursue a better life. Therefore, while the oppressed acknowledge the horrors of their enslavement, they also search out and embrace the good moments that sustain them spiritually and emotionally.

Wilson early on introduces Frado's free spirit into her text, describing her as "a wild frolicky thing" (18). Even after experiencing the brutal punishments later inflicted on her by Mrs. Bellmont, "[Frado's] jollity was not to be quenched by whipping or scolding. In Mrs. Bellmont's presence she was under restraint; but in the kitchen, and among her schoolmates, the pent up fires burst forth" (38). While she knows that her free-spirited attitude is bound to lead to Mrs. Bellmont punishing her, sometimes Frado, exhibiting the behavior of one who will always be resistant to her oppressed condition, just cannot help herself: "Occasionally, she would utter some funny thing for Jack's benefit, while she was waiting on the table, provoking a sharp look from his mother, or expulsion from the room. . . . Strange, one spark of playfulness could remain amid such constant toil" (53).

Jacobs notes a number of incidents of laughter within her story as well; her approach tends to focus more on laughter without real joy, however—on laughter used as a veil covering something else. Her citation of the following lines from Lord Byron's "The Lament of Tasso" sums up her perspective:

"Where laughter is not mirth; nor thought the mind;
Nor words a language; nor e'en men mankind.
Where cries reply to curses, shrieks to blows,
And each is tortured in his separate hell." (37)

There are two exceptions to this laughter-to-hide-the-pain focus in Jacobs's narrative: the heartfelt laughter slaves enjoy at outwitting the "massa" and laughter as a true celebration of freedom and the release of years of pent-up emotions. The first example occurs when the black cook in the Flint household reports to Linda that Dr. Flint has been tricked into selling Linda's brother and her two children to Mr. Sands, the children's real father, through a slave trader; she cannot contain her glee: "'Brudder, chillen, all is bought by de daddy! I'se laugh more dan nuff, tinking 'bout ole massa Flint. Lor, how he *vill* swar! He's got ketched dis time'" (108;

Jacobs's emphasis). The second incident happens after Linda finally arrives in New York and meets up with other black people from her Southern home. There is a culmination of emotions represented by various wordless expressions of joy: "[T]here was quite a company of us, all from my grandmother's neighborhood. These friends gathered round me and questioned me eagerly. They laughed, they cried, and they shouted" (165).

Slaves found many such nonverbal ways by which to communicate and signal to each other. For instance, Jacobs's Linda describes how her grandmother communicated not only when she wanted to speak to her granddaughter but also the nature of the meeting: "She had four places to knock for me to come to the trap-door, and each place had a different meaning" (147). The sad occasion of Aunt Nancy's death offers another example of the power of nonverbal communication, as Linda describes her grandmother's vigil by the bedside of her last surviving daughter: "Before she lost the power of utterance, she told her mother not to grieve if she could not speak to her; that she would try to hold up her hand, to let her know that all was well with her" (145).

Nonverbal, often defiant communication is at the core of an African American mother tongue, as we note with many of the tools of subtle resistance. Wordless communication also includes the use of physical antics and actions, some of which are expressions of grief or pain, such as Frado's silent weeping or a slave woman's "wringing of hands" at the selling off of her children. Others are calculated acts of misdirection.

Jacobs gives a number of examples in her narrative of the use of misdirection as an act of resistance. She describes, for example, the time Aunt Marthy dispels suspicion that she might be concealing her runaway granddaughter by actually inviting townspeople into her home for Christmas dinner, even though Linda is hidden above their very heads: "My grandmother had a motive for inviting them. She managed to take them all over the house. All the rooms on the lower floor were thrown open for them to pass in and out; and after dinner, they were invited upstairs to look at a fine mocking bird my uncle had just brought home. There, too, the rooms were all thrown open, that they might look in" (119). Through such apparently open actions, Aunt Marthy is able to quiet the suspicions of even the most skeptical regarding her possible involvement in concealing Linda.

Wilson does not emphasize misdirection so much in her narrative, but she does describe several instances where Frado seeks and receives relief from the oppressiveness and frustrations of her life through her physical antics. For instance, after she succeeds in tricking the willful sheep so that it falls into the stream, "she hopped about on her toes . . . with laughable grimaces" (55). Later, on the occasion of Mary's departure to visit with her brother, Lewis, Wilson writes that Frado cannot contain her happiness: "No sooner were they on their way, than Nig slyly crept round to Aunt Abby's room, and tiptoeing and twisting herself in all shapes, she exclaimed,—'She's gone, Aunt Abby, she's gone, fairly gone;' and jumped up and down, till Aunt Abby feared she would attract the notice of her mistress by such demonstrations" (80).

Of course, the old adage, "Actions speak louder than words" applies in appreciating the potential agency one can assume from the use of nonverbal communication. But the oppressor also found occasion to act out her or his anger and frustration at a slave or servant through the use of nonverbal physical communication. The difference was in the way the African American woman slave/servant was constantly able to change and remold the techniques so that they remained identifiably hers as a woman and as a black. White masters and mistresses, needing to vent their anger and frustration against their charges, found nonverbal ways to punish them besides whippings. Both Wilson and Jacobs, for example, describe incidents in which the oppressor cuts off the hair of the black woman out of rage and jealousy.

When the younger Bellmont son, Jack, returns home after being away for some time in *Our Nig*, he notes Frado's change in appearance:

"Where are your curls, Fra?" asked Jack. . . .

"Your mother cut them off."

"Thought you were getting handsome, did she?" (70)

Not only has Mrs. Bellmont nonverbally punished the black girl but also her actions suggest that she was jealous of and threatened by Frado's attractiveness and, presumably, sexual licentiousness. Similarly, in a fit of wordless anger at learning that Linda has become a mother for the second time, Dr. Flint attacks her: "[H]e was exasperated beyond measure. He rushed from the house, and returned with a pair of shears. I had a fine head of hair; and he often railed about my pride of arranging it nicely. He cut every hair close to my head" (77). Of course, both Frado's and Linda's

hair will grow back, but Wilson and Jacobs as black women autobiographers demonstrate through their narratives how the oppressor, when at a
loss for words, often resorts to physical actions to express emotional up-
heaval, whether that emotion be anger, frustration, sadness, or joy. The
particular act of cutting off the hair of these women recalls the prostitute/
whore image of black women and, merging text with context, alludes to
another biblical image—the act of cutting off the hair of whores and harlots.[4] Here, Wilson and Jacobs each goes beyond merely employing biblical allegory to shape the content within her text; each also uses this particular biblical theme to step outside of her text and address the
stereotypical belief of nineteenth-century European Americans that black
women are wanton, sexual animals.

We find in Jacobs's *Incidents* a reference to the slaves' Christmastime
festival of the "Johnkannaus," a physical dancing and masking activity
that seemed to serve a number of purposes. It was a release of frustration
and probable anxiety at the approach of the New Year's day sale of slaves;
it embodied a shared communal experience for slaves as they embraced
what was an obvious carryover of an African tradition;[5] and it allowed the
slaves, under the guise of this celebration, to go begging from door to door,
obtaining money, food, and beverages from whites, for, as Jacobs writes,
"It is seldom that any white man or child refuses to give them a trifle"
(119).

There is little use of physical antics as a tool of masking in either *Behind the Scenes* or *Reminiscences*. Again, this is the type of resistance tool
that was more likely to be employed by those writers highlighting the
need to fight ongoing oppression; in other words, it was a strategy that
better served the needs of antebellum autobiographers. However, a technique that all four autobiographers found a need for was dissembling, that
is, putting on an appearance, pretending, and playing make-believe,
whether to deceive others or—as perhaps in the case of Keckley—one's
self.

In a form of dissembling, Taylor is careful to balance her criticisms of
the dominant culture with conciliatory statements, much like the technique found in Wilson, Jacobs, and Keckley, but for a different reason.
Writing that she does not condemn all European Americans, she attempts
to create a healing tone conducive to the major themes in her narrative—
love of country, unity, and nationalism. Although she remains critical of
American justice, she interjects a note of optimism in her final chapter:

"We hope for better conditions in the future, and feel sure they will come in time, surely if slowly" (75). Whether Taylor is seriously optimistic here or demonstrating again her ironic humor, it is difficult to say.

An excellent example of dissembling on the part of slaves is noted by Jacobs in *Incidents* when Luke, a runaway, tells Linda Brent how he got his hands on his dead master's money. When the brutal "Massa Henry" finally died, Luke put his plan into action: "'Massa Henry he lib till ebery body vish him dead; an ven he did die, I knowed de debbil would hab him, an vouldn't vant him to bring his money 'long too. So I tuk some of his bills, and put 'em in de pockets of his ole trousers. An ven he was buried, dis nigger ask fur dem ole trousers, an dey gub 'em to me.' With a low, chuckling laugh, he added, 'you see I didn't *steal* it; dey *gub* it to me'" (193; Jacobs's emphasis). Jacobs demonstrates here the masking tool of dissembling rather than the flagrant tool of lying; Luke does not tell an untruth, but, in the way of the trickster, he outwits his oppressors by distorting and masking his true intentions.

Keckley's seemingly wistful thinking about most of her Southern slavery experience represents an attempt to cast a positive light on that past, thereby precluding overtly sarcastic statements about the antebellum South. However, there are a few covert hints that periodically emerge from the pages of *Behind the Scenes* that belie the Southern myth Keckley attempts to sustain and which suggest a certain amount of dissembling on Keckley's part as well. A telling example that reveals one of the apparent cracks in Keckley's fantasy slips out late in the narrative when she speaks to Mary Todd Lincoln about the letters the former First Lady is writing to a broker in an effort to relieve her finances. The broker, Mr. Brady, tells Mrs. Lincoln to write letters describing her economic straits so that he can threaten to publish them, thereby pressuring Congress into providing her with funds so as to avoid embarrassment: "When writing the letters I stood at Mrs. Lincoln's elbow, and suggested that they be couched in the mildest language possible" (294). This incident is an excellent example of the cracks and ruptures that must appear in women's autobiography, especially in the autobiography of black women who are attempting to juggle so many sociopolitical balls in the air. It is my premise that Keckley has taken her own advice to heart in the shaping of *Behind the Scenes* and has "couched" the words of her autobiography in the "mildest language possible." Such "couching" took on the form of dissembling by allowing this black woman writer to claim, when necessary, that her words were, perhaps, misinterpreted by the reader.

Juggling of the language also led to black women autobiographers' use of satire and sarcasm in addressing the racial attitudes of whites. While most whites who lived in Northern states presented themselves as being more open-minded than their Southern neighbors regarding the issues of race, it was obvious to both Wilson and Jacobs that the tolerance many Northern whites felt was limited to blacks residing in the distant South; many Northern whites who did treat blacks with kindness still considered those blacks to be of an inferior race. Wilson presents the Bellmonts, with the exceptions of Mrs. Bellmont and Mary Bellmont, as being the "tolerant" type of Northerner. However, even the members of the family who like Frado and are kind to her do not see her as being quite on their level; they treat her like a "pet Negro," failing to acknowledge her equality in humanity and intelligence, or seeing such positive traits as exceptions for the Negro.[6]

In one satirical episode, Wilson writes that Mrs. Bellmont complains to her husband about Frado's presumptions of Christianity and is resentful of Frado's attendance at church meetings: "'[W]ho ever thought of having a nigger go [to church], except to drive others there? Why, according to you and James, we should very soon have her in the parlor, as smart as our own girls'" (89). Contrary to the prevailing opinion that blacks were intellectually inferior to whites, Wilson has Mrs. Bellmont not only acknowledging Frado's intelligence but also showing fear of the equality of that intelligence, and, therefore, fearing the black race as an equal in society to the white race—"as smart as" her own. In other words, Mrs. Bellmont is threatened by Frado (and the race she represents), even while minimizing and oppressing her. This is a prime example of Wilson using her narrative to address a topic of her time. The oppression that Frado suffers at the hands of Mrs. Bellmont and her daughter Mary—and Frado's resistance to that oppression—form the core of Wilson's dramatic use of an African American mother tongue. Underlying all of her verbal and nonverbal techniques is the hint of satire, sarcasm, or ironic humor.

While Wilson's *Our Nig* revolves around the racial bias Frado suffers in the North, Jacobs also makes racism and hypocrisy in the Northern states important subjects in her autobiography. Using the literary tool of sarcasm, she writes about the disappointment Linda experiences after she reaches free soil. As a matter of fact, when Linda first sets foot on the dock in Philadelphia, Jacobs's sarcastic voice is clearly heard, hinting that the North which Linda expects to find will not be the North that she will soon encounter: "The next morning I was on deck as soon as the day dawned. I called Fanny to see the sun rise, for the first time in our lives, on free soil; for such I *then* believed it to be" (158; Jacobs's emphasis). Jacobs later writes about that first evening in the free states: "That night I sought my pillow with feelings I had never carried to it before. I verily *believed* myself to be a free woman" (161; my emphasis). Jacobs's emphasis and mine combine to show that Jacobs is using her text retrospectively, emphasizing not the elation that Linda feels in stepping on free soil, but gearing the tone of the narrative to address, from a distance, the hollowness of that elation.

In the chapter she calls "Prejudice Against Color," Jacobs continues in this sarcastic vein as she relates how Linda, traveling under white protection as a nurse for Mrs. Bruce's baby, is, under those conditions, able to avoid the racial bias that she had not expected to encounter when she had envisioned freedom in the Northern states: "Being in servitude to the Anglo-Saxon race, I was not put into a 'Jim Crow car,' on our way to Rockaway, neither was I invited to ride through the streets on top of trunks in a truck; but every where I found the same manifestations of that cruel prejudice, which so discourages the feelings, and represses the energies of the colored people" (176). Recalling apparent color-blindness she had noted on the part of the English during "A Visit to England," Linda is further disheartened by knowing that she must upon returning home once again face an American racism that continues to oppress her and her people: "During all that time, I never saw the slightest symptom of prejudice against color. Indeed, I entirely forgot it, till the time came for us to return to America" (185).

Keckley demonstrates a careful, studied use of the masking resistance technique of sarcasm, although more infrequently than either of the antebellum autobiographers or Taylor. Again, Keckley's greater need to mollify her readers, to engage their support, limits the amount of vigor with which she expresses her moments of discontent. Almost all of Keckley's uses of sarcasm and reader-directed rhetorical questions relate to her years of enslavement or to specific actions in which she calls attention to the exclusion or minimization of the contributions of blacks in general. Twice she uses sarcasm in noting slavery's reduction of blacks to the level of animals, an image regularly found in slave narratives of the antebellum period.

All slave narrators write that the majority of slave traders and slave owners, satisfied that African Americans were not as human as whites, persisted in treating blacks as if they were soulless and had the sensitivities of the common farm animal. One common belief was that slave women had no particular attachment to their own children, paying their offspring no more attention than a female animal pays to its litter. Consequently, many Southerners also believed that the relationship between the black man and the black woman was just as insignificant, that it was based purely on the sexual desires of both. Keckley's former mistress, the senior Mrs. Burwell, seeing the sorrow of Keckley's mother at the removal of her husband to a distant location, discounts the human, emotional connection that is being severed by this separation. Keckley writes the following sarcastic passage about Mrs. Burwell's stereotypical, insensitive reaction, but with no personal statement accompanying it: "My old mistress said to her: 'Stop your nonsense; there is no necessity for you putting on airs. . . . There are plenty more men about here, and if you want a husband so badly, stop your crying and go and find another'" (24). Although she has provided herself with the chance to do so, Keckley seems to shy away from taking this opportunity to attack racial sociopolitical beliefs and constructs. Keckley records a second incident that forces her, perhaps unwillingly, to note the inhumane treatment of slaves at the will of slave owners. In this particular incident, Keckley records how a slave owner, short of funds, decides to sell one of his slaves so that he will have enough money to cover the purchase of his winter hogs. In trying to determine the value of the slave, the slave owner adopts the same valuation system he uses to determine the purchase price for hogs. The young slave brought to him "was placed in the scales, and was sold, like the hogs, at so much per pound" (28).[7]

Because she is recalling incidents from her distant Southern past, Keckley is perhaps more forthcoming in her masked criticisms than she is in addressing oppressive acts perpetrated against her and members of her race by the postwar Southerners and Northerners she is attempting to court for economic reasons. We need to look at *Behind the Scenes*'s very brief "Thirty Years in Slavery" to visit Keckley's more overt and telling descriptions of masking, showing the slaves' need to veil their true feelings in the presence of their oppressors. At one point she sarcastically writes, "Colonel Burwell never liked to see one of his slaves wear a sorrowful face, and those who offended in this particular way were always punished. Alas! The sunny face of the slave is not always an indication of sunshine in the heart" (29). This passage recalls Jacobs's and Taylor's discussion on the successful use of laughter as masking. Is it possible that Keckley's pleasant, romanticized rhetoric is a mask?—a "sunny face" put on for the benefit of the new "massas" of her time?

Of these four black women autobiographers, perhaps Keckley is the most adept at manipulating her mother tongue after all. There is an ambiguity in Keckley's writing that allows her to confound the tone and rhetoric of her text; it is an ambiguity that I celebrate in that it forbids the reader to establish, without reservation, a cubbyhole into which to place her. She is operating very much from "behind the scenes," subversively orchestrating her text, much like the peddler in "Wizard of Oz"—except no one has yet managed to pull back the curtain to reveal the mechanics of her techniques.

Flagrant Resistance,
and Punishment Be Damned

> Surely thought requires language—how can you, without lan-
> guage, think or conceptualize? What happens to a language that is
> withheld or only used in a particular way with its users—does it
> become dissociated?
> —**Philip,** *She Tries Her Tongue*

In virtually all secular nineteenth-century black women's autobiographies written by formerly enslaved women, there are moments when the
author, the protagonist, and other oppressed blacks that these women
present in their narratives fight back, deliberately letting the oppressor
know that they retain a voice and that attempts to suppress that voice
have not been successful. Often, these moments of flagrant resistance lead
to severe punishment, or even death. These moments, however, also keep
the oppressor a bit unsure, not knowing when and under what circumstances the oppressed might strike back. The four autobiographers I treat
here make substantial use of the tools of flagrant resistance as these tools
further the goals of their narratives. I address specifically irony, sass/inso-
lence/impudence, backtalking, rage, and invective.

Wilson's mother tongue subversive techniques include the use of
irony and ironic humor as well as the masking tools of sarcasm and satire
in the structuring and presentation of *Our Nig.* In addition to the episodes
of resistance involving the protagonist Frado within the text, Wilson displays "double consciousness and double vision" in structuring the title
page, the epigraphs, and the various themes of her story to resist hegemonic oppression. According to Bernard Bell, the title and author's pseudonym, "By 'Our Nig,'" are an ironic play on the paternalistic identity
imposed on some black family servants by the master class. As Wilson's
use of the quotation marks indicates, she does not accept uncritically her
white-ascribed identity (Bell 47). Wilson is not only criticizing those who

carelessly use the deprecating term "nig" (or nigger) for blacks (or Negroes) but she also criticizes those who would dare claim ownership of another person when she highlights the possessive pronoun "our." Wilson, thus, turns the tables on her readers, bringing them shame and embarrassment when she embraces and simultaneously subverts the term "Our Nig." A number of scholars, including Phyllis Cole and Henry Louis Gates Jr., make note of the demeaning connotation attached to the term "nigger." Gates writes in his introduction to Our Nig, "We are free to speculate whether the oblivion into which Harriet Wilson disappeared for well over a century resulted from the boldness of her themes and from turning to that hated epithet, 'nigger,' both for title and authorial, if pseudonymous, identity" (xxix). Cole calls "nig" a "racial slur that is the book's title" (38).[1] Wilson proceeds to weave "ironic play" in and out of her narrative, sometimes making its presence felt in the actions of her characters, but more often using it as the vehicle for her voice as author to emerge.

While Wilson's irony may have escaped the perception of many of her nineteenth-century European American readers, it would not have been lost on African American readers. Unfortunately, I would surmise that her use of the term "nig" probably brought more shame and embarrassment to black readers in the nineteenth century than it did to white readers, as they probably would not have appreciated the irony in its usage nor thanked Wilson for placing it in such a public light. There is no evidence that there was any cry of outrage on the part of the white reading public about Wilson's book or about its use of the word "nig." On the contrary, as noted by Eric Gardner, many of the copies of Our Nig that were sold in the New England area were purchased by whites and used to educate their children about the virtues of faith. In researching the nineteenth-century publication history and distribution patterns of Our Nig, Gardner notes that the first readers for the narrative were not the black readers that Wilson addresses or the abolitionists, who may have shunned the book because of its attack on their character and behavior, but were "white, middle-class readers . . . under the age of twenty when Our Nig was printed" (227–28). The vast majority of the readers of Our Nig were not Wilson's "colored brethren," as she intimates in her preface, but were young white boys and girls just entering their maturity. Gardner concludes that "the book's purchasers either interpreted or deployed Our Nig as a book geared toward the moral improvement of young readers" (228). If that is true, then the irony contained in the narrative and in its title was clearly missed by the members of the white middle-class society who were actually its target.

In addition to the flagrant use of the "Nig" epithet, Wilson uses each section of her title as an indictment of Northern racial hypocrisy: reference to the protagonist as a "Free Black"; the image of the "Two-Story White House"; the geopolitical location of the oppression as being "North"; and Wilson's concluding words, "Even There." The irony of Frado's "free" status becomes obvious as Wilson details the slavelike treatment that Frado receives at the hands of Mrs. Bellmont; however, the irony of Wilson's depiction of the "white house" is two-fold. Not only does it evoke the image of the "big house" on the Southern plantation but also calls to mind the residence of the President of the United States, a site of white political power that has failed to protect this black child. Frado, perhaps, can be viewed as a metaphor for all blacks brutalized and/or enslaved in the New World. Wilson's reference to the "North" is also ironic, suggesting that while it is a supposed site of power and freedom, it has not fulfilled its promise of equality for blacks. This criticism is particularly telling because it challenges the commitment to providing freedom and equality that the abolitionists boasted were available to runaway slaves. Her use of the term "even there" conveys her belief that the kind of oppression traditionally represented by the supporters of Southern slavery can exist in any heart, anywhere; she determines to use her narrative to prove this thesis.

Wilson pointedly writes that her narrative is not intended for the eyes of the "refined and cultivated" and that "it is not for such these crude narrations appear" (3). As with her ironical use of the term "white house" in her title, Wilson again plays with her intended audience. First, if, as Wilson has stated, economic support is her intent, she cannot have expected there to be a sufficient enough number of "colored brethren" in her limited New Hampshire vicinity to guarantee such a financial return. Barbara A. White writes that the "colored brethren" noted by Wilson was "only . . . a small group" at the time she published her narrative (45). Therefore, the audience she is addressing in reality is not just the collection of her "colored brethren," but also, and more likely, European Americans residing in the New England states. Her use on more than one occasion of the term "gentle reader" within the narrative also suggests that the target audience of her text is a white readership and one that is decidedly *female*—her appeal to her "colored *brethren*" notwithstanding. Second, then, if her text is indeed aimed at Northern whites, there is the veiled suggestion that these readers are, contrary to Wilson's salutation, not as "refined and cultivated" as they presented and believed themselves to be if such "crude narrations" in fact are intended for their eyes. Wilson, in effect, is making "refined" Northern whites the butt of her ironic joke while appearing humbly to praise them. Wilson's pattern for the use of irony to mask more overt expressions of rage and frustration is firmly established in her preface. She goes so far as to state that she does not intend to draw attention away from the crime of Southern slavery "by disclosures of its appurtenances North" (3). Yet her entire text, from the title page on, focuses on Northern racism and its unique form of enslavement—black indentureship.

Jacobs makes little use of irony in the writing of *Incidents*—relying more heavily on sarcasm. But there is a great deal of irony in both Keckley's and Taylor's postbellum autobiographies. Taylor's use of irony, although almost nonexistent in the early chapters of her text, becomes more overt as her narrative progresses. One of her early uses of this literary tool deals with a role reversal and occurs upon the occasion of the fall of Charleston, South Carolina. In this passage, Taylor cleverly shows how the positions of Southern whites and Southern blacks reverse themselves: "I had quarters assigned me at a residence on South Battery Street, one of the most aristocratic parts of the city" (42). Here, she finds herself, a former slave, ensconced in rich and luxurious surroundings, while the Southern members of the white aristocracy, those made rich by having enslaved and persecuted her people and who had previously owned these dwellings, are homeless and wandering. Such reversals of fortune between the black enslaved and the white enslaver also emerge in Keckley's *Behind the Scenes* and in Jacobs's *Incidents*. Keckley notes that upon her visit to the fallen Richmond with the Lincoln entourage some years after the South's defeat, she enters the Senate chamber and sits "in the chair that Jefferson Davis sometimes occupied" (166). This episode, with its subtle irony, represents an instance where Keckley claims power, quietly and without a fuss, for herself—and perhaps for all former slaves. Using this same concept of reversals, Jacobs includes an incident wherein the stereotypical image of blacks being illiterate, dirty, and poor is reversed. With the Nat Turner insurrection came the opportunity for poor whites to join the militia in search of other evidence of black rebellion. These poor, illiterate whites were angered at the refinement of Aunt Marthy and her household: "My grandmother had a large trunk of bedding and table cloths. When that was opened, there was a great shout of surprise; and one [of the poor whites] exclaimed, 'Where'd the damned niggers git all dis sheet an' table clarf?' . . . 'White folks oughter have 'em all'" (65).

An incident loaded with even more irony is Taylor's reproduction, in its entirety, of the mustering out orders that the members of the black regiment receive from their former commander, Lt. Colonel C. T. Trowbridge. These General Orders are full of hope and promises for the black men and women who had fought for their freedom. However, the irony of the situation becomes evident to Taylor as she pens her narrative thirty-six years later, leading to her inclusion of this document in the latter pages of her text. Quoted below are some of the optimistic statements that Taylor records from Trowbridge's 1866 speech: "[Your] valor and heroism has [*sic*] won for your race a name which will live as long as the undying pages of history shall endure. . . . The flag of our fathers, restored to its rightful significance, now floats over every foot of our territory, from Maine to California, and beholds only free men! The prejudices which formerly existed against you are well-nigh rooted out. . . . The nation guarantees to you full protection and justice" (47, 48, 49). While these words gladdened Taylor's heart at that time, she realized years later, as she experienced the lynching and disenfranchisement of black Americans, how hollow these statements were. But at the time they were spoken, these words lifted the hearts of the black soldiers of the First South Carolina Volunteers.

In four incidents, Keckley also uses an ironic but subtle voice to criticize the European American culture that allowed slavery and its accompanying racist attitudes to exist. The first, addressing the mixed-blood heritage of her child, comes after Keckley hesitatingly tells of her rape and pregnancy: "Suffice it to say, . . . I—I—became a mother" (39). She then goes on to speculate about the humiliation that her son might suffer because of his mixed-blood status: "[H]e could not blame his mother, for God knows that she did not wish to give him life; he must blame the edicts of that society which deemed it no crime to undermine the virtue of girls in my then position" (39). Because of Keckley's subtleties, I find it necessary to emphasize a term in this passage that suggests an alternative reading. While Keckley indirectly addresses the sexual brutalities that slave girls suffered during their enslavement, her determination to move beyond this sense of victimization is most evident in this passage. By using "then," Keckley does two things: she exonerates her current readers from responsibility for the atrocities she suffered under Southern slavery in the past, and she firmly establishes her forward momentum into a new life of self-reliance, leaving the role of victim behind her.

In the second incident, Keckley introduces an example of the hypocrisy found in the actions of many Southern slave owners as she describes the events surrounding her very traditional American wedding in the home of her last owners, the Garlands (Mr. Garland had married one of the Burwell daughters some years past and received Lizzie in the bargain). One might think from the lavishness of these festivities that Keckley was a beloved daughter of the Garlands. She even has the same pastor who performed the weddings of Mr. Garland's own children performing her ceremony. What makes this occasion ironic is that Mr. Garland has stead-fastly refused Keckley's requests that she be allowed to buy freedom for her son and herself. However, Keckley writes that at her wedding, "Mr. Garland *gave* me away" (49; my emphasis). Whether or not Keckley in-tentionally shades this passage with irony is debatable; but intentionally or not, the technique is effective. What Garland has literally refused to sell—Keckley—he now figuratively gives away.

The two final passages exhibiting irony show Keckley's awareness that racism continues to be a factor in the lives of nineteenth-century African Americans, even after the war and even in the North—realities with which Wilson and Jacobs were very familiar. While Keckley writes about the celebrations that surround Lincoln's election to a second term as presi-dent, including celebrations by blacks who supported and spoke in favor of his efforts, she informs her readers that blacks were denied entrance to the official reception, the "levee," for Lincoln's second inauguration: "Many colored people were in Washington, and large numbers had desired to at-tend the levee, but orders were issued not to admit them" (158). She makes no acrimonious comment here, knowing that merely stating this historical fact will have an effect on her more perceptive readers—the black fighting men who were responsible for turning the tide of the war and guaranteeing a victory for the Union army were not welcome in the White House. To add to this irony, Keckley tells her readers that among those blacks refused admittance was Frederick Douglass, who had worked tirelessly to recruit black men for the Union army. When he was eventu-ally recognized by a member of the Congress, Douglass was brought into the levee and presented to President Lincoln. Keckley writes, "Mr. Douglass was very proud of the manner in which Mr. Lincoln received him. On leaving the White House he came to a friend's house where a reception was being held, and he related the incident with great pleasure to myself and others" (160). The fact remains, however, that the blacks who had fought in the war and/or had campaigned for the re-election of Mr. Lincoln, were not a part of the official celebration and had to plan a separate reception for themselves, a point that Keckley wants her readers to note.

Finally, some time after Lincoln's assassination, Mary Todd Lincoln found herself nearly penniless. Keckley writes that blacks in Washington, upon hearing about Mrs. Lincoln's financial condition, offered to assist her, as she had been unsuccessful in convincing Congress to absorb her debts: "The colored people were surprised to hear of Mrs. Lincoln's poverty, and the news of her distress called forth strong sympathy from their warm, generous hearts. Rev. H. H. Garnet, . . . and Mr. Frederick Douglass proposed to lecture in behalf of the widow of the lamented President, and schemes were on foot to raise a large sum of money by contribution" (313–14). However, while Mrs. Lincoln was petitioning white congressional members for aid and was selling personal items so that she could provide room and board for her children and herself, she "promptly replied, declining to receive aid from the colored people," Keckley writes (314). Failing in her appeal to Congress, Mrs. Lincoln later decided to accept aid from African Americans; however, those "colored people" she had previously refused now declined to pursue their earlier proposal. Since no whites came forward to assist her, Mrs. Lincoln remained destitute. What Keckley leaves unsaid in her narrative is just as relevant as her stated record. Keckley ends the presentation of this incident abruptly with the words, "so nothing was ever done," to suggest that perhaps Mrs. Lincoln deserved to have her poverty prolonged as a punishment for her racialist and classicist attitudes in refusing aid from "the colored people."

Another primary example of Wilson's and Jacobs's flagrant resistance to oppression is their assumption and then reversal of critical appellations assigned to them as blacks and as women. In *Our Nig*, Wilson illustrates the use of the terms "saucy" and "impudent" as they are used by Frado's oppressors to devalue her. On one occasion, Mrs. Bellmont says to her husband, "'[J]ust see how saucy she was this morning. She shall learn her place'" (47). When Mary Bellmont feels that Frado has dared to talk back to her, she screams at the girl, "'Saucy, impudent nigger, you! is this the way you answer me?'" (64). Both the terms "saucy" (or "sassy") and "impudent" are examples of minimizing terms used by white masters and mistresses to demean and reduce African Americans to childlike, voiceless stations in society. Referring to black men as being "saucy/sassy" was also a tactic to feminize and emasculate them. In addition to being called "saucy/sassy," black women were also subjected to the term "impudent." While the term was, and is, generally used to suggest that a person is being bold or cheeky, its origins are tied to sexual behavior, thereby targeting black women (reducing them) by reinforcing their supposed primitive sexuality.[2] Many black women have claimed these terms as their own, boastfully identifying themselves as sassy and impudent to let those who minimize them know that they cannot be injured by language and that those attempting to invalidate them had best beware the sassy and impudent tongues of black women. By reversing the polarity, black women nullify the words' power to hurt them while demonstrating that they are a power with which to be reckoned.[3] Wilson's purposeful characterization of Frado as being "saucy" and "impudent" demonstrates her refusal to allow this character to be rendered voiceless. In the same way, Wilson, the writer, was being more than a little "saucy" and "impudent" herself in giving power to the seemingly powerless Frado.

In Jacobs's *Incidents*, Linda practically tells her master, Dr. Flint, that she is claiming the demeaning attitude he applies to her for the express purpose of reversing its power over her. After Linda has challenged his statement that he has the right to do with her as he chooses, Dr. Flint attempts to remind Linda of her place: "'Do you think any other master would bear what I have borne from you this morning? Many masters would have killed you on the spot. How would you like to be sent to jail for your insolence?' 'I know I have been disrespectful, sir,' I replied; 'But you drove me to it; I couldn't help it'" (40). She lets him know that it is he who is responsible for her insolence, an attitude she fully accepts and acknowledges. The challenge in Linda's reply and her refusal to be silenced and disempowered cannot be mistaken.

The mother tongue technique of "talking back" or "backtalk" is the communicative tool that Jacobs uses to challenge the presumptions of veracity in the texts of white writers writing about blacks; she accomplishes her goal through the use of subtle, indirect, suggestive language.[4] In her preface, for instance, she gently suggests that those who have not experienced the Southern system of slavery cannot possibly have a full understanding of its cruelties: "Only by experience can any one realize how deep, and dark, and full is that pit of abominations" (2). Jacobs uses mother tongue's veiled terms to address white writers, such as Harriet Beecher Stowe, who write about slavery without having experienced it or, as in the case of Stowe, without even having personally witnessed it. We read a great deal of backtalk in most nineteenth-century African American women's autobiographies, and Jacobs, like the other black women autobiographers, also uses her narrative, that is, the text itself, to talk back to and, thereby, challenge the truthfulness of the portrayals of blacks in European American–produced texts. She suggests that in writing about an experience based solely on hearsay or conjecture, these writers cannot present a complete or accurate representation of the horrors of slavery.

For instance, when Jacobs began writing *Incidents* in 1853, she may have taken exception to the portrayal of African American women in Stowe's very popular *Uncle Tom's Cabin*, published in novel form in 1852:[5] both Jacobs and Wilson took the occasion of their own work to talk back to Stowe's text by developing more fully the powerful personalities and communicative maneuverings of African American women. Phyllis Cole recognizes in her article, "Stowe, Jacobs, Wilson: White Plots and Black Counterplots," that Jacobs and Wilson engage the weaknesses in Stowe's portrayal of blacks in her novel: "Jacobs' and Wilson's narratives are powerful counters to *Uncle Tom's Cabin*, rewritings that follow upon it both historically and textually. . . . Clearly Stowe would have gained substantially if she had been able to use Jacob's [*sic*] story or accept the offer of 'some facts'" (24, 31). Stowe, obviously, did not take advantage of her proximity to Jacobs to enter into a dialogue with her about areas in which Jacobs was clearly superior. One can only theorize that Stowe might have been intimidated by Jacobs's superiority in the area of first-hand knowledge of slavery and, by attempting to appropriate Jacobs's story for use in her own text, *The Key to Uncle Tom's Cabin* (Yellin, *Incidents*, xix), aimed to silence her. At this point in her life, however, Jacobs will not allow herself to be silenced by Stowe or anyone else.

The cardboard, two-dimensional blacks that people *Uncle Tom's Cabin* were meant to be nonthreatening figures for Stowe's predominantly white, Northern audience. Amy Schrager Lang writes that for Stowe, "the slave was a blank screen on which the white writer could project any image she pleased" (138). After all, there was no prominent African American woman novelist to contradict her. When the women characters in Stowe's narrative were not mulattos, Stowe most often chose to portray them as characters reminiscent of those found in American minstrelsy. Black-face American minstrelsy had its origins in the 1830s and is known for its broad strokes of racial humor, stereotypes, distortions, and exaggerations. It was to these characterizations that Jacobs reacted; not only did she add flesh and bone to Stowe's black sketches but, according to Harryette Mullen, she also stressed the power of the orality of the black female slave—"the sass, spunk, and infuriating impudence of slaves who individually and collectively refused to know their place" (245). Mullen shows, for instance, how a strong African American woman figure in Jacobs's *Incidents*, like "'Aunt' Betty," had earlier been reduced to the comical, mammylike "Chloe" in Stowe's novel.

Chloe's recounting to young George Shelby of an incident in which she claims domestic priority over her white mistress in the kitchen is an example of how Stowe waters down the black woman's "sass" and reduces her to a minstrel caricature: "'I got kinder sarcy, and, says I, "Now, Missis, do jist look at dem beautiful white hands o' yourn with long fingers, and all a sparkling with rings, like my white lilies when de dew's on 'em; and look at my great black stumpin hands. Now, don't ye think dat de Lord must have meant *me* to make de pie-crust, and you to stay in de parlor?" Dar! I was jist so sarcy, Mas'r George'" (21; Stowe's emphasis). Mullen specifically challenges the impotent orality with which Stowe endows the character of Chloe in that scene from *Uncle Tom's Cabin:* "This rendering of the black woman's speech is not an example of a textual representation of resistant orality, but rather an instance of jocular acquiescence, owing more to the conventions of minstrelsy . . . than to African American women's traditional deployment of sass as verbal self-defense. . . . Stowe's evocation of the sassy black woman settles for a comic representation" (255). Mullen accurately asserts that the mother tongue tool of sass in the hands of a fully developed, resistant black woman character becomes a discursive weapon, while in the hands of another writer, like Stowe, who is not cognizant of the nuances in black women's communicative styles and subversive actions, it is merely a device for humor at the black woman character's expense.

Jacobs's depiction of Betty, also a slave-cook, restores the power of black women's sass. "Betty's vernacular," writes Deborah Garfield, "is that of a combatant whose enterprising caginess, womanly fealty, and urge for freedom will never be hobbled by enforced illiteracy" (278). Betty's inability to read and write does not keep her from claiming and using her powers of speech to resist the oppressions of slavery. Her oral expressions subvert the label of illiteracy and then give power to the sassiness of the African American woman's voice. Jacobs writes that from her hiding place under Betty's kitchen floor, Linda Brent listens to the black woman's speech acts: "'If dey comes rummagin 'mong *my* tings, dey'll get one bressed sarssin from dis 'ere nigger" and "'Dis nigger's too cute for 'em dis time'" (103; Jacobs's emphasis). Such statements indicate that the sass of African American women is serious business and is not for the amusement of the dominant society. Garfield further writes that "Betty realigns the kitchen's cozy associations with incendiary resolve and underwrites many of those in Stowe's *Uncle Tom's Cabin*" (279). The slave kitchen for the black woman in Jacobs's narrative is not akin to the warm, homey, domestic environs presented in Stowe's text—it is a site of battle, a site of oral resistance where the black woman's mother tongue asserts itself.

Aunt Nancy in *Incidents* represents another fully developed black woman who maintains a sense of dignity and is not merely reduced to a comic or peripheral position in Jacobs's narrative. Aunt Nancy worked in Dr. Flint's home and is described by Jacobs as "the good aunt who had served his family twenty years" (101). She was one of the few in whom Linda could confide regarding her plans to escape, and Aunt Nancy said to her, "'I shan't mind being a slave all *my* life, if I can only see you and the children free'" (129; Jacobs's emphasis). One senses the strength of character reflected in this full, three-dimensional representation even as she approaches death: "My aunt had been stricken with paralysis. She lived but two days, and the last day she was speechless. Before she lost the power of utterance, she told her mother not to grieve if she could not speak to her; that she would try to hold up her hand, to let her know that all was well with her. Even the hard-hearted doctor was a little softened when he saw the dying woman try to smile on the aged mother" (145). The dignity with which Jacobs endows her aunt counters the frivolous, superficial words, thoughts, and actions of Stowe's black women characters.

In addition to criticizing writers of other texts, such as Stowe, who exist within the sociopolitical locus of her time but have no direct experience with the atrocities of slavery, Jacobs also makes a point of criticizing a particular character within her narrative who presumes to write about the virtues of slavery. Near the end of her autobiography, Jacobs drives her point home by targeting an Englishwoman, the Honorable Amelia Matilda Murray, who has written a favorable statement about the American slave system: "I do not deny that the poor are oppressed in Europe. I am not disposed to paint their conditions so rose-colored as the Hon. Miss Murray paints the condition of the slaves in the United States. A small portion of *my* experience would enable her to read her own pages with anointed eyes. If she were to lay aside her title, and, instead of visiting among the fashionable, become domesticated, as a poor governess, on some plantation in Louisiana or Alabama, she would see and hear things that would make her tell quite a different story" (184–45; Jacobs's emphasis). Meanwhile, Jacobs assures her readers on a number of occasions that they can trust her narrative: "You may believe what I say; for I write only that whereof I know. I was twenty-one years in that cage of obscene birds. I can testify, from my own experience and observation" (52). Jacobs wants her readers to know the difference between second- and third-hand reports about the conditions of Southern slavery, reports that come from monied, privileged whites who have never suffered or witnessed the brutalities and indignities of that peculiar institution, and this truthful account of a former slave that she is laying before them.

There is also the suggestion in *Our Nig* that Wilson, like Jacobs, employs the mother tongue technique of talking back to criticize Stowe's *Uncle Tom's Cabin*, particularly Stowe's characterization of Topsy. As many have noted, Stowe limited the power of her black characters, making them less than lifelike and softening or shutting down their resistance to their oppressors. One exception might have been her treatment of Topsy, had Stowe not stripped Topsy of her defiant nature by "taming" her under the strict Christian instruction of Miss Ophelia. The Topsy first brought into the St. Clare household shows an outspokenness and insightfulness regarding her treatment as a slave, as evidenced in her following exchange with the pure, white Eva St. Clare:

"But, Topsy, if you'd only try to be good, you might—"

"Couldn't never be nothin' but a nigger, if I was ever so good," said Topsy. "If I could be skinned, and come white, I'd try then."

"But people can love you, if you are black, Topsy. Miss Ophelia would love you, if you were good."

Topsy gave a short, blunt laugh that was her common mode of expressing incredulity. (409)

Topsy, as young as she is, has experienced enough of life as a black slave to conclude that the white culture under whose power she lives is totally vested in the ideology that names whiteness superior and blackness inferior. The incredulity of her laugh comes from her amazement that Eva is so blinded to the fact that goodness, within this American society, will always be equated with whiteness and, more important, that blackness must always equal evilness. So, Topsy decides to be as good at being evil as she can be.

Under similar circumstances in Wilson's *Our Nig*, the pure James Bellmont tries to convince Frado that life would be wonderful if she would only be good; but Frado, like Topsy, expresses her disbelief:

"Are you glad I've come home?" asked James.

"Yes; if you won't let me be whipped tomorrow."

"You won't be whipped. You must try to be a good girl," counselled James.

"If I do, I get whipped;" sobbed the child. "They won't believe what I say." (50–51)

Both Topsy and Frado know that their goodness has nothing to do with the way they will be treated, and they express this knowledge to Eva and James, first with words to try to make their companions understand the impossibility of these requests for "goodness," and then Topsy with a "blunt laugh" and Frado with tears of frustration. Their resorting to wordless dismissals of the discussions embody the power of the mother tongue's use of wordless communication.

There are many other similarities between the thoughts, words, and physical antics of these two characters—at least, until the point that Stowe turns Topsy into a black replica of the now-dead Eva, destroying the willfulness, energy, and resistance that had characterized her struggles as a child of slavery. No one, including myself, would suggest that life for Topsy was better when she was a slave. My point is that Stowe's emphasis is on the unacceptability of a black in any position but one of tameness under the tutorship of white society—it is the act of taming Topsy, as if she was a wild animal being groomed for the circus, that reduces her to a two-dimensional character.

Stowe effectively re-creates Topsy in the image of her own racialist beliefs in the superiority of white society. Even so, Topsy was apparently not sufficiently civilized to remain in the United States. As a number of scholars note regarding Stowe's colonizationist views suggested in *Uncle Tom's Cabin*, by the end of the text, all of the principal black characters

were either dead or had left the country to settle in Canada or Africa—
Topsy is traveling to Africa to become a missionary. In his debates with
Frederick Douglass on the positives and negatives of Stowe's contributions to the cause of blacks in the United States, black scholar and essayist
Martin Delaney sarcastically asked, "'[I]s not Mrs. Stowe a Colonizationist? Having so avowed, or at least subscribed to, and recommended
their principles in her great work of Uncle Tom'" (quoted in Levine 82).
Robert Levine goes on to note that Stowe was so apparently stung by the
criticism of her exile of all of the blacks in her novel that "she sent a note
to the New York meeting of the American and Foreign Anti-Slavery Society declaring, in the paraphrased words of the proceedings, 'that if she
were to write "Uncle Tom" again, she would not send George Harris to
Liberia'" (83). Of course, this statement only verifies that, in Stowe's eyes,
George's possible acceptability is specifically attached to his obvious white
features; Stowe offers no change in her dispensation of other blacks in her
text. Topsy is still not an acceptable "American."

Unlike Stowe's Topsy, Wilson's Frado—even as an adult mother figure—maintains her willfulness, her energy, and her voice, despite those
who try to tame and subdue her. This determination is evidenced by her
ill-fated drive for self-reliance (as an itinerant saleswoman) and economic
independence after the desertion of her husband. Wilson takes the model
of Topsy that Stowe puts forth in her 1852 narrative and re-shapes that
image so that Frado (as Wilson) continues to resist attempts to control and
repress her spirit. By talking back to Stowe, Wilson empowers herself as
an author—she presents a willful, resistant Frado; she rejects the false
coating of compliance that Stowe has applied to the character of Topsy;
and she assures future black women readers and writers that oppressed
nineteenth-century black women never relinquished the fight for agency.
Wilson makes no attempt to make Frado palatable for white readers.

About four-fifths of the way through her autobiography, Wilson presents the sketch that embodies the deep-seated need for all people, no
matter how oppressed and presumably powerless, to have a voice—to talk
back. Through the combination of the word and the physical force behind
it, Frado discovers the power of her voice. This is the pivotal scene in the
narrative: while Frado understands that, as an indentured servant, she is
obligated to serve the Bellmonts, she realizes, for the first time, a sense of
self and a sense of her own human power, just as young Frederick
Douglass did in his pivotal confrontation with Mr. Covey.[6] In this particular scene, Mrs. Bellmont is angry that Frado has not brought wood from

the shed quickly enough, and she determines to beat Frado: "'Stop!' shouted Frado, 'strike me, and I'll never work a mite more for you;' and throwing down what she had gathered, stood like one who feels the stirring of free and independent thoughts. . . . Frado walked towards the house, her mistress following with the wood she herself was sent after. She did not know, before, that she had a power to ward off assaults" (105). Frado learns (as Wilson has learned) that even though she has been cast in the role of victim, she is not powerless—even though Jill Jones erroneously interprets Wilson's difficulty in maintaining the "I" narrative voice as evidence that "Frado is so completely powerless" (39). Both Frado the protagonist and Wilson the autobiographer learn that they can claim sanctuary and authority under certain circumstances and that there are gaps of resistance that they can occupy, no matter how brief and short-lived those moments are.

When Taylor writes in the preface to *Reminiscences* that she hopes that her text will offer "instruction for its readers," she introduces a sarcastic tone that does not fully develop into the rage of flagrant resistance until the reader encounters her chastising verbal barrage in chapter 13, "Thoughts On Present Conditions." Taylor has lived through the Civil War, through the programs (and failures) of the Freedmen's Bureau, through Reconstruction, and through continuing segregation. Not only does the young Susie talk back in the context of her narrative but also the mature Susie King Taylor steps outside her narrative and uses her text to talk back to the dominant culture that continues its attempt to oppress African Americans. Taylor is no longer as optimistic in her language near the end of her autobiography as she appeared to be at its beginning; nor does she appear to be as confident in her beliefs for social justice as Keckley was in the years immediately following the North's victory.

Early contextual examples of Taylor's youthful directness and sense of self-worth include her response to a Yankee captain during the first stages of the war who shows surprise at her literacy, suggesting that she is different from other Southern blacks he has encountered. She responds, "'[T]he only difference is, they were reared in the country and I in the city'" (9). While the captain's comment might simply have been a result of his knowledge that most Southern states prohibited slaves from being taught to read and write, it is also characteristic of the racialism prevalent in nineteenth-century European America.[7] Since that racialism was based on the belief that blacks were essentially inferior to whites, someone thus indoctrinated would assume that a literate black person was an anomaly. Taylor, in her response, attempts to dispel such an assumption by implying that had they been permitted the opportunities to pursue their education—opportunities more readily available in the city than in the country—blacks could be as literate as whites. Already, by considering the implications of the captain's remarks as they might impact her "community," Taylor, even as a child of fourteen, assumes a position that is characteristic of the African American woman who speaks on behalf and in defense of her African American community. At the same time, her response sets the tone for her later challenges of American racism and classism. Taylor's continued efforts to engage, challenge, and educate her readers are evident throughout her narrative. Yet these efforts really blossom as she turns talking back into backtalk and rage in the narrative's next to the last chapter.

In "Thoughts on Present Conditions," Taylor delivers an old-fashioned tongue-lashing—or perhaps, mother-tongue-lashing—to white Americans, whom she sees as not only tolerating but also supporting the racism and classism that continue to minimize the contributions of black Americans and to deny blacks the dignity to progress as a people. She writes, "I *must* say a word on the general treatment of my race, both in the North and South, in this twentieth century" (61; my emphasis). Her use of the term "must," as opposed to "want to" or "would like to," indicates that she feels a responsibility, a need, to speak out on certain points; it also indicates that she has, up to this point, "held her tongue" (as women, children, and blacks were expected to do) but that she can no longer deny her voice. And that voice is now dripping with anger: "They say, 'One flag, one nation, one country indivisible.' Is this true? . . . No, we cannot sing, 'My country, 't is of thee, Sweet land of Liberty'! It is hollow mockery" (61, 62).

Taylor's criticism of America's exclusionary position, especially as it applies to the racism and classism that she as a black woman has witnessed in America, can be more fully appreciated when we look at the angry statements she makes regarding the favored status of America's white immigrants and regarding America's involvement in Cuba during the "Spanish War." About the status of immigrants, she writes: "All we ask for is 'equal justice,' the same that is accorded to all other races who come to this country, of their free will (not forced to, as we were), and are allowed to enjoy every privilege, unrestricted, while we are denied what is rightfully our own in a country which the labor of our forefathers helped to make what it is" (63–64).[8] Entering into the international political arena, a very outspoken Taylor uses her narrative to address American racism in the following statement about Cuba: "With the close of the Spanish war, and on the entrance of the Americans into Cuba, the same conditions confront us as the war of 1861 left. The Cubans are free, but it is a limited freedom, for prejudice, deep-rooted, has been brought to them and a separation made between the white and black Cubans, a thing that had never existed between them before; but to-day there is the same intense hatred toward the negro in Cuba that there is in some parts of this country" (63). Taylor thus identifies this peculiar color prejudice as a sickness born within the white American society and suggests that white America infects other areas of the world with its sickness. Aside from the nineteenth-century blacks who were prolific writers on sociopolitical issues in this country—Douglass, Ida B. Wells Barnett, Martin Delaney, and others—Taylor is perhaps the only "nonwriter" (having written only this one work) to address these issues so forcefully in a text that Thomas Wentworth Higginson patronizingly refers to as "this little volume" in his introduction to *Reminiscences* (xi).[9]

Stepping outside of her own story, as she does on a number of occasions, Jacobs uses her author's voice to express her rage at the continued destruction of black families; this new destruction was caused by the enactment of the Fugitive Slave Act of 1850. Jacobs uses rhetorical questioning to chastise her passive white audience and angrily writes, "Every where, in those humble homes, there was consternation and anguish. But what cared the legislators of the 'dominant race' for the blood they were crushing out of trampled hearts?" (191). Former slaves who had enjoyed freedom for years and who had begun new families on Northern soil were no longer safe in their new lives. Jacobs's bitterness about the failure of Northerners to squelch this act and about many Northerners' active participation in the re-enslavement of blacks for financial gain is clear in her narrative. Like Wilson, she addresses racism and hypocrisy in the North as a primary theme, using the flagrant tools of rage and irony as she addresses Linda's fear of enslavement even on free soil.

Wilson also comments on how the Fugitive Slave Act affected all blacks, including free blacks of the North such as Frado. Even though Frado was not and had never been a slave, Wilson knows that the enforcers of the Fugitive Slave Act are not particular. As the now-mature Frado travels in search of employment in the states of New Hampshire and Massachusetts, she is "watched by kidnappers," hunters anxious to earn a few extra dollars and not averse to waylaying any black found unprotected in the North (129). Wilson exposes the hypocrisy of Northerners regarding their treatment of members of the black race in general; she writes that Frado, in addition to fearing kidnappers, is "maltreated by professional abolitionists," those professing sentiments of racial equality for blacks but who in actuality have no love for them on a personal level: "Faugh! To lodge one; to eat with one; to admit one through the front door; to sit next one; awful!" (129).

The chastisement of European American readers for their complacency and lack of response to the abhorrent conditions of African Americans is more or less characteristic of the secular autobiographies written by these black women autobiographers. However, their statements directed at African American readers vary. Keckley rarely addresses blacks specifically at all,[10] while Jacobs addresses them indirectly by presenting their actions of resistance to oppressions within her text. Wilson asks in her preface that her "colored brethren . . . not condemn this attempt of their sister to be erudite" (3). Of the four, Taylor is the most direct in speaking to her black readers, and she does not leave them unscathed in her criticisms of America's postwar behavior toward black veterans. Turning her gaze upon young African Americans, she chastises them for forgetting the sacrifices made on their behalf: "We do not, as the black race, properly appreciate the old veterans, white or black, as we ought to. . . . I look around now and see the comforts that our younger generation enjoy, . . . and see how little some of them appreciate the old soldiers. . . . Let the younger generation take an interest also, and remember that it was through the efforts of these veterans that they and we older ones enjoy our liberty today" (51–52). I want to emphasize Taylor's use of "we" and "our" in this passage because they harken back to black women's community-centered focus; as a member of that community, Taylor includes herself as one responsible for the vitality and cohesiveness of that community. Her scolding of young blacks aside, however, the primary targets of Taylor's invective remain the white-male leaders of the white American establishment. She injects linguistic power into her narrative through her critique of those who minimize the humanity of blacks. Her position is firm and her voice assumes authority through the self-assured, public stand that she takes in the final chapters of her autobiography.

Whenever a black person in nineteenth-century America spoke out publicly against the white establishment, the possibility of severe punishment was always a concern. However, as we see in the autobiographies of these four black women, even in Keckley's linguistically veiled narrative, black women's refusal to succumb to total victimization at times triumphed over any fear of retribution. At these times, their tongues were sharp and cut to the core of the system that sought to crush their spirits. And their actions were flagrant, calling for the use of a biting mother tongue that could aggressively convey their rage. It was during these times that Wilson, Jacobs, Keckley, and Taylor said: punishment be damned. They had something to say, and what they had to say was not pretty and was not sugar-coated. From Maria W. Stewart's 1831 *The Productions of Mrs. Maria Stewart* to the present, black women autobiographers shaped their personal narratives as social discourse, utilizing various aspects of an African American mother tongue to resist sociopolitical and literary oppression.

Linkages

Continuation of a Tradition

> praise-song poem ululation utterance
>   one song would bridge the finite in silence
> syllable vocable vowel consonant
>   one word erect the infinite in memory
> —**Philip,** *She Tries Her Tongue*

African American mother tongue techniques not only shape the nine-teenth-century personal narratives of black women like Wilson, Jacobs, Keckley, and Taylor but also they continue to play a major role in con-temporary African American women's search for voice. I noted in my introduction that while I focus specifically on a deep study of just four nineteenth-century black women's autobiographies, these four are rep-resentative of the variety of tone, style, and unique communicative tech-niques of other black women's life-writings. I note in this chapter the tex-tual and contextual similarities that link black women's autobiographies together as mother tongue statements of resistance to sociopolitical con-structs and as affirmations of selfhood. I consider the personal narratives of Maria W. Stewart, Anna Julia Cooper, Ida B. Wells (Barnett), Zora Neale Hurston, Maya Angelou, and Alice Walker, as we move from the dis-courses of the early nineteenth century to those into the second half of the twentieth century.

The search for voice always returns to the politics of language. As bell hooks writes, "Our words are not without meaning, they are an action, a resistance. Language is also a place of struggle" ("Choosing the Margin" 16). In Jill Nelson's 1997 text, *Straight, No Chaser: How I Became a Grown-up Black Woman,* the author shows how the line of descent con-tinues to connect black women through their unique use of language (and nonlanguage). Her closing chapter, "The Niggerbitchfit," gives specific examples of the communicative power of the African American mother tongue, acknowledging its gender as well as its racial implications:

> Crossing the street on the way to work early in the morning, a man in a four-wheel-drive vehicle wants to turn right, but we are crossing the street, black women. . . . He does not allow us the right of way, but turns rapidly in front of us so that we must stop or be run over. A sister turns toward me and cuts her eyes, I suck my teeth, behind me a woman mutters, "Typical!" In seconds the eight of us in the cross-walk connect, acknowledge the man's lack of courtesy, pass judg-ment. All the while we keep stepping toward the curb, reach it, and scatter in various directions. "You all have a nice day," a woman singsongs, and each of us laughs, nods, briefly united by her affirma-tion of his blindness and of our visibility, her positive wish. (199)[1]

This encounter and Nelson's description of it demonstrate several aspects of the mother tongue and of black women's acts of resistance. Here we have a man's refusal to see or acknowledge black women; we have black women communicating without the use of words ("cuts her eyes," "suck my teeth," "nods"); we have black women instantaneously forming a community of women in mutual understanding; we have black women continuing their respective "journeys"; we have music ("singsongs"), we have laughter, and we have affirmation of their "visibility."

To deny the existence of special ways of communicating within the black woman's collectivity would also be to deny the existence of the prejudices that have forced women and people of color to find alternative and subversive ways of communicating—away from the gaze of the dominant power. Both denials suggest attempts by those espousing these positions to forge the semblance of unity through the recognition of common American bonds, bonds, however, that history shows us are so threadbare at times as to be nonexistent. Except for times of national emergencies, white-male America still tends to resist acknowledgment of its female and nonwhite components. The rhetoric of black women's auto-biographies continues to chip away at that resistance with a resistance of its own. Perhaps the earliest black woman's voice to be heard from the pages of an autobiographical discourse belongs to Maria W. Stewart.

As Marilyn Richardson writes, Stewart did something in 1832 Boston that no woman born in the United States had ever done before: "She mounted a lecture platform and raised a political argument. . . . Stewart spoke out against the colonization movement, a controversial scheme to expatriate certain black Americans to West Africa" (xiii). Why was this action so monumental? It represented the movement of a woman—and even more significantly, a black woman—into a public arena traditionally restricted to men—to white men. Stewart is an important subject of my analysis because she spoke in public on public issues and because she made a public, written record of her words and left "extant copies of her texts" (xiii). In 1835, Stewart published *Productions of Mrs. Maria W. Stewart, Presented to the First African Baptist Church & Society, Of the City of Boston.* Forty-four years later, she re-issued her narrative of speeches, essays, and religious meditations to which she added "a group of letters from friends and colleagues, including one called by its author a biographical sketch, and a memoir detailing the experiences she referred to as her 'sufferings During the War'" (Richardson 79). The full, laborious title of this 1879 edition is *Meditations From The Pen Of Mrs. Maria W. Stewart, (Widow of the late James W. Stewart), Now Matron of The Freedman;s* [sic] *Hospital, and Presented in 1832 to the First African Baptist Church and Society of Boston, Mass., First Published by W. Lloyd Garrison and Knap* [sic]*, Now most respectfully Dedicated to the Church Militant of Washington, D.C.*

Both of Stewart's autobiographical narratives are characterized by the merger of genres and literary styles we also encounter in the works of black women autobiographers like Wilson, Jacobs, Keckley, and Taylor, among others. However, we also see Stewart easily moving between the characteristics of the secular and the spiritual autobiography. Richardson notes that Stewart, in writing about feminist issues, "cit[ed] feminist precedents drawn from biblical, classical, and historical sources" and that her "synthesis of religious, abolitionist, and feminist concerns places her squarely in the forefront of a black female activist and literary tradition" (xiii, xiv). Richardson especially singles out Stewart's 1879 narrative as being an innovation in black women writers' autobiography through its "inventive use of narrative technique [which] presents us with a significant and previously unexplored resource in the study of black women's literary history" (xiv). While the early part of her narrative is primarily memoir in nature and is devoted to political and social issues as they relate to the black community in America, her inclusion of incidents of a more personal nature, specifically "Sufferings During the War," allow her to merge memoir with personal narrative. In addition, her inclusion of "Letters and Commendations" in this 1879 edition is reminiscent of the slave narrative genre "when whites of some prominence and reputation frequently were called upon to write introductory paeans vouching for both the character and ability of a particular author, and dispelling any doubt that the volume at hand was the authentic work of a black writer" (Richardson 79). I find it interesting that Stewart would use this slave narrative tactic in a post–Civil War edition but not in the 1835 edition. It is so unexpected that it suggests a purposeful bit of ironic humor on the part of Stewart—a personal chuckle at the expense of white society.

Stewart's 1835 publication did evidence some literary characteristics of the slave narrative—there is a humble tone suggesting the unworthiness of the writer's abilities and there is a statement, an apologia, that addresses the writer's purpose for presuming to write: "I hope my friends will not scrutinize these pages with too severe an eye, as I have not calculated to display either elegance or taste in their composition, but have merely written the meditations of my heart as far as my imagination led; and have presented them before you in order to arouse you to exertion, and to enforce upon your minds the great necessity of turning your attention to knowledge and improvement" (quoted in Richardson 28).

In her lectures, Stewart challenges blacks to "demand their human rights from their white oppressors" (Richardson xiii) and "warned white Americans that the souls of black Americans 'are fired with the same love of liberty and independence with which your souls are fired'" (Foster, *Written* 3). Since Stewart was not a slave and was speaking from Boston, a city with a growing black population, she had a freer voice than that enjoyed by formerly enslaved or oppressed black women. But she was still a woman in a society dominated by patriarchal controls. In order for her voice to be heard, it had to free itself from those controls. That freedom came in the form of an African American mother tongue that blurred and blended a variety of styles and tones. Stewart's narrative blends literary genres (the sentimental, the slave narrative, the memoir, and the personal narrative) and employs mother tongue characteristics of subtle, masking, and flagrant resistance.

Stewart uses both the excessive literary stylings of American romanticism and the mother tongue communicative technique of masking in the following passage: "All the nations of the earth are crying out for liberty and equality. Away, away with tyranny and oppression! And shall Afric's sons be silent any longer? Far be it from me to recommend you either to kill, burn, or destroy. But I would strongly recommend to you to improve your talents; let not one lie buried in the earth. Show forth your powers of mind" (quoted in Richardson 29). As noted before, the use of rhetorical questions is an act of subtle resistance because it suggests resistance without actually advocating it. In this particular case, however, Stewart has cleverly instilled in her text a suggestion of overt action on the part of blacks in resisting oppression; while she writes "far be it from me to recommend" any type of violent action, her mere mention of the possibility and types of forceful resistance that might be employed is an advocacy in itself.

In her blending of the spiritual with the secular, Stewart often uses biblical allusions and allegories, as she does in this passage extolling God's love for the black man: "He hath made you to have dominion over the beasts of the field, the fowls of the air, and the fish of the sea [Genesis 1:26]. He hath crowned you with glory and honor; hath made you but a little lower than the angels [Psalms 8:5]; and according to the Constitution of these United States, he hath made all men free and equal. Then why should one worm say to another, 'Keep you down there, while I sit up yonder; for I am better than thou?' It is not the color of the skin that makes the man, but it is the principles formed within the soul" (quoted in Richardson 29). Stewart cleverly uses two documents that whites celebrate and revere, the Bible and the Constitution of the United States, to attack their practices of racially oppressing and suppressing black people both spiritually and physically.

In another passage, not only does Stewart offer a series of rhetorical questions; she answers them as well: "How long shall the fair daughters of Africa be compelled to bury their minds and talents beneath a load of iron pots and kettles? Until union, knowledge and love begin to flow among us. How long shall a mean set of men flatter us with their smiles, and enrich themselves with our hard earnings; their wives' fingers sparkling with rings, and they themselves laughing at our folly? Until we begin to promote and patronize each other" (quoted in Richardson 38). This passage speaks to union/unity among women, to the freeing of the minds of black women, and to women assuming "place" within the sociopolitical activities and policies of America. Foster notes that "Stewart believed passionately that women had the responsibility of speaking out and into history" (*Written* 4). Stewart exhorted her black and white sisters, from the public venues of podium and print, chastising them for their inactivity but encouraging them now to rise up: "Stewart addressed her black sisters directly saying, 'O, ye daughters of Africa, awake! Awake! Arise! No longer sleep nor slumber, but distinguish yourselves.' . . . She challenged her 'fairer sisters, whose hands are never soiled, whose nerves and muscles are never strained, go learn by experience!' what it is like for other women" (*Written* 4). Similar words of exhortation and chastisement appear in the personal narratives of black women throughout the nineteenth century. Harriet Jacobs implored white women to come to the aid of their black sisters of the South and pointed out to her white women readers that something as basic as New Year's day held such different meanings for white women and for slave women. At the turn of the century, Susie King Taylor scolded blacks of the younger generation for taking so much of their freedom for granted with little regard for the struggle of the black generations before them that had paved their way.

Like Taylor, Stewart also points to remembrances from the Civil War, but from the vantage point of 1879. While Taylor's *Reminiscences* records her actual involvement in the war and is often told in the voice of a war correspondent, Stewart "wove references to events of national import into detailed accounts of her private difficulties, sorrows, and successes. . . . She chose to locate her reminiscence at the very matrix of change, the years when the transformations she had called for decades earlier . . . were coming into being. . . . She chose . . . to persist in her determination to offer the academic and religious training she felt young blacks would need to successfully meet the challenges of post-emancipation life" (Richardson 83). Richardson also notes a textual similarity between Stewart's establishment of point-of-view in her narrative and that used by Harriet Wilson in *Our Nig*—both experiment with and shift from first- to third-person narration:

> Moved to compose a more imaginative document than the straightforward recitation of her recollections, Stewart experimented with a variety of narrative techniques . . . telling her story at time in the first person, at times in the third. . . . Through references to herself as 'our heroine' . . . and the deliberate disruption of the chronological sequence of the events she recounts, Stewart displays a decided impulse toward the construction of an autobiographical tale reminiscent of *Our Nig*, that work of controversial authorship and genre. . . . Exploiting techniques popularized in the sentimental novels and drama of the day, Stewart introduced cliff-hanging moments of uncertainty, cruel misunderstandings which compromise the heroine's reputation, . . . prayers answered in the fullness of time. (82)

In the style of Wilson, Jacobs, and Keckley, Stewart both uses and disrupts the expectations of the sentimental narrative. Richardson references the friendship that developed between Stewart and Keckley, which might account for some similarities in the blending of literary genres and writing styles as noted by Mary Helen Washington: "Like her friend, the early black autobiographer Elizabeth Keckley, Stewart undertook a sequence of forays in search of 'specific language, specific symbols, specific images with which to record [her life]'; the result is a rare and valuable experimental work by a nineteenth-century black woman gathering her resources to attempt the telling of a portion of her life story" (quoted in Richardson 84). Stewart's search, as well as those of Wilson, Jacobs, Keckley, and Taylor, of course, all led to the discovery and employment of an African American mother tongue.

Most of these black women autobiographers advance the belief that women's nurturing natures and their concerns for moral lessons are paramount to the growth and advancement of the country. Anna Julia Cooper writes in *A Voice From the South by a Black Woman of the South*, "Now let us see on what basis this hope for our country primarily and fundamentally rests. Can any one doubt that it is chiefly on the homelife and on the influence of good women in those homes?" (12). Cooper's use of "we" and "us" attempts to create the type of bonding we have seen earlier, especially in Jacobs's *Incidents*, and her use of rhetorical questions is one of the more effective employments of this subtle resistance technique. *A Voice From the South* supports the existence of a black woman's way of speaking. In her preface, "Our Raison D' Etre," Cooper suggests the reality of this black woman's speech in the following passage: "[A]s our Caucasian barristers are not to blame if they cannot *quite* put themselves in the dark man's place, neither should the dark man be wholly expected fully and adequately to reproduce the exact Voice of the Black Woman" (iii; Cooper's emphasis). The development of this voice grew out of nineteenth-century black women's need for creative expression, and to that end, Martha J. Cutter writes that "Cooper employs a musical, heterogenous speech that releases the plethora of repressed discourses trapped within the Law of the Father" (77).

Other similarities between Cooper's autobiography that link her to her predecessors include evidence of counterculture, a justification for writing, and the need for genre blurring and language manipulation. Cutter regards *A Voice of the South* as a narrative of counterculture and determines that Cooper "strategically marshals the ideology of the cult of domesticity while simultaneously coopting many of its principles" (76). We have noted the same act of embracing while rejecting sentimental ideology in the narratives of Wilson, Jacobs, and Keckley. For instance, while Cooper celebrates a woman's role as moral stabilizer of the home, she also speaks in favor of women's entry into the public arena; Cooper thereby confounds the myth of the cult of true womanhood that discourages such entry: "It is not the intelligent woman vs. the ignorant woman; nor the white woman vs. the black, the brown, and the red,—it is not even the cause of woman vs. man. Nay, 'tis woman's strongest vindication for speaking that *the world need to hear her voice.* . . . Woman in stepping from the pedestal of statue-like inactivity in the domestic shrine, and daring to think and move and speak,—to undertake to help shape, mold, and direct the thought of her age, is merely completing the circle of the world's vision" (121–22; Cooper's emphasis). This passage embodies Cooper's view of the importance of unity (woman-to-woman, woman-to-man) in building a strong nation and woman's vital part (her voice) in accomplishing that task, similar to the postwar comments of Susie King Taylor. The sociopolitical implications of Cooper's words support woman's resistance to being minimized or repressed and state her intention to "speak."

Also reminiscent of Taylor is Cooper's engagement of international ideas. Her statements at times represent her entrance into an international sociopolitical arena as she uses her "woman-of-color" voice in speaking to the oppressions under which women of color live in other areas of the world: "In Oriental countries woman has been uniformly devoted to a life of ignorance, infamy, and complete stagnation. The Chinese shoe of to-day does not more entirely dwarf, cramp, and destroy her physical powers, than have the customs, laws, and social instincts, which from remotest ages have governed our Sister of the East, enervated and blighted her mental and moral life" (9). This passage not only speaks to attempts by men to render women of color—in this case Chinese women—voiceless but it also shows the power of Cooper's assumption of a narrative voice on their behalf and for the entire community of women of color. So, while the Chinese women in this scenario are silenced, Cooper takes up their cause and makes their silence a tool with which to challenge the silencing agency.

As with black women writers of autobiography before her, Cooper feels a need to justify why she is putting pen to paper, and also like many before her, she does so in an apparent apologia: "If these broken utterances can in any way help to a clearer vision and a truer pulse-beat in studying our Nation's Problem, this Voice by a Black Woman of the South will not have been raised in vain" (iii). By appearing to minimize her worth, in the style of the slave narrative, Cooper uses the impression of unworthiness as a transcultural tactic that ingratiates her with her intended readers. The irony lies in the textual act of capitalizing "Voice," "Black," and "Woman," indicating her belief in her worthiness.

The guise of humility of the slave narrative is but one indication of Cooper's blurring and merger of literary genres. Frances Smith Foster states that "African American women continued to experiment with the literary techniques that would most effectively help them bear witness" (*Written* 5), and Cutter writes:

> In form and content, *A Voice of the South* straddles a number of rhetorical and thematic divisions, adding to its ability to create new forms of language. The work is both autobiographical and expository; in the eight essays that make up the text, Cooper draws heavily on personal experience, but her overall focus is an argument about the equality of all African American women supported through the rhetorical practices of deduction, logic, and classical argument. The text is both oral and written. . . . The voice marshaled is communal and individualistic. . . . The text therefore represents a diversity of voices, genres, and formats. (77)

Cooper's text is a heteroglossic continuation of the mother tongue experimentations of earlier nineteenth-century black women's personal narratives and acts as a link to an African American women's literary tradition that continues into the twentieth century.

Foster states that in the year *A Voice of the South* was published, 1892, we entered into a "new era in African American women's literary tradition. It became less discreet, more visible [and] writers such as Ann Petry, Margaret Walker, Gwendolyn Brooks, and Lorraine Hansberry were building both consciously and unconsciously upon the foundations of their literary foremothers" (*Written* 6, 8). Published ten years prior to Taylor's very direct discourse, Cooper's narrative took the subtle challenges that Keckley wove into her autobiography and spoke more openly. Foster names Cooper as someone "clearly in the tradition of Maria W. Stewart and others before her who had refused to be silent or to confine their comments to subjects deemed appropriate to their race, gender, and class" (*Written* 187). This determination firmly situates Cooper in the mode of those black women who use the African American mother tongue to shape their texts as well as develop the content of those texts. I offer now a few examples of African American mother tongue techniques in Cooper's *A Voice from the South* representing the categories of subtle, masking, and flagrant resistance.

Cooper recognizes that black women can create gaps of empowerment for themselves through subtle techniques of silence and whisperings: "[I]t may be woman's privilege from her peculiar coigne of vantage as a quiet observer, to whisper just the needed suggestion or the almost forgotten truth. The colored woman, then, should not be ignored because her book is resting in the silent waters of the sheltered cove" (138).

I have noted earlier Cooper's use of the subtle technique of rhetorical questioning, a staple in black women's resistive arsenal. Another example interestingly combines a rhetorical question with the flagrant tool of rage. On behalf of women, Cooper angrily asks, "Why should woman become plaintiff in a suit versus the Indian, or the Negro or any other race or class who have been crushed under the iron heel of Anglo-Saxon power and selfishness?" (123).

In another merging of mother tongue categories, Cooper uses both the flagrance of irony and the masking of biblical allegory to challenge power-hungry white, male politicians: "If woman's own happiness has been ignored or misunderstood in our country's legislating for bread winners, for rum sellers, for property holders, for the family relations, for any or all the interests that touch her vitally, let her rest her plea, not on Indian inferiority, nor on Negro depravity, but on the obligation of legislators to do for her as they would have others do for them were relations reversed" (124).

The final example I offer of Cooper's use of mother tongue techniques is a form of backtalk—the technique of talking back to other texts—and in this case, to texts that attempt to portray Negro characters. Cooper, like Jacobs and Wilson, is critical of white literary figures and their threadbare, two-dimensional portrayals of black characters in their narratives. She writes the following passages:

[William Dean] Howells has recently tried his hand . . . at painting the Negro, attempting merely a side light in half tones, on his life and manners; and I think the unanimous verdict of the subject is that, in this single department at least, Mr. Howells does not know what he is talking about. (201)

And,

> I am brought to the conclusion that an authentic portrait, at once
> aesthetic and true to life, presenting the black man as a free Ameri-
> can citizen, not the humble slave of *Uncle Tom's Cabin*—but the
> *man*, divinely struggling and aspiring yet tragically warped and dis-
> torted by the adverse winds of circumstance, has not yet been
> painted. (222–23; Cooper's emphasis)

And finally,

> I once heard Henry Ward Beecher [brother of Harriet Beecher
> Stowe] make this remark: "Were Africa and the Africans to sink to-
> morrow, how much poorer would the world be? A little less gold and
> ivory, a little less coffee, a considerable ripple, perhaps, where the
> Atlantic and Indian Oceans would come together—that is all; not a
> poem, not an invention, not a piece of art would be missed from the
> world." (228)

Of course, Cooper, those African American writers and artists who pre-
ceded her, and those who will follow all "talk back" to Mr. Beecher in
voices that prove him wrong. Cooper was optimistic about the destiny of
blacks in America. As Foster writes, "*A Voice From the South* was a manifestation of Anna Julia Cooper's belief that the twentieth century would
see a new America, one more prosperous and powerful than ever before
[and] that the touchstone for this new society would be the African
American woman . . . for as Cooper had explained before, 'Only the
BLACK WOMAN can say "when and where I enter, in the quiet, undis-
puted dignity of my womanhood, without violence and without suing or
special patronage, then and there the whole *Negro race enters with me*"'"
(*Written* 7; Cooper's emphasis).

Cooper's *A Voice From the South* is social discourse and establishes
black women's relevance in the advancement of society, although she recognizes that black women continue to face resistance to their presence and
to their voices. Nonetheless, of the "colored woman" Cooper asserts "that
great social and economic questions await her interference, that she could
throw any light on problems of national import, that her intermeddling
could improve the management of school systems, . . . that she has a word
worth hearing on mooted questions in political economy, that she could
contribute a suggestion on the relations of labor and capital, or offer a
thought on honest money and honorable trade" (135). In other words,

Cooper's "colored woman" is not chained to the domestic sphere, but manipulates her movements as she maneuvers between the private and public worlds just as she manipulates the insertion of her mother tongue ideology into the spaces and gaps of American literary and sociopolitical society.

Foster compares Cooper to the next black woman autobiographer I want to address—Ida B. Wells: "Like Ida B. Wells, Cooper essayed to defend her race by intervening into the political process through deeds of defiance and with sharply worded arguments that marshaled facts and examples from history and from current events" (*Written* 186). Wells's narrative, *Crusade for Justice: The Autobiography of Ida B. Wells* published in 1970, is unique on its own merits, yet similar to the communicative approaches of other black women writers. What is particularly noteworthy is the extended period of time addressed in her narrative and the related social and political changes occurring in America that accompany this era.

Wells was born a slave in 1862, although she was too young when slavery ended to have much of a recollection about it. In this, however, she does share some commonalities with Susie King Taylor—they both experienced and share their views about the traumatic post–Civil War changes in the South: Reconstruction, American imperialism, and struggles of blacks as free men and women in a dominant white American society. Also like Taylor, much of Wells's focus is away from herself and aimed at the history of African Americans and their struggles to obtain justice and fair treatment. A big difference is that Wells is an integral part of the struggles about which she writes. Between her introductory personal items, some of which suggest the literary style of the slave narrative, and the second half of her text which deals more with her personal world and domestic life, Wells attempts to write a primarily historical narrative with powerful sociopolitical implications.

She began writing her autobiography in 1928 after realizing that the history books were not addressing the role of blacks in American history. Like most black women writers, she begins by justifying why she is writing: "It is . . . for the young people who have so little of our race's history that I am for the first time in my life writing about myself. I am all the more constrained to do this because there is such a lack of authentic race history of Reconstruction times written by the Negro himself" (4). This brief introductory passage plays with the standard phrase of many slave narratives, "written by himself," and also ironically challenges the authenticity of the black history written by whites, ironic because questions of authenticity had been generally attached to texts written by black slave narrators. Wells continues: "[B]ecause our youth are entitled to the facts of race history which only the participants can give, I am thus led to set forth the facts contained in this volume which I dedicate to them" (5). The suggestion here echoes that of Harriet Jacobs when she states that those outside of the experience of slavery are less qualified as accurate chroniclers of its realities. Other characteristics that mirror the genre of the slave narrative include the opening establishment of humanity—"I was born" (5); the rape of slave women—"My father . . . was the son of his master" (8); and the cruelty and jealousy of her father's white mistress, such as we have seen in the narratives of Jacobs and Keckley, as Wells's father explains to his mother why he refuses to allow any contact between his children and the white wife of his dead white father—"'Mother,' said he, 'I never want to see that old woman as long as I live. I'll never forget how she had you stripped and whipped the day after the old man died'" (10). From these beginnings, Wells's commitment to family (raising her young siblings with little help after their parents died of the fever) and community (arousing Southern blacks, Northern whites, and the international theater to the horrors of the lynching of Southern black men) form the basis of her writing as social discourse in the literary stylings of an African American mother tongue.

Akiko Ochiai writes that *Crusade for Justice* claims a special place as a "protest against oppression" because of its unique perspective and literary style—it is "an historical record from an African American point of view and . . . a contribution to the African American literary tradition" (365). As I have noted, a black woman's self-writing in the African American literary tradition is firmly attached to her relationship to community and family. Wells recalls learning from her mother the importance of familial connections, although the relevance of this experience did not register until later in her life: "My mother . . . was born in Virginia and was one of ten children. She and two sisters were sold to slave traders when young, and were taken to Mississippi and sold again. She often told her children that her father was half Indian, his father being a full blood. . . . She often wrote back to somewhere in Virginia trying to get track of her people, but she was never successful. We were too young to realize the importance of her efforts, and I have never remembered the name of the county or people to whom they 'belonged'" (8). This statement embodies the regret Wells feels for the loss of an important ancestral link. It speaks to the belief that the loss of memory must eventually lead to the loss, to a certain degree anyway, of culture. Black women have always been the primary purveyors of culture within the African American community, and culture is preserved through our links with past ancestors. Wells's loss of this link in her heritage creates a painful gap that she, as an adult, is more able to appreciate than she had appreciated it as a child.

From her father Wells learned the importance of activism and resistance to oppression, even with the threat of bodily harm or death. She writes that her father "was interested in politics and I heard the words Ku Klux Klan long before I knew what they meant. I knew dimly that it meant something fearful, by the anxious way my mother walked the floor at night when my father was out to a political meeting" (9).

As a newspaper woman, Wells later employed her position and her gift for language to continue the fight against legal inequalities for black men in the South. She used her pen as well as her voice, both in America and in Great Britain, to denounce the failure of the American legal system to guarantee due process for all. Like Jacobs, Wells found the people of England (and Scotland) to be receptive to her, women dignitaries from both countries inviting her to speak on numerous occasions. The particularly horrific torture and burning death of a black man in Texas accused (but never tried) of raping and murdering a five-year-old white girl in 1893 drew international attention. Wells writes, "The fire lighted by this human torch flamed around the world. . . . Mrs. Isabelle Fyvie Mayo, a Scottish authoress . . . wanted to know . . . why the United States of America was burning human beings alive in the nineteenth century. . . . Mrs. Mayo asked if [Miss Catherine Impey, editor of *Anti-Caste*] knew anyone in the states who could come over and tell them about it. She thought that if this could be done, they might arouse public sentiment against such horrible practices. . . . Thus it was that I received the invitation to go to England" (85). Not only does this passage imply that a more humane attitude existed on the part of the British, it also supports two characteristics of the mother tongue—it shows the formation of an extended community of women and it employs a bit of the masking technique of sarcasm in displaying surprise on the part of a Scottish woman that America is still so uncivilized.

In a chapter titled "Breaking the Silent Indifference," Wells details the many meetings at which she spoke throughout England, opportunities that gave her voice a freedom that she had not experienced on American soil and a freedom which allowed her to chastise those in a position to have freedom of voice, but who chose not to exercise it. Not one to be silent herself, and often employing irony as a mother tongue tool of flagrant resistance, Wells writes that on the occasion of the 1892 World's Fair in Chicago (actually held in 1893 because the buildings were not completed on time), she worked with Frederick Douglass and the church women in the city to print "a creditable little book called *The Reason Why the Colored American Is Not in the World's Columbian Exposition*. It was a clear, plain statement of facts concerning the oppression put upon the colored people in this land of the free and home of the brave" (117).

Wells received much support from the community of black women in America. Ochiai notes that her publications about lynching "corresponded with the rise of the African American Women's Club Movement," which provided financial backing for Wells's antilynching pamphlets (367). As a result of international pressures, the financial and sociopolitical support of the black women's clubs, and extensive newspaper coverage from Northern presses, Wells began to see a decrease in (although not an elimination of) lynchings taking place in the United States. However, as Ochiai notes, Wells continued to fight against injustices in her crusade, and she used a number of literary genres to write a personal narrative reflective of her battle: "In incorporating confessional elements, Wells tries to show her life not as a mere response to conditions at the turn of the century, but as an active career that changed and reshaped American society" (380).

Confessional elements come into play as Wells, after she becomes the married Mrs. Wells-Barnett, tries to balance her private, domestic life with her public, activist program: "Even though I was quite content to be left within the four walls of my home, it seems that the needs of the work were so great that again I had to venture forth. . . . I took a nursing baby and fared forth to do the bidding of the colored citizens of Chicago" (252). Later, her ten-year-old son eased her conscience as she debated whether or not to become involved in protests surrounding a lynching in Cairo, Illinois: "'Mother if you don't go nobody else will.' I looked at my child standing there by the bed reminding me of my duty, and I thought of that passage of Scripture which tells of the wisdom from the mouths of babes and sucklings. I thought if my child wanted me to go that I ought not to fall by the wayside" (311–12). Here Wells incorporates a biblical reference to strengthen her connection with her readers, particularly her connection with other mothers.

In addition to the genre of the confessional, *Crusade for Justice* strongly embodies characteristics of the testimonial autobiography—a text which "focuses on the community and the 'self' as a member of the community" (Ochiai 365). Although the "self" is present, its presence is usually subordinated by the presentation of overriding themes that have a community focus, themes that are offered in a logical, objective fashion. While similar to Taylor's autobiography on this count, Ochiai writes that Wells's "purpose is not mere reminiscence, but rather to publicize her political positions, to raise a call to arms, and to inspire readers to action" (369). Taylor's *Reminiscences* also urges action; however, her call comes primarily at the end of her narrative while Wells makes a call for action the central focus of hers. A final characteristic of a testimonial autobiography, one that we see in Keckley and Taylor as well as in Wells, is the act of quoting "lengthy documents or newspaper accounts" (371–72) as another statement of objectivity and authenticity.

The structure of *Crusade for Justice*, while primarily chronological, also focuses on specific highlights that affect the life and work of the writer. Consistent with the "incidents" of Jacobs life and the incidents that "moulded" Keckley's character, the "vignettes" that shape Wells's autobiography represent "autobiographical turning points" in her life (Ochiai 368). The memoirlike approach that Wells, Keckley, and Taylor use grows out of personal experience, but focuses less on the personal and more on "the external events and figures who occupy some important place in the affairs of the world" (Olney, introduction xxxiii).

Wells died before completing *Crusade for Justice*, literally stopping not only in mid-sentence, but in mid-word, as she was writing about being thanked for bringing to light a racist episode involving the American Citizenship Federation: "I also received some beautiful letters from members of the board of directors thanking us for calling attention to what was go—" (419). It is not clear why Wells stopped writing so abruptly. Obviously she had more to say, but while her legacy is incomplete, her narrative shows the continuation of the characteristics of black women's sociopolitical discourses and their unique manners of expression. Zora Neale Hurston, who began writing not long after the era of Ida B. Wells-Barnett, wrote an autobiography that to many also appeared to be incomplete, not because the writer was physically unable to complete it, but because it seemed to omit so much pertinent autobiographical information.

As a student said to me recently, when most people read an autobiography, they expect to find out some truthful information about the writer, so it was a bit disconcerting for this student to walk away from an autobiography with more questions in his head than answers. It is not that Hurston's *Dust Tracks on a Road* (1942) does not provide answers, but you really have to dig for them, and even after finding them, you are not really sure how reliable they are. Mary Helen Washington characterizes *Dust Tracks* as being "a strangely disoriented book which Alice Walker calls 'oddly false-sounding.' Zora used all sorts of manipulative and diversionary tactics in the autobiography to avoid any real self-disclosure. The sections on her adult life are a study in the art of subterfuge" (19–20). There are instances within *Dust Tracks* where Hurston all but says that certain pieces of information are none of the readers' business. I am thinking particularly of the chapter titled "Love" in which she introduces her relationship with A.W.P. She reveals that here was "the man who was really to lay me by the heels," and she acknowledges, "I did not just fall in love. I made a parachute jump" (183). It obviously was a relationship of many highs and many lows, and not only does Hurston suggest that she does not know how it will end, she bluntly tells the readers, "And even if I did know all, I am supposed to have some private business to myself. Whatever I do know, I have no intention of putting but so much in the public ear" (189).

Hurston was always forthcoming, however, about her hesitation in writing the autobiography in the first place, noting that "her career was hardly over" (Hemenway 275), and in that hesitation, I feel that she is letting the reader know that she will not be forthcoming at all. To entice her to write the autobiography, her editor at Lippincott, Bertram Lippincott, allegedly proposed that what she would be writing was to be the "first volume of a multivolume work" (275). If this is true, it goes a long way toward explaining the rambling, "disoriented" nature of the narrative. Of course, another, or perhaps an additional, explanation might have to do with the legacy of the African American mother tongue approach to autobiography, with its gaps, its inconsistencies, and its challenges to expected linguistic styles.

Dust Tracks is indeed an atypical autobiography, but in its uniqueness we can see the links that connect it with black women's personal writing of earlier times. For instance, there seemingly is a tone of humility as she addresses what appears to be a predominantly white audience/readership. While Robert Hemenway describes *Dust Tracks* as "an autobiography at war with itself," he also notes Hurston's mastery with figurative language, a talent that allows her to "charm with transparently posed humility" (275, 276). Hurston's war with the autobiography (mirrored by her conflict with America's movement toward World War II at the time of its writing) makes her appear hesitant at times as she struggles to fool her readership into overlooking some of the powerful masked messages of her text. Hemenway sees a narrative that "illustrates the contradictions, ambivalence, and disappointment of Zora Hurston's personal and professional life in the 1940s" (278), and that is partially true.

Hurston maneuvers within a literary tradition where she must dodge attacks from a number of fronts, to return to war terminology. She disrupts the black-male-dominated literary tradition that emerged during the New Negro Era by writing a text within the unique genre of African American autobiography that takes on an even greater degree of uniqueness. Stephen Butterfield argues that the typical black autobiographer "is generally not an individual with a private career, but a member of an oppressed social group with ties and allegiances to the other members. . . . [This autobiography] is characterized by political awareness, empathy for suffering, knowledge of oppression, and a sense of shared life, shared triumph, and communal responsibility" (quoted in Hemenway 278). There is a bit of all of these elements in *Dust Tracks*, but they are not the focus of Hurston's text. Hurston is not writing an autobiography specifically to protest a political issue, although the narrative does manage to do that.

Contrary to Butterfield's assessment, Hurston is indeed "an individual with a private career"; she is a professional author, and as such, she is using this narrative to advance the development of her text as an artistic work. This reality establishes a point of departure from the nineteenth-century black women's autobiographies we have thus far reviewed—those which black women wrote with the purpose of raising money for personal needs or with the purpose of broadly challenging the oppressions created by slavery and racism. These autobiographers are different from Hurston in that they were not professional writers and their aims were not to become professional writers. We will see this same point of departure in the autobiographies of Maya Angelou and Alice Walker, who are also professional writers engaged in the "private careers" of literature. But rather than disconnecting these three black women's personal narratives from the earlier women's texts, this difference reinforces the power and variety of the manner in which the techniques of an African American mother tongue can be used.

I have already indicated that Hurston's expected audience appeared to be members of the white American society. Hurston, as Hemenway has noted, was a master of figurative language, and she filled her work with metaphors that grew out of the black vernacular tradition. It becomes obvious that she is addressing a white audience when she pauses to explain the meaning of some of her metaphors, metaphors that would require no explanation for a black audience. Hurston writes of her father, "A little of my sugar used to sweeten his coffee right now. That is a Negro way of saying his patience was short with me" (19). And when young Zora tells her father that she wants a saddle horse for a Christmas present and he responds that she "'ain't white,'" Hurston explains in a footnote: "That is a Negro saying that means 'Don't be too ambitious. You are a Negro and they are not meant to have but so much'" (29). Again, Hurston takes this opportunity to explain the meaning of the metaphor to her white readers, but here she does much more than use the metaphor as a masking technique. She also uses it as an indirect criticism of white racialism and oppression that shows evidence of the more flagrant techniques of rage and irony.

In addition to rage and irony, Hurston makes use of sass, impudence, and backtalk as a technique of flagrant resistance in *Dust Tracks*. Hurston's mother had encouraged all of her children to "jump at de sun," and young Zora took that advice literally, developing early a strong sense of her importance in the universe. Others, however, did not appreciate her assertiveness and free spirit. When Zora's father complained that "dire things" would befall her because of her "sassy tongue," Mama would intervene: "She conceded that I was impudent and given to talking back, but she didn't want to 'squinch my spirit'" (13). After Mama died and Zora was sent to school in Jacksonville, many attempts were made to "squinch" her spirit: "In the classroom I got along splendidly. The only difficulty was that I was rated as sassy. I just had to talk back at established authority and that established authority hated back talk worse than barbed-wire pie" (70). Finally, Hurston paints a very unflattering picture of a jealous, mean-spirited stepmother who "threatened to beat me for my impudence" and who called Zora "a sassy, impudent heifer" (75, 76). Rather than feeling demeaned by the use of these terms, Hurston feels empowered by them, just as slaves claimed the same demeaning labels and reversed their negative meanings by embracing them; she takes them into herself, reshapes them to fit the special person she already believes herself to be, and flagrantly defies those who try to restrain her. So the stepmother, as was the case with southern slave owners, found her power blunted by the very words she intended to be weapons.

Hurston also uses a great deal of humor as a masking technique in her autobiography. Some of the humor is merely for amusement; however, some of it takes on an ironic edge, placing it in the flagrant mother tongue category. The ongoing melodrama that young Zora creates involving Miss Corn-Shuck, Mr. Sweet Smell, Miss Corn-Cob, and the rest of the cast is wonderfully amusing and imaginative. But if one looks deeper, a case can be made for gender conflicts, racial and "colorism" issues between Miss Corn-Shuck and Miss Corn-Cob, and class issues surrounding the "Spool People," who "couldn't do a thing unless they saw somebody else doing it" (54–58). Young Zora realizes that what is imagined is usually more interesting than the reality. For instance, although the truth about Mr. Pendir establishes the fact that he does not turn into a "'gator," young Zora rejects the evidence placed before her: "My phantasies were still fighting against the facts" (61).

The subtle mother tongue techniques of silence, whispering, and secrecy also play prominent roles in *Dust Tracks*. Hurston tells the story of the murder of her mother's favorite nephew: "It was whispered that he had been shot in the head by a white man unintentionally, and then beheaded to hide the wound" (64). A black man told Hurston's family these facts several years later—after he had moved to Texas: "There was never any move to prove the charge, for obvious reasons" (64). Chances were, the white man would not have been charged anyway, and those who broke their silence were subjecting themselves to possible retaliation from the white community.

Hurston learned first-hand the importance of secrecy when, while working as a house servant, she found herself having to fend off the advances of her white-male employer. Finally, she followed through with her threat to report him to his wife. The woman "began to cry without moving anything in her face," and Hurston writes, "Right then I learned a lesson to carry with me through life. I'll never tell another wife" (95). As was true with many of the white slave mistresses of the nineteenth century, this white woman was another victim in a white man's act of lusting after a black servant, and the picture Hurston paints reinforces the continuation of the myth of the black woman as Jezebel.

Another incident addressing silence applies to the silencing of Hurston on the occasion of her mother's death. Her Mama knew that she was dying, so she entrusted her voice to Zora: "I was not to let them take the pillow from under her head until she was dead. The clock was not to be covered, nor the looking-glass" (64). The black women of the community, however, were steeped in tradition. Hurston writes that during her mother's final moments, "she could not talk. But she looked at me, or so I felt, to speak for her. She depended on me for a voice" (65). When Zora tried to stop the women from covering the clock and from removing the pillow, "Papa pulled me away. Others were trying to silence me. [. . .] I was to agonize over that moment for years to come" (66).

In her foreword to *Dust Tracks,* Maya Angelou celebrates Hurston's humor, speech, and uniqueness as a writer: "Her books and folktales vibrate with tragedy, humor and the real music of Black American speech" (viii). Angelou notes the unsatisfactory results of attempts by white writers to capture the special nuances of black speech and black personalities: "[A] large number of white writers have felt they were not only capable but called upon to write the 'Black person's story.' It is rather astounding that so many noninformed, or at best partially informed, yet otherwise learned personages have felt and still feel that although they themselves could not replicate the grunts, moans, and groans of their black contemporaries, they could certainly explain the utterances and even give descriptions, designs and desires of the utterers" (vii). Angelou notes, as had Jacobs and Cooper before her, that there was and is an assumption among many white intellectuals that literacy alone qualifies them to replicate the rhetoric and other communicative devices found in the ways that blacks communicate among themselves. Of course, the nuances I have described as characteristic of an African American mother tongue belie that assumption. I agree with Angelou when she states that Hurston talks back to those outside of the black community and chooses "to write her own version of life in *Dust Tracks on a Road*" (viii), a version more representative of the African American mother tongue than it is of the traditional autobiographic form and content.

When Maya Angelou published the first of her autobiographical texts in 1970, *I Know Why the Caged Bird Sings,* she continued the tradition of merging literary genres—autobiography, travel adventure, historical text, ethnography—and blurring lines between fiction and nonfiction, between fact and Hurston's "phantasy." *Caged Bird,* like Hurston's *Dust Tracks* is the product of a private career and thus focuses on the personal and professional life of the author. While both Hurston and Angelou experience incidents that sever their connections with community, Hurston's communal separations leave her disjointed and isolated, much like the lack of community ties negatively impacted Harriet Wilson. Angelou, however, in demonstrating the sustaining power of community, shows

Marguerite capable of forming new ties and forming new communities throughout the text.

Marguerite's first community is that of Stamps, Arkansas, with "Momma's" store standing at its center. Like the front porch of Joe Clark's store in Hurston's Eatonville, Momma's store represented stability and safety for Stamps's black community. This is where its members gather one night to listen as Joe Louis retains his title as heavyweight boxing champion, and it is from this location that they form safety nets against Southern whites who would be angry and vengeful after Louis's victory: "It would take an hour or more before the people would leave the Store and head for home. Those who lived too far had made arrangements to stay in town. It wouldn't do for a Black man and his family to be caught on a lonely country road on a night when Joe Louis had proved that we were the strongest people in the world" (136). Even though this incident ends with an awareness of the oppressions still plaguing blacks in the South, Angelou also shows here, as she does throughout the autobiography, the various ways that blacks resisted oppression—a resistance steeped in African American mother tongue communicative techniques. The masking technique of laughter often mixed levity with a recognition of the sorrow, regret, or anger floating beneath its surface. When the fight announcer says that Joe Louis is trying to fight his way out of a clench, Angelou writes that "some bitter comedian on the porch said, 'That white man don't mind hugging that niggah now, I betcha'" (133).

Laughter was generally a salvation for black children in the South: "Laughter so easily turns to hysteria for imaginative children" (45). Angelou captures the power of imagination in the lyrical composition of her personal narrative as well as through the characters of the story. Using ironic humor, Angelou writes about one of Marguerite's fantasies in which she is really a little white girl: "Wouldn't they be surprised when one day I woke out of my black ugly dream, and my real hair, which was long and blond, would take the place of the kinky mass that Momma wouldn't let me straighten? My light blue eyes were going to hypnotize them.... Then they would understand why I had never picked up a Southern accent, or spoke the common slang, and why I had to be forced to eat pigs' tails and snouts. Because I was really white and because a cruel fairy stepmother, who was understandably jealous of my beauty, had turned me into a too-big Negro girl" (2–3). Note that Hurston's *Dust Tracks* and Angelou's *Caged Bird* both introduce a cruel stepmother who tries to control and minimize them. Angelou's evil stepmother is purely imaginative, however, while Hurston's is real (maybe; with Hurston, it is sometimes difficult to determine what is real and what is imagined).

Marguerite, even when faced with the facts of a situation, generally finds her imaginative versions of reality much more interesting. In Momma's confrontation with the white dentist who refuses to treat Marguerite—"I'd rather stick my hand in a dog's mouth than in a nigger's" (189)—Momma maintains her dignity in showing the dentist that his behavior is shameful by forcing him to pay her interest on money she had lent him during the depression. However, Marguerite's version turns Momma into an avenging angel (perhaps Lucifer):

> Momma walked into that room as if she owned it.... Her eyes were blazing like live coals and her arms had doubled themselves in length.... Her tongue had thinned and the words rolled off well enunciated. Enunciated and sharp like little claps of thunder.
>
> "You knave, do you think you acted like a gentleman, speaking to me like that in front of my granddaughter? ... Leave Stamps by sundown.... You will never again practice dentistry.... You will be a vegetarian caring for dogs with the mange.... Is that clear?"
>
> The saliva ran down his chin and his eyes filled with tears. "Yes ma'am. Thank you for not killing me. Thank you Mrs. Henderson."
>
> Momma pulled herself back from being ten feet tall with eight-foot arms. (190–91)

When Angelou writes, "I preferred, much preferred, my version" (193), she echoes the sentiments of Hurston whose fantasies were constantly "fighting against the facts."

The creation of fantasies is equivalent to storytelling, and storytelling in the black community is a highly rated art. The more creative the story—that is, the more creative the "lie"—the more celebrated is the storyteller. Like storytelling, lying is a performance perfected by blacks in their dealings with a white system that denies them entrance. It is an act of flagrant mother tongue resistance that Angelou demonstrates in her account of the resistance Marguerite encounters when she attempts to secure a job as a streetcar "conductorette" in San Francisco. Marguerite enters into the performance with the white receptionist who is determined that she will deny Marguerite's application. Angelou writes, "[T]he standard questions reminded me of the necessity for dexterous lying" (269). After reviewing the questions, Marguerite's "lying" begins: "Sitting at a side table my mind and I wove a cat's ladder of near truths and total lies. I kept my face blank (an old art) and wrote quickly the fable of Marguerite Johnson, aged nineteen, former companion and driver for Mrs. Annie Henderson (a White Lady) [in reality, Momma] in Stamps, Arkansas" (269).

Another mother tongue tool of flagrant resistance involves the use of the term "impudent." Since to be impudent is an obvious act of resistance to and defiance of authority, those in positions of authority—whites over blacks, men over women, adults over children—often hold it to be an undesirable characteristic. Angelou writes, "'Thou shall not be dirty' and 'Thou shall not be impudent' were the two commandments of Grandmother Henderson upon which hung our total salvation" (27). According to Momma, "The impudent child was detested by God and a shame to its parents and could bring destruction to its house and line" (28). Of course, a child with an imagination and a sense of self such as those possessed by Marguerite cannot help but be defiant, so impudence for her becomes necessary and desirable.

Marguerite searches for and finds many outlets for her creativity, including the Southern act of creating mosaics of the front yard: "I raked the yellow-red dirt, and made half-moons carefully, so that the design stood out clearly and mask-like. . . . Momma was admiring the yard, so I joined her. It truly looked like a flat redhead that had been raked with a bigtoothed comb. Momma didn't say anything but I knew she like it" (29). Since masking is a significant weapon in the mother tongue arsenal of black women and since black women were limited in their outlets for creative expression, the image that Angelou creates here reinforces the black woman's (and black girl's) surreptitious entry in the world of expression. This incident also speaks to the comradery found in the silent woman-to-woman appreciation of another black woman's creative expression and resistance to a life without options. Neither of these black "women" has to say anything, as each recognizes the power of this creative release. Other examples of silence in *Caged Bird* are less fulfilling, however.

One of the most painful incidents in *Caged Bird* centers around Mr. Freeman's rape of Marguerite and her uncles' subsequent murder of Mr. Freeman. The subtle mother tongue techniques of silence and secrecy emerge as Mr. Freeman, the oppressor, uses them as weapons to force Marguerite into secrecy by threatening the life of her brother: "'If you ever tell anybody what we did, I'll have to kill Bailey'" (74). After Marguerite realizes that her words of accusation against Mr. Freeman in court led to his beating death, she retreats behind a wall of silence as an act of self-protection and to protect others from what she determines is the power of her voice: "I could feel the evilness flowing through my body and waiting, pent up, to rush off my tongue if I tried to open my mouth. . . . The only thing I could do was to stop talking to people. . . . Just my breath, carrying my words out, might poison people and they'd curl up and die" (86, 87). It took Mrs. Bertha Flowers and her love of language, voice, and literature to end Marguerite's silence: "'Words mean more than what is set down on paper. It takes the human voice to infuse them with the shades of deeper meaning'" (98). This deeper meaning emerges with the application of mother tongue techniques, or what Angelou calls "mother wit"—"[T]hose homely sayings . . . couched [in] the collective wisdom of generations" (100).

Finally, let me address Angelou's appreciation of music and song as elements of rejoicing and release in the black community. She notes how the voice of the Southern preacher turns a narrative (the prayer) into music—into a song for the soul: "It was the usual prayer. Only his voice gave it something new. After every two words he gasped and dragged the air over his vocal chords, making a sound like an inverted grunt. 'You who'—grunt—'saved my'—gasp—'soul one'—inhalation—'day'—humph" (125). The combination of words, wordlessness, and musicality create a sense of the old Negro spirituals (DuBois's "sorrow songs") that is at once joyful and mournful. This same musicality drives the sermon that forges an antiphonal relationship between preacher and churchgoers:

"Aaagh. Raagh. I said . . . Charity. Woooooo, a Charity. It don't want nothing for itself. It don't want to be bossman . . . Waah . . . It don't want to be headman . . . Waah . . . It don't want to be foreman . . . Waah . . . It . . . I'm talking about Charity . . . It don't want . . . Oh Lord . . . help me tonight . . . It don't want to be bowed to and scraped at." (127–28)

The music of the sermon then merges with the music of the spirituals: "'Before this time another year, / I may be gone, / In some lonesome graveyard, / Oh, Lord, how long'" (130). As the worshipers leave the revival tent, they hear "the ragged sound of honky-tonk music" (131). Angelou writes that while this sinners' music disturbs those newly emerged from a celebration of God, the music of each addresses the fact that they are all "needy and hungry and despised and dispossessed," finding release through musical forms that are different, yet the same: "A stranger to the music could not have made a distinction between the songs sung a few minutes before and those being danced to in the gay house by the railroad tracks. All asked the same questions. How long, oh God? How long?" (132). The implication here is that the mother tongue technique of masking does not allow one outside of the black community—"a stranger"—to penetrate beyond the mask in order to recognize the subtle differences between the spirituals and the blues. The music, instrumentation, and wailing voices are similar. Both musical forms spring from a well of need—the need of freedom of the soul and freedom in life. However, while the spirituals call upon God and Christ for this release, the blues (even when they invoke the name of the Lord) want healing to come from earthly sources—that is, from a lover, from the bossman, from the landlady, and so on.

Music, as a tool of empowerment, at times becomes a weapon of defiance, taking on the characteristics of flagrant resistance. When Marguerite's graduating class sings the Negro National Anthem (James Weldon Johnson's "Lift Ev'ry Voice and Sing"), despite the principal's instruction to eliminate it because of the presence of a white politician, that is a flagrant act. The voice that the white politician (through the black principal) tries to deny them is reclaimed: "We were on top again. As always, again. We survived. The depths had been icy and dark, but now a bright sun spoke to our souls. . . . Oh, Black known and unknown poets, . . . who will compute the lonely nights made less lonely by your songs. . . ? [We] survive in exact relationship to the dedication of our poets (include preachers, musicians and blues singers)" (184). The children in this case, using the lessons of selfhood passed on to them through generations of black struggle and resistance, transcend attempts to silence them.

The last autobiography I treat, Alice Walker's *In Search of Our Mothers' Gardens* (1984), is a fitting end to my analysis, not just because of its chronological positionality, but because of its tribute to our ancestral linkages. In citing the work of Deborah McDowell, Matthew A. Fike writes that "Walker engages in a wholistic act of completion by seeking connections with literary foremothers" (142). As I noted with my own "foremothers" and as we have seen in Angelou's autobiography, these black women nurtured their creativity through the outlets available to them—music, gardening, cooking, quilting, storytelling—and made their impact on society in subtle ways. Walker writes in *Our Mothers' Gardens:* "I notice that it is only when my mother is working in her flowers that she is radiant, almost to the point of being invisible—except as Creator:

hand and eye. She is involved in work her soul must have. Ordering the universe in the image of her personal conception of Beauty" (241). In much the same way, Walker "orders" her autobiographical text in a way that allows her to be the "Creator" of her space.

In Search of Our Mothers' Gardens is not a chronological narrative but is a marvelous collection of essays, articles, lectures, reviews, poetry, and personal statements penned by Alice Walker. It is autobiography, it is anthropology, it is history, and it is literature. Walker demonstrates with this collection the continuation of black women's merging of genres and their embrace of creative outlets that free their art and voices, centering her text around the lecture, "In Search of Our Mothers' Gardens," that she delivered at Jackson State University (Mississippi) in 1974.

Early on, Walker establishes the debt today's African American literary tradition owes to slave narratives "where escape for the body and freedom for the soul went together" (5). She also acknowledges the struggle faced by prior generations of women for a place within which to create (specifically referencing Virginia Woolf) as a precursor to her own success: "I sat down at my desk one day, in a room of my own, with key and lock, and began preparations for a story about voodoo, a subject that had always fascinated me. Many of the elements of this story I had gathered from a story my mother several times told me" (9). Walker goes on to note her discovery of the folklore work of Zora Neale Hurston as she researched her story, a connection that, she gloats, linked "Zora, my mother, and me": "She had provided, as if she knew someday I would come along wandering in the wilderness, a nearly complete record of her life. And though her life sprouted an occasional wart, I am eternally grateful for that life, warts and all. . . . I wrote . . . 'The Revenge of Hannah Kemhuff' based on my mother's experiences during the Depression, and on Zora Hurston's folklore collection of the 1920s, and on my own response to both out of a contemporary existence. . . . I would not have written the story . . . had I not known that Zora had already done a thorough job of preparing the ground over which I was then moving" (12–13). Here Walker pays homage to the importance of a continuing African American oral tradition that Hurston has captured as part of the black literary tradition; she also pays homage to the pioneering works of black foremothers that allow for a dialogue between these ancestors and the works of contemporary black women.

Like her predecessors, Walker highlights the positive influences of community in general and of a woman's community in particular. She writes, "What the black Southern writer inherits as a natural right is a sense of community. . . . It went without saying, in my mother's day, that birth and death required assistance from the community, and that the magnitude of these events was lost on outsiders" (17). She remarks about the legacy of black women's strength and passion exemplified by memories of her aunts: "When I was a child, my aunts . . . were the most independent people I knew. . . . At family reunions they would reminisce about the old days when each of them had been able to fish and hunt and trap, to shoot 'straight as a man,' and to defend themselves with their own fists. After telling of a typical day's work on the farm, . . . my favorite aunt would add: 'And then I'd come to the house, bathe, put on my *red* dress, put a little *red* rouge on my lips, put a dusting of talcum down my bosom, do up my hair, and wait for my "fella" to come calling'" (184–85; Walker's emphasis).

This black woman's creation of self (the self of a real woman, not a "true" woman) again emphasizes black women's need to step outside of the expected parameters of creativity. According to Walker, "[T]he duty of the writer is not to be tricked, seduced, or goaded into verifying by imitation or even rebuttal, other people's fantasies" (312). The original paths the black women forged in the literary arena, however, made it easy for members of the dominant white culture to minimize their contributions: "Critics seem unusually ill-equipped to discuss and analyze the works of black women intelligently. . . . And, since black women writers are not, it would seem, very likable—until recently they were the least willing worshipers of male supremacy—comments about them tend to be cruel" (260–61). Not only does Walker offer an explanation for white-male rejection of black women and their texts, she manages to inject a healthy dose of sarcasm into her text by implying that (1) white U.S. literary critics are not equipped to engage the intelligence of black women writers and (2) that these critics (most of whom are white-male) resent black women's failure to "properly" acknowledge white-male superiority. Since Walker made these comments in the early 1980s, the quality of the analyses of black women's writing by white-male scholars has greatly improved—perhaps because of criticism from black women writers like Walker. Regardless, it would be illogical to dismiss out-of-hand white-male critical comments. Robert Hemenway is still the author of the most comprehensive text on Zora Neale Hurston, although he does admit that Hurston's canon needs additional analysis, one written by a black woman. That is not to minimize white men's scholarly and intellectual abilities to write this text, but it does suggest that there exists within a black woman's community an understanding of communicative techniques, that is, the African American mother tongue, to which others (specifically white men) remain unaware.

Before specifically noting other examples of Walker's use of African American mother tongue techniques, let me offer some indications of her text as social discourse as she engages both national and international issues that affected blacks. She ironically analyzes the position that white liberals took as they heralded the death of the Civil Rights Movement: "[White liberals] have apparently never stopped to wonder why it is always the white man . . . who says that the Movement is dead. . . . The Movement is dead to the white man because it no longer interests him. [H]e can afford to be uninterested: he does not have to live by it, with it, or for it, as Negroes must" (121). Writers of slave narratives encountered the same disinterest on the part of Northern abolitionists regarding the plight of blacks after the Civil War.

On the international front, Walker recounts a 1977 visit she made to Cuba after the Cuban Revolution. She writes that "color remains, but beyond color there is a shared *Cuban-ness*. . . . Unlike black Americans, who have never felt at ease with being Americans, black Cubans raised in the revolution take no special pride in being black. They take great pride in being Cuban. . . . Young white Cubans seem equally unaware of themselves as white. (Though older white Cubans certainly retain the racism they grew up with, the revolution does not permit them to display it, except by attitude)" (210–11; Walker's emphasis). I cannot help but relate this observation to a comment that Susie King Taylor made in her *Reminiscences*—that Cubans showed no awareness of color differences—that is, racial superiority or inferiority—until the arrival of American soldiers in the late nineteenth century. Walker's observation supports Taylor's comment in that it is the older Cubans, those whose parents were exposed to those racial distinctions, who continue to exhibit the taint of racism.

Racial minimization is one of those byproducts of slavery that continues to haunt African Americans in the United States and that leads to a continued attempt to lessen the effects of racial epithets by claiming them intraculturally. Walker includes in *Our Mothers' Gardens* an anecdote about black acquaintances who use the term "nigger" to refer to each other and who justify its use by denying its derogatory nature. When Walker was visiting her friends Joe and Mabel, Joe asked his young sons, "'Where've you two little niggers been?'" A discussion followed about whether or not the term is offensive and hurtful, as Walker insisted it was. When Joe stated that he was just preparing his sons, Walker challenged him: "'You are preparing them to *be* "niggers"?'" (188). The conclusion they reached was that no matter how one "prettied it up" and no matter how much it was used by blacks in jest, the term "nigger" was imbued with a racial offensiveness that constant use merely perpetuated. Many blacks continue to use the term among themselves, perhaps in an effort to deflate its power to wound. Ironically, however, young middle-class white men have jokingly begun to refer to each other as "nigger" and as "bitch." While many blacks and women are attempting to claim these appellations in order to minimize their negative effects, white men (the originators of the terms as epithets) are reclaiming the words and the power they originally wielded by using them to address each other. For instance, I have heard young white men call each other "nigger" or "bitch" in joking ridicule of blacks and women. The ability to then deflate the power of those words is compromised.

African American women, being both black and female stand to be most disenfranchised by this reversal of power. Jill Nelson's rhetorical evaluation of these terms, however, suggests that black women are again holding the upper hand; rather than being doubly disenfranchised, some black women are adding the word "fit" to "nigger" and "bitch" and creating one word—"niggerbitchfit" (198). The addition of "fit" suggests rage, insanity, or physical confrontation. It occurs when a black woman has exhausted all avenues of dealing reasonably with those who continue to deny her selfhood. No one in his or her right mind would want to face a black woman who is about to have a "niggerbitchfit."

Walker suggests that the tenacity of our mothers and grandmothers in passing on the spirit of self prepares black women for their battles within a society that often does not see them: "We will know beyond all efforts to erase it from our minds, just exactly who, and of what, we Black American women are" (235). Walker reminisces back to her childhood and recalls the pride she felt reciting her Easter speech at the age of six: "When I rise to give my speech I do so on a great wave of love and pride and expectation. People in the church stop rustling their new crinolines. They seem to hold their breath. I can tell they admire my dress, but it is my spirit, bordering on sassiness (womanishness), they secretly applaud. 'That girl's a little *mess*,' they whisper to each other, pleased" (385; Walker's emphasis). In this one incident, Walker gives us evidence of all three categories of mother tongue communication: her flagrant resistance to authority through her "sassiness" and the fact that she is a "mess"; the community's subtle embrace of her rebelliousness through their "secret" applause and their "whispers" of pride; and masking suggested in her motion of "rising," an action that represents more than just the physical act of standing—it suggests the spiritual act of transcending.

Michael Fike writes that *Our Mothers' Gardens* demonstrates that "slavery and patriarchy, though fatal to some, did not eradicate women's artistic ability but did rechannel it into quilting, hymn singing, and gardening" (153). Music, specifically the singing of hymns, jazz, blues, and rhythm and blues, is an ever-present tool and weapon in black women writers' arsenals and embodies so much of black women's creative art. Walker writes: "[T]he majority of our great-grandmothers knew, even without 'knowing' it, the reality of their spirituality, even if they didn't recognize it beyond what happened in the singing at church—and they never had any intention of giving it up. . . . Listen to the voice of Bessie Smith, Billie Holiday, Nina Simone, Roberta Flack and Aretha Franklin among others, and imagine those voices muzzled for life" (46, 49).

Walker's *Our Mothers' Gardens* is not an ending but a continuation of the celebration of ancestral linkages that fortify African American women's sociopolitical and literary occupation of places, spaces, and gaps in American society: "[P]erhaps in Africa over two hundred years ago there was . . . a mother; Perhaps she painted vivid and daring decorations in oranges and yellows and greens on the walls of her hut; Perhaps she sang—in a voice like Roberta Flack's—sweetly over the compounds of her village; Perhaps she wove the most stunning mats or told the most ingenious stories of all the village storytellers. Perhaps she was herself a poet—though only her daughter's name is signed to the poems that we know" (243). Those daughters include Maria W. Stewart, Anna Julia Cooper, Harriet Wilson, Harriet Jacobs, Elizabeth Keckley, Susie King Taylor, Ida B. Wells (Barnett), Zora Neale Hurston, Maya Angelou, Alice Walker, and all those black women who occupy places in this tradition—before, between, and beyond.

Afterword

Piecing It All Together

Slip mouth over the syllable; moisten with tongue the word.
Suck Slide Play Caress Blow—Love it, but if the word
gags, does not nourish, bite it off—at its source—
Spit it out
Start again
—**Philip,** *She Tries Her Tongue*

Literate nineteenth-century African American women autobiographers who could actually write their own stories found themselves in possession of the knowledge and ability to use and manipulate the written language of their oppressors. Power is inherent in such knowledge, and black women autobiographers used that power to outwit the white-male literary hegemony. As I noted earlier, the combined acts of manipulating language and eliminating language, that is, the use of silences and "body language," gave power to black women writers through the emergence of a unique body of mother tongue communicative techniques. By creating linguistic "gaps" within the lines of their discourses, as well as within the linguistic spaces that already existed between those lines, they made powerful statements about their lives and about the societal conditions with which they had to contend.

Although Michel Foucault states that it is not "our task . . . to give voice to the silence that surrounds [statements]" (*Archaeology* 119), we must acknowledge and recognize the import of silences as they have historically characterized women's writing—as they speak to the historical, political, and social constraints that led to their existence. Foucault declares that everything in a particular discourse can never be said, that "each discourse contains the power to say something other than what it actually says, and thus to embrace a plurality of meanings" (118), yet he later contradicts himself: "Each statement occupies in it a place that belongs to it alone. The description of a statement . . . consist[s] in discovering what *special place it occupies,* what ramifications of the system of formations make it possible to map its localization, how it is isolated in the general dispersion of statements" (119; my emphasis). The suggestion that a "statement" occupies a "place" implies that there is a certain amount of stability within and around that particular statement. Although Foucault's theories do recognize the existence of what he describes as "discontinuities, ruptures, gaps, entirely new forms of positivity, and of sudden redistributions" (169), his suggestion that any statement has the ability to occupy a specific place (which implies a permanence) belies the actuality of the shifting plates of discursive structures.

Such shifting within American literary tradition—a shifting that recognizes the spaces that women and people of color occupy, a shifting that forces the emergence of gaps and ruptures, a shifting that alters meaning and makes discourse malleable in the hands of nineteenth-century African American women autobiographers—allowed for the emergence of the suggestive nuances of an African American mother tongue. This mother tongue defies the sociopolitical, historical, and literary constraints inherent in the limiting legacies of race, gender, and class. When Wilson, Jacobs, Keckley, Taylor, and other black women autobiographers employed the many communicative techniques they found at their disposal, they realized a freedom of form—and voice—that allowed them to resist and deflate the obstacles that nineteenth-century white America had placed in their paths. While they may not be part of the "big picture" that the National Association of Scholars proposes as the focus of American literary study, they are a big part of the historical and literary development of American literature, for they bring to light black women writers' alternative approaches to the genre of autobiography.

Returning to the primary focus of *Rhetoric and Resistance in Black Women's Autobiography,* that is, the emergence of nineteenth-century black women's autobiography as social discourse, let me suggest that a black woman's discovery of agency frees her public voice. This premise also works in reverse—the discovery that she has a public voice gives her agency. Both discoveries involve a challenge to existing patriarchal structures. And no matter how powerful and repressive those patriarchal structures might be, they have great difficulty in suppressing a black woman who has assumed agency. Sidonie Smith writes that "the pressure of androcentric discourse, including autobiography itself, to repress the feminine and to suppress woman's voice, betrays a fundamental fear and distrust of woman's power, which while repressed and suppressed continues to challenge the comfortable assertions of male control" (*Poetics* 40–41). Just as many African American slaves stole their education, many black women appropriated words from the language of those who strove to keep them silent, disguised those words, and re-shaped them to fit their mouths. Frances Smith Foster, although writing specifically about Keckley's *Behind the Scenes,* makes an important point that applies generally to the narratives of nineteenth-century African American women autobiographers when she notes that "rather than elaborating upon the weight of their oppression, the women emphasize the sources of the strength with which they met that force" ("Respect to Females" 67). To that end, the principle autobiographers I analyze—Wilson, Jacobs, Keckley, and Taylor—each wrote a personal narrative that did more than focus on injustices. Each of their autobiographies contains admonishments regarding the cruelties and brutalities perpetrated not only against the autobiographer herself but also against the African American community as a whole. And each also states or hints at movement toward a more inclusive American society.

Nineteenth-century African American women autobiographers used no single African American mother tongue strategy in creating their personal narratives. They used the various communicative tools I identify in my earlier chapters in combinations and variations that have not previously been noted by scholars of autobiography, women's studies, or African American literature. This flexibility of narrative technique makes mother-tongue-influenced African American women's autobiography difficult to define and defend—but not impossible. It is this very flexibility that makes resultant nineteenth-century African American women's autobiography consistent with the fluid, blurred incompleteness that must characterize the countergenre that these black women writers devised.

When Bakhtin notes that heteroglossia is prominent in the "low genres" of street songs, folk sayings, fairs, and so forth, he paves the way for the inclusion of other areas of expression that had previously fallen outside of the dominant white culture's definition of a literary system. For instance, African American forms of expression such as black folktales, signifying, playing the dozens, and an infinite variety of subversive uses of language—sass, invective, impudence, backtalking, just to name a few—demonstrate Bakhtin's criteria for heteroglossia. The African American mother tongue is heteroglossic.[1]

By appropriating and then subverting the accepted literary and linguistic systems of the dominant society, African American women autobiographers use, according to Bakhtin, not only "a heteroglossia consciously opposed to this literary language" but one that is "parodic, and aimed sharply and polemically against the official languages of its given time" (273). Members of society situated outside of the established literary power structure found themselves in a position to use their voices to decry the oppressive conditions of their lives. While they were generally conscious of the need to veil or soften their expressions of outrage, they were nonetheless not reluctant to find the means to voice those expressions, and the language of the oppressor became their weapon:

> The internal stratification of any single national language into social dialects, characteristic group behavior, professional jargons, generic languages, languages of generations and age groups, tendentious languages, languages of the authorities, of various circles and of passing fashions, languages that serve the specific sociopolitical purposes of the day . . .—this internal stratification present in every language at any given moment of its historical existence is the indispensable prerequisite for the novel as a genre. The novel orchestrates all of its themes, the totality of the world of objects and ideas depicted and expressed in it, by means of the social diversity of speech types [raznorecie] and by the differing individual voices that flourish under such conditions. (262–63)

Sometimes the "I" voice in black women's personal narratives is not a single voice at all, but one representative of many, sometimes conflicting, voices.[2] While the literary obstacles that the oppressed encountered varied, usually those obstacles were driven solely by gender or race or, in the case of black women writers, by the combination of the two.

The patchwork autobiographies that nineteenth-century black women produced demonstrated multivocality, not only because these narratives emerged from both black and white novelistic predecessors but also because they contain "modes of figuration lifted from the black vernacular," from a black way of speaking.[3] They embody the European linguistic stylings of texts written according to Germanic and Romantic language structures, the African stylizing that represented the emerging literary tradition found in the slave narrative, as well as the everyday linguistic stylings—the vernacular—found within the black community. African American women autobiographers merged and subverted the literary tools that were available to them (or stolen by them) and introduced a unique and distinctive voice into the American literary tradition.[4] Resultant black women autobiographers' discourses, in many cases, look different and sound different from the discourses of white men, white women, and black men. Even when black women's autobiography appears to mimic the white form, if one reads what is inscribed in the gaps of these narratives and the stories that they appear to tell, the complex, multifaceted nature of black women's autobiography emerges.

Wilson, Jacobs, Keckley, and Taylor used African American mother tongue strategies in both the framing of their texts and the presentation of their contexts. But they represent only four examples of enslaved nineteenth-century black women autobiographers who found ways to subvert existing literary paradigms. They are members of a community of innovative black women communicators, a community that stretches back to West Africa and forward into the twenty-first century and beyond.

By looking critically at the autobiographies of Wilson, Jacobs, Keckley, and Taylor, one will note that the type, the degree, and the intensity of the various communicative techniques selected, finally, depended upon a number of factors: the proximity of the autobiographer's publication date to the years of the Civil War; the intended audience of the autobiography; and the author's primary reason(s) for writing, that is, the author's anticipated goal(s). Overriding all of these factors was the determination to nullify the constraints of race, gender, and class on nineteenth-century African Americans, specifically on black women.

Because of the nature of enslavement and because of the scars left by particularly vicious acts of oppression, nineteenth-century African American women autobiographers, in an effort to make changes for themselves and for their black brothers and sisters, chose to make public their stories of personal hardship. By applying the special communicative techniques that characterize the African American mother tongue, and by subverting and re-molding existing American literary genres, these black women established positions from which they could express resistance to the oppressions they suffered. They carve out enough room for their social, political, and literary voices to resonate. The volatile atmosphere of the pre–Civil War years made antebellum black women's autobiographies, including Wilson's *Our Nig* and Jacobs's *Incidents*, simultaneously

enticing and suspect as the country moved closer and closer toward a violent clash between North and South. The aftermath of that war greatly
influenced the way postbellum black women autobiographers used their
African American mother tongues. Keckley's *Behind the Scenes* and
Taylor's *Reminiscences* attempt to create a physical, emotional, and social
distance between the authors and the taint of victimization that they had
experienced under American slavery.

The closer the publication date of the autobiography to the Civil War
years, the more the autobiographers rely on popular narrative paradigms
and the literary techniques most appealing to nineteenth-century white
women readers. This is especially obvious in Wilson's *Our Nig*, Jacobs's
Incidents, and Keckley's *Behind the Scenes*, with their heavy reliance on
the sentimental style. Taylor is far enough removed from the Civil War
years that she can and does exercise more independence in her choices of
literary genres and language. Because of the influence of the sentimental
narrative, the language in the earlier three personal narratives is descriptive, emotional, metaphorical, and colorful. At the same time, however,
these three black women autobiographers use sentimental language to
obscure much of the harshness and/or bitterness the texts address. One
might expect to discover such subversive literary techniques in Wilson's
and Jacobs's antebellum autobiographies, narratives influenced by the
heightened emotions attached to the political and social tensions between
the North and South, by the widespread popularity of the sentimental,
captivity, and seduction novels, and by each author's need or desire to
conceal her real identity. These two African American women autobiographers found it imperative at times to dissemble. They were usually covert
in their choices of language and tone. At other times, however, they were
extremely outspoken and flagrant, evidently desiring to jolt their readers.
Of the three categories of mother tongue usages I identified earlier—tools
of subtle resistance, masking tools (saying one thing but meaning another), and tools of flagrant resistance—Wilson and Jacobs make ample
use of all three, although Wilson employs more techniques of flagrant
resistance in her narrative than does Jacobs. Their need to use a broad
range of literary strategies drawn from African American culture mirrors
their need to appropriate an equally broad range of traditional American
literary genres that they could subvert in the shaping of their personal
texts.

As might be expected, because of its appearance during the heyday of
sentimental literatures, Keckley's *Behind the Scenes* also exhibits the

flowery, romanticized language of the sentimental novel. More interesting, however, given the fact that slavery is no longer an issue for this postbellum autobiographer, is Keckley's heavier reliance on subtle indirection than either Wilson or Jacobs, who were publishing under the shadow of possible retaliation from slavery's supporters (North and South). The flagrant techniques of backtalk, impertinence, impudence, insolence, invective, irony, rage, and sass appear sparingly and subtly in Keckley's autobiography. I might have expected Keckley's personal narrative, coming after the war as it does, to be more direct and unrestrained, especially in its depiction of the hardships of her thirty years in slavery. Keckley's narrative moves in a different direction, however, forsaking an explicit emphasis on the powers of her oppressors and embracing instead a literary approach through which she celebrates her empowerment through self-reliance. As such, her autobiography serves a unique function. While the autobiographical texts of both the antebellum and postbellum eras address sociopolitical issues, Keckley's narrative acts as a bridge between the very descriptive, metaphorical literary techniques of Wilson's and Jacobs's antebellum narratives and the more historical, activist memoir form of the later African American women's autobiographies, exhibiting characteristics of both eras. Keckley's *Behind the Scenes* thus reveals rhetorical and discursive traits of both pre–Civil War African American women's personal narratives and the narratives produced by black women autobiographers in late-nineteenth-century America.

Although Taylor's 1902 *Reminiscences* makes little use of the romantic model of sentimental fiction that still characterizes Keckley's memoir, it shares a literary connection with this earlier postbellum narrative by also combining the techniques of the historical text and memoir with the cultural and literary conventions of the slave narrative. Taylor then stretches the boundaries of the autobiography even further, incorporating the thrilling characteristics of the adventure novel into her narrative.[5] What makes Taylor's autobiography even more singular during this time is that she re-embraces the flagrant resistance tools that were most evident in Wilson's *Our Nig* and that are missing from or softened in Keckley's narrative. While both Keckley and Taylor aim at being independent, self-reliant women, Keckley remains socially, politically, and somewhat emotionally dependent on European American society for acceptance; her indirect and veiled language reflect this dependency. On the other hand, Taylor, several decades removed from the Civil War and having earned her stripes in that battle itself, demands social and political restitution for the black race from the white American society, and she does very little narrative dissembling in making her dissatisfactions known. Like Wilson and Jacobs, Taylor more obviously uses aspects of all three categories of the mother tongue communicative techniques. Yet her narrative exhibits more personal and political agency than either of the antebellum autobiographies. As a matter of fact, while the other three autobiographers are still painfully aware of the gaze of their white readers, Taylor declares a more independent voice. She guides her readers, rather than letting them guide her, picking and choosing the appropriate tone according to the impression she wants to make on them.

Taylor's minimal use of the sentimental fiction model reflects the type of readership she anticipates. Her text is not one to be read and discussed at tea time or at ladies' garden parties. It is a fact-filled historical narrative and sociopolitical commentary designed primarily to reach the ears of the white-male leaders of America who are responsible for effecting changes that would counteract the racial prejudice and bias she saw oppressing the members of her black community. Keckley's primary anticipated audience, on the other hand, remained white Northern women readers as well as white Southern women readers who were still consumers of the sentimental novel and who might respond to Keckley's intimate details of her life with Mary Todd Lincoln. Her financial needs made it imperative that she entice these readers with the promise of such intimacy, since the end of slavery had led to a decline in the popularity of the traditional slave narrative.

African American mother tongue strategies address connections between the "I" of the writer and the "we" of family and community. Wilson and Jacobs focus much more attention and energy than do Keckley and Taylor on the subject of family—Wilson having been abandoned by hers and trying to create one of her own, and Jacobs trying to preserve and protect hers. Our Nig and Incidents address motherhood and its central locus within the family and within nineteenth-century American society. Motherhood empowers Linda because of the support she receives from her grandmother and the "other mothers" in her life. They prepare her for the ordeal she will encounter as a black mother in nineteenth-century America. Frado's experiences with mothers, mother figures, and motherhood are less empowering—her mother abandons her, Mrs. Bellmont brutalizes her, and she finds herself, as a mother, financially and physically unable to provide for her own child. Although Keckley and Taylor were also mothers, their postbellum autobiographies do not dwell on that aspect of their lives. However, this omission speaks less to the minimization of the role of mother and more to the determination of these postslavery black women autobiographers to redirect their narratives toward public as opposed to private topics. Each chose not to make motherhood—such an intimate part of her life—a topic in her public discourse. Beyond the births and deaths of their sons, little else is written about Keckley's and Taylor's roles as mothers, each author choosing to draw a curtain around her private life while focusing the reader's attention on her public, sociopolitical agenda.

This redirection moves the reader's gaze away from the individual, the "I," and forces it to consider the "we," and for Keckley and Taylor, that "we" is the larger black community. Keckley and Taylor each decided to concentrate her discursive energies on the struggles of the newly freed members of the African American community, although that effort appears more obvious in Taylor's narrative. Keckley is more ambiguous about her commitment to the African American community in general. As a matter of fact, there are times when Keckley appears to care only about the Lincolns, when she is almost dismissive of the struggles of the freedmen and freedwomen finding their way to Washington, D.C.[6] However, once we get beyond her masking and conciliatory posturing for the sake of her white readership, we note her numerous mentions about her acquaintance with Frederick Douglass, her alliances with black clergymen in the cause of improving the plight of former slaves, and her work on behalf of newly freed slaves in Washington as well as in New York. She makes it clear that she supports economic advancement and self-reliance for the black community and that she takes part in programs that lead toward these ends.

Of the four autobiographers featured in my analysis, Jacobs and Wilson make the strongest appeals to, and indictments of, their white-female communities. Jacobs's *Incidents* most obviously challenges white women readers of the North to stand up and cry out, as sisters, against the destruction of black family units. Jacobs was particularly successful in couching very critical statements in a language that was designed to catch her white readers unaware. She orchestrated her narrative to "play on them, to disarm them, to manipulate them; to soften them up, only to melt them down to acceptance of her" (Kafka 124). The sometimes biting tone of Wilson's narrative and her pointed use of rhetorical questions make it clear that *Our Nig* was meant for the eyes of those Northern whites whose racism blinded them to the oppressions she suffered, yet who simultaneously claimed to feel compassion for the slaves of the South. The anger and rage of her narrative, represented by her primary use of the mother tongue techniques of flagrant resistance, mirror the rage she felt toward her intended audience—not her "colored brethren," but a passive, Northern, white audience—basically the same audience targeted by Jacobs, Keckley, and Taylor.

Wilson, Jacobs, Keckley, and Taylor were successful in thwarting many oppressive acts, including the denial of access to literary and public arenas, by employing gender- and race-specific acts of resistance. The autobiographies that these women wrote drew narrative powers from the verbal and nonverbal linguistic systems of resistance found in the African American slave communities—systems that retained linguistic characteristics found in the Yoruba culture. Even though Wilson's experiences were set in the Northern states, away from the slave quarters that sustained the storytelling tradition, I suspect that in her early years, she was influenced by Southern black traditions of communication—and, thereby, by West African traditions—either through her father or by observing other blacks within her small community.

The differences in literary style and technique between antebellum and postbellum African American women's autobiographies are grounded in the social, political, and economic changes effected by the Civil War, with all of its implications. William L. Andrews takes a rather negative view of the changes that emerge in the later African American women's autobiographies, characterizing the postbellum narrative as "a studied refusal to explore the kinds of moral problems attendant to the slave woman's sexuality that surface often in the discourse of the antebellum antislavery movement" ("Changing Moral Discourse" 227). Veiled within this criticism is the suggestion that postbellum black women autobiographers deserted the concerns of their antebellum sisters. But postbellum African American women autobiographers merely took another step, perhaps along a different path, toward minimizing past oppressions that often reduced them to no more than victims of sexuality; they empowered themselves and their autobiographies by denying those oppressions agency within their narratives.

Claudia Tate's scholarship supports these conclusions. She notes that while antebellum texts "inscribe black women's moral indignation at the sexual and maternal abuses associated with slavery," the writings of postbellum black women "construct, deconstruct, and reconstruct Victorian gender conventions in order to designate black female subjectivity as a most potent force in the advancement of the race" ("Allegories" 107). Joanne Braxton further states that the postbellum autobiographies of former slave women "reflect a shift from the preoccupation with survival found in the slave narratives to a need for self-expression and self-identi-fication [creating] vital and sometimes hybrid forms . . . as they grappled with the challenges of freedom and the problem of attaining a public voice" (10). In their narratives, these postbellum black women autobiog-raphers move away from re-living a past that focused on survival and moved toward a present and a future that focused on social, cultural, po-litical, literary, and economic advancement.

By employing their African American mother tongues to assume agency, Wilson, Jacobs, Keckley, and Taylor all resist various conditions of oppression that members of the dominant culture bring to bear against them. While none of these four women is successful in all efforts of resis-tance, each is able to change the course of many events through the power of her African American woman's voice. Each constructs a self that is not a victim but an empowered agent. I think, therefore, that the concept of nineteenth-century African American women as victim is and always has been false—a way to perpetuate the sense of black women's powerless-ness. I build my argument around the term "victim" itself as defined in *The Random House Dictionary of the English Language:* "1. a person who suffers from a destructive or injurious action or agency; 2. a person who is deceived or cheated, as by his or her own emotions or ignorance, by the dishonesty of others, or by some impersonal agency; 3. a person or animal sacrificed or regarded as sacrificed; 4. a living creature sacrificed in religious rites." As I review these definitions, keeping in mind that they are created based on someone's perceptions, that they have passed through oral usage, and that they have been set down in writing and are informed by subjective interpretations, I suggest that all of these defini-tions apply to Wilson, Jacobs, Keckley, and Taylor—at one time or an-other—as substantiated by their personal narratives. But, none of them apply to these women consistently or definitively. That is because each of these women was able, through her writing, to diffuse the power that sought to make her a victim in all things, in all ways, and at all times. Using the techniques of their African American mother tongues, these black women writers resisted European American oppression, denied Eu-ropean American attempts to minimize and silence them, spoke out for and in defense of their broader African American communities, and preserved the sense of their cultural heritage as it grew out of their West African and African American ancestries.

Through her resistance to oppression, each of these women weakened the hold of the oppressor. Their victim's status was not a constant; it was a psychological tool wielded by members of the dominant white power structure to control and check the resistance of those they had enslaved. Once the so-called victims—Wilson, Jacobs, Keckley, and Taylor—recognized the falsehood of their status as victims, they were able to speak out and "talk back." Were they always successful in finding ways to avoid their victimization? No, but they were successful more often than not, as evidenced by the final step each took toward claiming agency for herself—the writing and publishing of a personal narrative that not only took on the guise of social commentary, challenging established ideologies, but also inadvertently led to the creation of a countergenre to conventional autobiography. Wilson, Jacobs, Keckley, and Taylor avoided ultimate victimization by consistently resisting oppression; by occupying places within the American social, political, and literary arenas; by assuming ownership of the subversive spaces in which they survived; and by creating their own "black-woman" gaps in the inevitable cracks in the public sphere. They used their African American mother tongues to release the power of their voices for their black communities, for themselves, and for the generations of black women writers yet to come.

Notes

Introduction: Life-Writing and Subversion

1. See Courtney Leatherman's article in *Chronicle of Higher Education*, "English Curriculum Favors Morrison Over Swift, Report Says."

2. To my way of thinking, the term "black," like the term "Negro," is a societal construct generally used to refer to peoples having certain physical characteristics. Normally, I prefer to use the term "African American" (no hyphen) to denote a group of people whose cultural ancestry places their origins in Africa but who, primarily because of the slave trade to the New World, adopted other cultural characteristics as well, creating a unique blend of "Africa" and "America" (the connotation of America also being in question). For the sake of simplicity and because little attention or consistency have been exercised in the application of these terms, I will use them interchangeably throughout my text. The same justification for simplicity applies to my use of the terms "white" and "European American."

3. Even though Taylor's autobiography was actually published in the early twentieth century, I include her in this study because her text presents the life that she lived as an African American woman in nineteenth-century America.

4. Akiko Ochiai references Gates in a like manner in his analysis of Ida B. Wells's *Crusade for Justice*, which he claims as "neither fiction nor totally objective history, but a recreation of history through one particular person. Henry Gates calls this intermediate discourse between history and literature 'fictive'" (380).

5. The metaphorical places, spaces, and gaps that I reference throughout this text have figurative meanings regarding literary and sociopolitical positioning. The "places" represent the definitions and ideologies determined by the white male hegemony; the "spaces" are those areas of resistance that women and nonwhite men occupy, areas that the dominant white man recognizes and acknowledges, but minimizes regarding its power; the "gaps" also represent areas that women and nonwhite men occupy, but these areas were created by women and nonwhite men and kept hidden from the white male gaze, serving to further empower these "others."

6. See Braxton's *Black Women Writing Autobiography* for a well-documented, comprehensive listing of nineteenth-century African American women autobiographers.

7. Harriet E. Wilson, *Our Nig; or, Sketches from the Life of a Free Black, in a Two-Story White House, North. Showing that Slavery's Shadows Fall Even There*, 2nd ed. (London: Allison and Busby, 1984). All further citations are to this edition and will appear parenthetically within the text.

8. Harriet A. Jacobs, *Incidents in the Life of a Slave Girl, Written by Herself* (Cambridge: Harvard University Press, 1987), 232. All further citations are to this edition and will appear parenthetically within the text.

9. Elizabeth Keckley, *Behind the Scenes. Or, Thirty Years a Slave, and Four Years in the White House* (New York: Oxford University Press, 1988), viii. All further citations are to this edition and will appear parenthetically within my text.

10. Susie King Taylor, *Reminiscences of My Life in Camp, With the 33rd United States Colored Troops, Late 1st S.C. Volunteers* (Boston: Published by Author, 1902). All further citations are to this edition and will appear parenthetically within the text.

11. Several feminist theorists have addressed women's use and subversion of silence and secrecy. For instance, Sidonie Smith writes that, historically, woman's forced social role "condemned her to public silence" (*Poetics* 7). Mary Field Belenky notes in her 1986 research that women working in a public arena speak about "voice and silence," using terms like "being silenced" and "not being heard" in relation to the male voice (18).

12. Henry Louis Gates Jr., Bernard Bell, and many other theorists in African American studies programs extensively discuss the importance of secrecy and concealment in the communicative and literary practices of nineteenth-century African American men. Stephen Butterfield writes that guile and masking in slave communities are necessary tools in avoiding "arrest, capture, whipping, and possibly death," noting that these evasive actions offer a "partial explanation for the predilection toward irony and satire in black writing" (20).

13. Several experts in the study of African American women's autobiography discuss the covert methods these women employed to make their voices heard. Braxton notes that the female fugitive claimed "sass and invective as well as biblical invocation" as her "tools of liberation" (16). Darlene Clark Hine suggests that nineteenth-century African American women employed the tools of "secrets and dissemblance" because they understood that certain topics were "better left unknown, unwritten, unspoken except in whispered tones" (915–16). Hine continues by noting that concern about rape led to the "development of a culture of dissemblance among Black women," characterizing dissemblance as "the behavior and attitudes of Black women that created the appearance of openness and disclosure but actually shielded the truth of their inner lives from their oppressors" (912). In her evaluation of the texts of African American women, Harryette Mullen addresses what she calls the "verbal skills of runaway tongues: the sass, spunk, and infuriating impudence of slaves who refused to know their place" (245).

14. Gates explains why he differentiates between the traditional "signifying" and the "Signifyin(g)" of the black vernacular: "The bracketed *g* enables me to connote the fact that this word is, more often than not, spoken by black people without the final *g* as 'signifyin'.' This arbitrary and idiosyncratic convention also enables me to

recall the fact that whatever historical community of Afro-Americans coined this usage did so in the vernacular as spoken, in contradistinction to the literate written usages of the standard English 'shadowed' term. The bracketed or aurally erased *g*, like the discourse of black English and dialect poetry generally, stands as the trace of black difference in a remarkably sophisticated and fascinating (re)naming ritual graphically in evidence here. This (re)naming apparently took place anonymously and unrecorded in antebellum America. Some black genius or a community of witty and sensitive speakers emptied the signifier 'signification' of its received concepts and filled this empty signifier with their own concepts. By doing so, they (un)wittingly disrupted the nature of the sign = *signified/signifier* equation itself" (*Signifying* 46; Gates's emphasis).

15. It is difficult to discuss commonalities in black women's positions in society and in their approaches to communicative techniques without appearing to reify monolithic notions of black identity. However, at the risk of being so interpreted, I feel that I must establish the existence of these differences in the black woman's position and view from those of everyone else, differences that emerged as a result of society's attempts to codify black women in its own way.

16. William Bascom points out that while the mission schools in West Africa erroneously applied the name Yoruba indiscriminately, the people of Western Nigeria actually identified themselves by ethnic subgroups. The largest of these subgroups, the Oyo, were called Oyo Yoruba by other subgroups, "Yoruba" translated to mean "cunning" (5). The name stuck, however, being generally applied to over a dozen subgroups in much the same way that the appellation "Sioux" is used generally in America to represent the Dakota, the Lakota, Santee, and a host of other Plains Indian nations. For my purpose, I have chosen to use the general "Yoruba" identifier when discussing cultural linkages between blacks in the New World and peoples from western Africa.

17. Bentham's Panopticon Penitentiary called for the edifice to be circular with the prison cells "occupying the circumference" while the guards or "keepers" were situated in the center of the structure. The premise was that "by *blinds* and other contrivances, the keeper is concealed from the observation of the prisoners, unless where he thinks fit to show himself: hence, on their [i.e., the prisoners'] part, the sentiment of an invisible omnipresence" (194; Bentham's emphasis).

18. While feminist scholars regularly use the term "gaps" to represent the crevices that exist within the ideologies of a male-dominated society, crevices which the woman seeking agency occupied, I am using the term more specifically in my text to reference those loci unseen and/or unacknowledged by the white male eye. These deeper shadows provided the woman writer with an indestructible power.

Chapter 1. Autobiography, Authorship, and Authority

1. Regarding the history of autobiography, James Olney writes that "there is no evolving autobiographical form to trace from a beginning through history to its present state because man has always cast his autobiography and has done it in that form to which his private spirit impelled him, often, however, calling the product not an autobiography but a lifework" (*Metaphors of Self*, 3). I will consider the defini-

tional shadings of autobiography, lifework, and life-writing as they apply to the personal narratives of "others" later in this chapter.

2. Historian Jack P. Greene notes in the prologue to *The Intellectual Construction of America: Exceptionalism and Identity From 1492 to 1800* that some historians began to challenge the established interpretation of "America" in the latter part of the nineteenth and early decades of the twentieth centuries, "examining and condemning its uncritical underlying parochialism and chauvinism," thereby, already questioning the lack of serious consideration given to "other" Americans (3, 4).

3. Although St. Augustine is celebrated as having been the originator of the paradigm from which white male autobiography descended, Frances Smith Foster notes that most scholars continue to ignore "the African heritage of Augustine" and situate this originator of the model for the contemporary autobiography solely in a European theater ("Autobiography after Emancipation: The Example of Elizabeth Keckley" 34). St Augustine (A.D. 354–430) was one of the Latin fathers in the early Christian Church, author, and bishop of Hippo in North Africa, which is present-day Algeria. Foster further notes that prior to St. Augustine's *Confessions,* "Assyrians, Egyptians, and Babylonians customarily inscribed prayers and personal desires upon tombs and pillars," inscriptions that can be traced back to "as early as 2450 B.C." (33).

4. In *The Education,* Adams took the position of a national spokesman who "felt himself to be the fulcrum of historical and social forces, an elect representative of his unique place in his family's and nation's history" (quoted in Brodzki and Schenck 2). Likewise, Franklin's *Autobiography of Benjamin Franklin* attempts to establish him as a national example whose life is uniquely and singularly representative of American success.

5. The *OED,* in establishing the negative connotation of the term "nigger" and stating that its use is "colloquial and usually contemptuous," offers the following examples of its usage: "1786 Burns *Ordination* iv, 'How graceless Ham leugh at his Dad, Which made Canaan a nigger.' 1849 H. Coleridge *Ess.* (1851) I. 164 'A similar error has turned Othello . . . into a rank woolly-pated, thick-lipped nigger'" (137).

6. With the encouragement of Henry Louis Gates Jr., Starling published her dissertation, *The Slave Narrative: Its Place in American History,* as a book in 1988. William L. Andrews also notes Starling's contribution to autobiographical study in his 1991 essay, "African-American Autobiographical Criticism: Retrospect and Prospect," stating that it was in Starling's dissertation that *Incidents* was first acknowledged as the actual autobiography of Harriet Jacobs. Braxton also notes in her study that prominent black male critics of Starling's time, including Sterling Brown and Arna Bontemps, contested Starling's claim that Jacobs was the author and subject of *Incidents,* denying public recognition for Starling and her research for several decades (22).

7. Many prominent Washington, D.C., African Americans supported the idea that Redpath had written Keckley's text, not necessarily because they actually believed that rumor, but because they were upset that Keckley had betrayed the memory of Abraham Lincoln and the confidences of his widow by revealing such intimate details about Mary Todd Lincoln's economic and mental states. Even

Braxton refers to Keckley's text as being a "ghost-written autobiography" (43). Keckley's authorship was also called into question in 1935 when David Rankin Barbee, a student of the Lincoln/Civil War era, claimed to have discovered an article in which George Alfred Rownsend identified journalist Jane Grey Swisshelm as author of "the Madam Keckley book" (*Evening Star* A10). Barbee even concluded that Elizabeth Keckley never existed, but was merely a protagonist invented by Swisshelm. Very soon after Barbee had made his conclusions public, however, another student of the Lincoln era, John E. Washington, came forward with documented evidence on the life of Keckley, having spoken with people who were acquainted with her (*Evening Star* A12). He hints that Swisshelm's 1880 narrative, *Half a Century,* probably took much of its material from Keckley's 1868 *Behind the Scenes.* To further refute Barbee's claim that Keckley was fictional, the minister of the church that Keckley attended for thirty years and the man who delivered the eulogy at her funeral, Francis Grimke, wrote a letter that was published in the *Journal of Negro History (JNH)* in which he confirms the reality of Elizabeth Keckley (314). The question of whether Keckley actually wrote *Behind the Scenes* (or what parts of it) remains shrouded in mystery; however, an acquaintance of Keckley, Carrie Elizabeth Syphax Watson, asserts in the *JNH* that "aunt Keckley" wrote the book herself, aside from "corrections in construction of phrases and grammatical errors" (316). Further, according to Washington, Mrs. John Brooks, niece of a woman with whom Keckley had lived in New York, claimed that James Redpath "would spend several hours every evening with [Keckley]. Everybody in the house knew that Mrs. Keckley was writing a book on Mrs. Lincoln and that Redpath was helping her compile it" (*Evening Star* A12). While Ruth Painter Randall (*Mary Lincoln: Biography of a Marriage* 471) and Justin G. and Linda Levitt Turner (*Mary Todd Lincoln: Her Life and Letters* 430) believe that journalist Hamilton Busbey, whose signature appears on a copy of the first edition of Keckley's book, helped Keckley write her book, none of them question the authenticity of her life and her work. For the sake of argument, I will regard Elizabeth Keckley as the author of *Behind the Scenes.*

8. This statement excludes the 1789 *Narrative* of Olaudah Equiano who spent more time in England and on the sea than in the United States and whose focus was specifically on the outlawing of the slave trade as opposed to the abolition of slavery.

9. Citing from Rousseau's *Confessions,* Brodzki and Schenck note that Rousseau did not suffer any other man to stand above him regarding his honesty and the forthright nature of his narrative: "'let the numberless legion of my fellow men gather round me, and hear my confessions. Let them groan at my depravities and blush at my misdeeds. But let each one of them reveal his heart at the foot of Thy throne with equal sincerity, and may any man who dares, say, "I was a better man than he"'" (3).

10. Benstock's use of the term "gaps" refers to her recognition of the unavoidable omissions in all autobiographies; I later use the term "gaps" more formally to represent areas of subversion occupied by women and nonwhite writers that exist beyond the gaze of the white man.

11. A number of other critics notice an emphasis on community, family, and collectivity in nineteenth-century African American women's autobiographies, in-

cluding Frances Smith Foster who refers to the "viable and resourceful community of resisters" in Jacobs's *Incidents* (*Written* 95) and Gwendolyn Etter-Lewis who writes that the early African American women autobiographers "reconstructed their lives not from the perspective of an isolated self acting alone and unassisted but in conjunction with others such as family, mentors, and community" ("Work Place" 167).

12. While Braxton's statement appears tentative on this point, the African American black autobiographer's balancing of conciliatory and confrontational tones has always been an important masking tool, as evidenced in Equiano's *Narrative*. As I see it, this shifting is reflective of the struggle between the demand to have one's voice heard and the frustrating realization that one is dependent on the cooperation and assistance of the members of the dominant society to move one's private voice into a public setting.

13. Of African American autobiographers, Frederick Douglass is best known for his statements recounting the moment he recognized the connection between the denial of literacy to the black man and the white man's position of power: "I now understand what had been to me a most perplexing difficulty—to wit, the white man's power to enslave the black man. From that moment, I understood the pathway from slavery to freedom" (58).

14. Valerie Babb writes that "literacy validates the experience of one race or culture while making that of another all but invisible. In a culture dominated by literacy, the creation of literature by a slave forbidden to read or write or by a free Black writer marginalized because of his or her color made textual production itself a political act asserting equality" (39).

15. Black poet Phillis Wheatley is often cited as a black artist accused of doing no more than mimicking the Romantic lyrics of white poets. The editors of *The Norton Anthology of African American Literature* note, however, that Wheatley in eighteenth-century America "had first to write her way *into* American literature before she or any other black writer could claim a special mission and purpose for an *African* American literature" (167; editors' emphases). However, those who would claim that Wheatley made no political statements in her poetry overlook her brief chastisement of the white reading public who seemed to feel that the celebrated black Roman dramatist, Terence, was an exception for his race:

> The happier *Terence* all the choir inspir'd,
> His soul replenish'd, and his bosom fir'd;
> But say, *ye Muses,* why this partial grace,
> To one alone of *Afric's* sable race;
> From age to age transmitting thus his name
> With the first glory in the rolls of fame?
> ("To Maecenas" 169–70; lines 37–42; Wheatley's emphasis)

16. While in her preface Wilson names her "brethren" as the audience and purchasing group for her narrative, the sentimental tone of *Our Nig* and a number of ironic, sarcastic phrasings suggest a Northern, white target audience. Also, as many Wilson scholars have noted, most blacks were not of the economic level to be able to

provide the type of buying power that would be necessary to assist Wilson financially.

Chapter 2. Black Women Autobiographers' Encounter with Gender, Race, and Class

1. Barbara Welter in *Dimity Convictions* offers the following criteria for admittance into the "cult of true womanhood": "The attributes of True Womanhood, by
which a woman judged herself and was judged by her husband, her neighbors and
society, could be divided into four cardinal virtues—piety, purity, submissiveness
and domesticity. Put them all together and they spelled mother, daughter, sister,
wife—*woman*" (21; my emphasis). I emphasize "woman" because we must note
that the woman being described here is the European American woman, the black
female's perceived inhumanity making her ineligible for inclusion.

2. Quoted from Anne Firor Scott's *Southern Lady: From Pedestal to Politics,
1830–1930.*

3. Barbara Omolade writes, "Most white women sadistically and viciously punished the black woman and her children for the transgressions of their white men.
White women used the social relationship of supervisor of black women's domestic
labor to act out their racial superiority, their emotional frustrations, and their sexual
jealousies" (10).

4. Refer to Werner Sollor's *Neither Black Nor White, Yet Both* for an interesting
treatment of the stereotype of the "tragic mulatto."

5. Wilson's racial make-up is confounded in her text. As Henry Louis Gates Jr.
notes in his introduction to *Our Nig*, Wilson is herself identified as "black" on New
Hampshire's 1850 census, even though the option of "mulatto" was also available.
This is probably an excellent example of irony and "creative" writing on Wilson's
part as she plays with the construct of "race," knowing that a beautiful mulatto child
would engender more interest in her narrative than an "ordinary" Negro.

6. From Catherine Clinton's *The Plantation Mistress: Woman's World in the Old
South* (quoted in Gwin 45–46).

7. Braxton is not the only source that calls the paternity of Keckley's son into
question. Becky Rutberg writes in *Mary Lincoln's Dressmaker* that the white man
who fathered Keckley's child was Alexander Kirkland who died when George
Keckley was eighteen months old. Rutberg, however, does not specify the source of
her information. Both Rutberg and Braxton also identify Keckley's real father as her
mother's master, even though Keckley, with no obvious attempt to dissemble or
mislead, identifies her father as being a slave on a neighboring plantation where he
remained until his owner decided to relocate in the West (22).

8. The conclusion of Sorisio's article is so powerful in its determination as to why
Keckley's narrative was met with such anger that it is worth citing in its entirety:
"When Keckley ripped away the curtain to expose the private behavior of a white
middle-class woman in such a public forum, when she revealed what many readers
wanted so desperately to keep *behind the scenes*, it was an unforgivable violation of
gentility and an unacceptable assertion of racial worth. This combination was certain

to, and indeed did, generate an enormous amount of wrath" ("Unmasking" 36; Sorisio's emphasis).

9. Virginia Woolf suggested in *A Room of One's Own* that men reacted to such feminine involvement out of fear: "Possibly when the professor [white male] insisted a little too emphatically upon the inferiority of women, he was concerned not with their inferiority, but with his own superiority" (34).

10. Although many of these nineteenth-century constructs have been challenged almost to the point of eradication in some instances, Mary Field Belenky notes that even in current times, women continue to struggle with the labels and implied meanings attached to terms like femininity: "In everyday and professional life, women often feel unheard even when they believe that they have something important to say. Most women can recall incidents in which either they or female friends were discouraged from pursuing some line of intellectual work on the grounds that it was 'unfeminine' or incompatible with female capabilities. All women grow up having to deal with historically and culturally engrained definitions of femininity and womanhood—one common theme being that women, like children, should be seen and not heard" (5).

11. William L. Andrews notes the 1980s' interest that black self-representation aroused in white society: "[O]nce the public began to read the wealth of black autobiographies spawned by the upheavals of the 1960s, it didn't take long for scholars to start rediscovering black autobiography, first in reviews, then in critical essays, and eventually in ambitious attempts to define a tradition of Afro-American first-person writing" ("Toward a Poetics" 78).

12. Feminist scholars who address the polyvocal aspects of the woman writer include Joanne Braxton, Evelyn Higginbotham, Barbara Smith, Sidonie Smith, among others.

13. Mae Gwendolyn Henderson writes, "As gendered and racial subjects, black women speak/write in multiple voices—not all simultaneously or with equal weight, but with various and changing degrees of intensity" (36).

14. For important critical essays on the constructs of race, gender, and culture, see the following sources: Sandra Adell ("Writing About Race"); Kwame Anthony Appiah ("Race"); Houston A. Baker ("Figurations for a New American Literary History"); and James L. Gray ("Culture, Gender, and Slave Narrative").

15. See Barbara J. Fields's discussion about the historical link between the economics of class and the "emergence of and salience of different conceptions of race" in "Ideology and Race in American History."

16. While several black women writers and scholars make note of these creative outlets for black women—Alice Walker in *In Search of Our Mothers' Gardens* and Maya Angelou in *I Know Why the Caged Bird Sings*, to name two prominent examples—my reference is more personal. A native of the hard red dirt of Alabama, I watched my grandmother and other members of this Southern black woman's community patiently and creatively sew their quilts, make mosaics out of their grassless front yards (even creating walkways lined with pieces of colored glass), grow the most marvelous array of flowers and vegetables behind their houses, and make flavorful meals out of what many in white society called weeds.

Chapter 3. A Patchwork of Cultures: Journeys of African American Women Autobiographers

1. Although I want to avoid the assumption that all West African cultures can be lumped under one homogeneous umbrella, for the sake of simplicity in my study, I will use the terms West Africa and West African to represent all of these various cultures from which came the American slave unless I am specifically noting a tradition, belief, or custom of the Yoruba culture. The truth is that African Americans are descendants from a variety of cultures occupying the western areas of Africa. John Hope Franklin and Alfred A. Moss Jr.'s *From Slavery to Freedom: A History of Negro Americans* and Henry Louis Gates Jr.'s *The Signifying Monkey: A Theory of Afro-American Literary Criticism* and *Figures in Black: Words, Signs, and the "Racial" Self* all deal with the various West African cultures in great detail.

2. Refer to Bernard Bell's *The Afro-American Novel and Its Tradition* for a detailed discussion of African "sacred" time and Western "profane" time.

3. The concept of black women as gatherers, as harvesters, also had roots, literally, in the soil of Africa; Jacqueline Jones notes that "as members of traditional agricultural societies, African women played a major role in the production of the family's food" (39). The gathering of vegetables and herbs was regarded as woman's work, which probably accounts for her alleged understanding of and skill in working roots as a conjurer.

4. Wole Soyinka notes the influence of Yoruba gods on the New World's "socio-religious reality and in the secular arts," specifically, "Yemaja (Yemoja), Oxosi (Ososi), Exu (Esu), and Xango (Sango)" (1).

5. Gates further notes in *The Signifying Monkey* that "Esu," known as "Esu-Elegbara" in Nigeria and as "Legba" among the Fon in Dahomey, appears to be the mythical progenitor of "Exu" in Brazil, "Echu-Elegua" in Cuba, "Papa Legba" in the pantheon of the "loa" of "Vaudou" in Haiti, and "Papa La Bas" in the "loa" of "Hoodoo" in the United States. Gates characterizes "Esu" as the "guardian of the crossroads, master of style and the stylus, master of the mystical barrier that separates the divine from the profane worlds" (237). See pages 237–38 for Gates's comparison of "Esu" to his "Western relative," Hermes.

6. While the teachings and the practices of Christianity seemed to be in conflict as they related to slavery, Houston A. Baker notes in *Long Black Song* that what emerged as the "black" church in the slave community "provided a new basis of social cohesion for these displaced Africans—a nation within a nation for the black American folk" (43).

7. Bernard Bell examines the historical debate between Frazier and Melville J. Herskovits in which the anthropologist Herskovits "advanced the theory that through the processes of retention (the continuity of some African interpretations of phenomena), reinterpretation (the interpretation of white cultural patterns according to African principles), and syncretism (the amalgamation of African and American cultural patterns and sign systems), the African heritage—i.e., the culture of African peoples south of the Sahara, especially the Yoruba and Dahomeans—was a continuing force in black American life" (11). John Hope Franklin agrees with Herskovits, writing that "despite the heterogeneity characteristic of many aspects of

African life, the African peoples still had sufficient common experiences to enable them to cooperate in the New World in fashioning new customs and traditions which reflected their African background" (25).

8. To continue Gates's argument: "The full erasure of traces of cultures as splendid, as ancient, and as shared by the slave traveler as the classic cultures of traditional West Africa would have been extraordinarily difficult. Inadvertently, African slavery in the New World satisfied the preconditions for the emergence of a new African culture, a truly Pan-African culture fashioned as a colorful weave of linguistic, institutional, metaphysical, and formal threads" (3).

9. Houston A. Baker challenges the various attempts that European Americans have made to deny an African American link with beast/animal tales: "That [Joel Chandler] Harris and subsequently Ambrose E. Gonzales tried to identify the animal tales of black America with Aesop and an old Western tradition is indicative of the differentiation between black and white culture. Any black man reading about Brer Rabbit, any black man who knows that the rabbit tales were produced by his ancestors in slavery, realizes that this black American trickster has more to do with Denmark Vessey and Nat Turner than with Chauntecleer and Pertelote" (*Long Black Song* 12).

10. Thurstan Shaw notes that in attempting to trace the histories of African cultures, researchers find that they must rely on the unwritten documentation of "oral traditions, praise songs and traditional ceremonies" (12).

11. A. B. Ellis writes, "Some men make a profession of story-telling, and wander from place to place reciting tales. Such a man is termed an *akpalo kpatita,* 'one who makes a trade of telling fables'" (243).

12. William Bascom offers the following distinctions between myths, legends, folktales, riddles, and proverbs, the primary oral traditions of the Yoruba: "Of the prose narratives, myths about the deities and legends about past kings and war heroes are grouped together in a single category; both are considered to be factual accounts of past events, in contrast to folktales which are recognized as fiction. . . . [F]olktales are predominantly moralistic in intent; whereas the myths and legends impart information that is important because it is regarded as true. Riddles are recognized as sharpening the wits and training the memory of children; but they also impart knowledge; proverbs are the concern of adults. Because they express Yoruba morals and ethics, they are convenient standards for appraising behavior, and they are continually quoted in discussing an issue and in commenting on the behavior of others" (98). Such proverbs appear to be the forebearers of the African American tradition of Signifyin[g].

13. Oyěwùmí goes on to state that the "system of indirect rule introduced by the British colonial government recognized the male chief's authority at the local level but did not acknowledge the existence of female chiefs. Therefore, women were effectively excluded from all colonial state structures" (123).

14. Amadiume's study was conducted among the Igbo, considered a Yoruba subgroup, in the town of Nnobi, Nigeria.

15. Bell, relying on the published research of historian Ruth Finnegan, identifies four principal functions of oral narratives in African cultures: "They transmit

knowledge, values, and attitudes from one generation to another, enforce conformity to social norms, validate social institutions and religious rituals, and provide a psychological release from the restrictions of society" (16). See Finnegan's *Oral Literature in Africa.*

16. Gloria T. Hull and Barbara Smith also address the African American woman's "multilayered oppression," but are quick to point out that African American women have devised ways "in which [they] have created and maintained [their] own intellectual traditions as black women, without either the recognition or the support of white-male society" (xviii).

17. See Richard Dyer's "White" for an interesting discussion on whiteness being everything and nothing.

18. See Sandra M. Gilbert and Susan Gubar's *The Madwoman in the Attic* for a full discussion of "anxiety of authorship," the white woman writer's "dis-ease" within the white-male literary tradition.

19. Deborah Gray White also interrogates the prevalence of the "Jezebel" and "Mammy" stereotypes as they are applied to black women in *Ar'n't I a Woman: Female Slaves in the Plantation South:* "One of the most prevalent images of black women in antebellum America was of a person governed almost entirely by her libido, a Jezebel character" (28–29).

And: "Mammy was a woman completely dedicated to the white family, especially to the children of that family. She was the house servant who was given complete charge of domestic management. She served also as friend and advisor. She was, in short, surrogate mistress and mother" (49).

20. Robert Stepto is credited for initially using the term "articulate hero" to describe Frederick Douglass.

Chapter 4. The Emergence of an African American Mother Tongue

1. These same elements are found in such classic gothic narratives as Charlotte Bronte's *Jane Eyre* and Charlotte Perkins Gilman's *The Yellow Wallpaper.* See Greg Johnson's "Gilman's Gothic Allegory: Rage and Redemption in *The Yellow Wallpaper.*"

2. Richard VanDerBeets characterizes the captivity narrative as a tale wherein the hero experiences "Separation (isolation from one's culture and symbolic death), Transformation (a series of excruciating ordeals in passing from ignorance to knowledge and maturity, accompanied by ritualized adoption into a new culture), and Return (symbolic rebirth with a sense of moral or spiritual gain)" (*Indian Captivity* x). See also John Sekora, "Red, White, and Black."

3. Written under the pseudonym of Betsey Kickley, *Behind the Seams; by a Nigger Woman Who Took in Work from Mrs. Lincoln and Mrs. Davis* was published by National News in New York City in 1868.

4. This excerpt is taken from a lecture delivered in 1866 by General Clinton B. Fisk, head of Tennessee's Freedmen's Bureau, and published by the Library of Congress in "Plain Counsel for Freedmen."

5. According to Liberty County property records, the Grest plantation was located on the Isle of Wight. It is interesting to note that a number of scholars, notably

history professor James M. McPherson, identify Susie King Taylor's place of birth as "one of the Georgia Sea Islands" (introduction to the 1968 Arno Press edition of *Reminiscences*). While the Isle of Wight surveyed is currently not an island but is situated on the mainland of Georgia, there is speculation that, with changes in the Georgia coastline over the course of time, water levels have dropped so that some former Sea Islands are now a part of the mainland.

6. Even though Taylor indicates in her text that she escaped from her plantation at the onset of the war with an uncle, she does not identify him by name, so there is no way to determine if the John Baker identified in this passage is related to her father, Raymond Baker. If he is, it seems strange that Taylor would not say so; at the same time, however, her not identifying him as such is consistent with her tendency to provide little personal information in her narrative.

7. Although two former commanders of Taylor's regiment, colonels T. W. Higginson and C. T. Trowbridge, note her service with the 33rd, she received no military pension. Trowbridge states in his letter attached to her narrative, "I most sincerely regret that through a technicality you are debarred from having your name placed on the roll of pensioners, as an Army Nurse; for among all the number of heroic women whom the government is now rewarding, I know of no one more deserving than yourself" (xiii). He does not state what the "technicality" was.

8. Quoted from Gilbert and Gubar's "Sexual Linguistics."

9. Sidonie Smith writes, "Harking back to the phase before the symbolic logic of binary opposition insists on male privilege and superiority, the language of feminine desire—the *écriture féminine* of Hélène Cixous, the *womanspeak* of Luce Irigaray, the *jouissance* of Julie Kristeva—finds its voice in alliance with the mother and her milk, her body, her rhythmic and nonsensical language. Now the subject position from which woman speaks may be, like the voice of the mother, outside time, plural, fluid, bisexual, de-centered, nonlogocentric. Having returned to her origins in the mother and the silent and silenced 'culture' she shares with all women, the autobiographer manifests a different relationship to storytelling as a woman" (*Poetics* 58; Smith's emphasis).

10. I must note that in her entire essay, Barbara Smith uses the phrase "female language" only once while she uses the phrase "woman's language" and "woman's speech" numerous times. This fact suggests to me that her one use of "female" was in error and that she never meant to suggest a biological essentialism in black woman's language.

11. One need only look at the poems of Emily Dickinson to see the effectiveness of such structural techniques.

Chapter 5. Subtle Resistance in *Our Nig, Incidents, Behind the Scenes,* and *Reminiscences*

1. Elizabeth Fox-Genovese questions Harriet Jacobs's/Linda Brent's successful avoidance of rape at the hands of Dr. Norcom/Dr. Flint, stating that "it stretches the limits of all credulity that Linda Brent actually eluded her master's sexual advances" (*Within the Plantation Household* 392). While such successful resistance is hard to

credit, it is not totally outside of the scope of possibility. One need only recall the seductions taking place at the octoroon balls in Louisiana at the time. Since Dr. Flint specifically proposes taking Linda on a trip to Louisiana with him and later establishing her in her own cottage, it would stretch the limits of credulity not to recognize the doctor's familiarity with such balls and the history of sentimental seductions that occurred between white gentlemen and fair-skinned black women. Dr. Flint did not want to rape Linda; he wanted to seduce her.

2. Another act of concealment that Keckley does not mention is the fact that her son enlisted in the Union army as a white man (Rutberg 54).

3. Refer to the subversive tactics that Douglass employed to learn to read and write in his 1845 *Narrative*.

4. Refer to W.E.B. DuBois's *Souls of Black Folk* for an extended presentation of the concepts of double-consciousness.

5. Particularly amusing in its ridicule of those who attempt to isolate racial essences is the following excerpt from William Wells Brown's 1853 novel, *Clotel; or The President's Daughter,* as learned white men consider ways to keep nonwhites from voting: "'Lest the wisdom of our courts should be circumvented by some such men as might be named, who are so near being born constitutionally that they might be taken for white by sight, I would suggest that our court be invested with SMELLING powers, and that if a man don't exhale the constitutional smell, he shall not vote!'" (276; Brown's emphasis).

Chapter 6. Allusion as Hidden Discourse in Black Women's Autobiography

1. According to Yellin's note 3, chap. 12, on page 269 of *Incidents*, "abolitionists, who characterized slavery as 'the national sin,' routinely symbolized the institution as a serpent."

2. In much African American literature, Ethiopia symbolically represents all of "Mother Africa."

3. Zora Neale Hurston, among others, stresses the importance of the metaphor in Negro expression: "The metaphor is of course very primitive. It is easier to illustrate than it is to explain because action came before speech. Every phase of Negro life is highly dramatised" ("Characteristics" 224–25).

4. There are a couple of biblical allusions in Jeremiah that suggest shame attached to the hair being shorn, leaving the forehead exposed as an act of reduction: "2. thou hast polluted the land with thy whoredoms and with thy wickedness. 3. Therefore the showers have been withholden, and there hath been no latter rain; and thou hadst a whore's forehead, thou refusedst to be ashamed" (Jeremiah 3:2–3) and "29. Cut off thine hair, O Jerusalem, and cast it away, and take up a lamentation on high places; for the LORD hath rejected and forsaken the generation of his wrath. 30. For the children of Judah have done evil in my sight, saith the LORD: they have set their abominations in the house which is called by my name, to pollute it" (Jeremiah 7:29–30: Bible's emphasis).

5. See Yellin note 1 for chapter 22, "Christmas Festivities," for a thorough discussion of this transatlantic tradition.

6. Citing from what she calls the "Book of Dixie," Zora Neale Hurston writes that

"every white man shall be allowed to pet himself a Negro. Yea, he shall take a black man unto himself to pet and to cherish" ("The 'Pet' Negro System" 156).

7. In a reversal of this oppressive act, a runaway slave in William Wells Brown's *Clotel; or, The President's Daughter* outwits a Northern white train conductor who insists, regardless of his funds, that he ride in the "Jim Crow" car, which is also the luggage car. Brown writes, "Slavery is a school in which its victims learn much shrewdness" (274). Since William, this runaway slave, is being treated like an object, like a piece of luggage, he claims the same fare as a piece of luggage: "'What do you charge per hundred-weight for goods?' Inquired the negro. 'A quarter of a dollar per hundred,' answered the conductor. 'I weigh just one hundred and fifty pounds,' returned William, 'and will pay you three eighths of a dollar.' 'Do you expect that you will pay only thirty-seven cents for your ride?' 'This, sir, is your own price. I came in a luggage-van, and I'll pay for luggage.' After a vain effort to get the negro to pay more, the conductor took the thirty-seven cents, and noted in his cash-book, 'Received for one hundred and fifty pounds of luggage, thirty-seven cents'" (274).

Chapter 7. Flagrant Resistance, and Punishment Be Damned

1. The *OED* traces the origin of "nigger," demonstrating its use as an offensive term as early as the eighteenth century.

2. The following definitions from the *Random House Collegiate Dictionary*, second edition, shed light on the minimizing and sexually demeaning nature of these terms: "Sass" (1)—1) stewed fruit; fruit sauce; 2) fresh vegetables [1765–75, New England, Midland, South]. "Sass" (2)—1) impudent or disrespectful backtalk; 2) to answer back in an impudent manner [1855–60 American from "sassy," uncertain origin]. "saucy"—1) impertinent; insolent; 2) pert, boldly smart. "Impudent"—1) of, pertaining to, or characterized by impertinence or effrontery; 2) [obsolete] shameless or brazenly immodest [from Latin "impudens" (shameless) from the base "pudere" (to be ashamed)]. "Pudendum" [usually pl. pudenda]—(anatomy) the external genital organs, esp. those of the female; vulva [from Latin "pudendus," gerundive of "pudere" (to be ashamed). The *OED* sheds further light on the term "sassy" tracing its possible origins back to Africa: "'sassy-tree,' the African 'Erythrophlaum guineense' the bark of this tree, a decoction of which is used in West Africa as an ordeal poison."

3. More often than not, especially with the advent of the powerful black women's clubs in the final decade of the nineteenth century and continuing to the present time, these terms (like "nigger") are more often used intraculturally to deflate the intended minimization inherent in their use by the dominant society.

4. See bell hooks's *Talking Back: Thinking Feminist, Thinking Black* and Henry Louis Gates Jr.'s "James Gronniosaw and the Trope of the Talking Book."

5. Jean Fagan Yellin notes in her introduction to *Incidents* that "Jacobs felt Stowe had betrayed her as a woman, denigrated her as a mother, and threatened her as a writer" (xix).

6. The realization of selfhood—that one is an independent, valuable individual with a mind and soul—serves as a pivotal point in Frado's life when she verbally challenges Mrs. Bellmont as it also proves to be in the life of a young Frederick

Douglass when he physically fights the slave-breaker, Mr. Covey, and decides at that point that he would never again be a slave in spirit: "My long-crushed spirit rose, cowardice departed, bold defiance took its place; and I now, resolved that, however long I might remain a slave in form, the day had passed forever when I could be a slave in fact. I did not hesitate to let it be known of me, that the white man who expected to succeed in whipping, must also succeed in killing me" (79).

7. I define racialism here as a system in which a member of one racial group, while not denying the rights of equality due to other racial groups, still considers her or his own race superior in intellect, appearance, and social behavior.

8. Many black writers of the nineteenth century make comment about the favored status received by European immigrants arriving in America compared to the oppressions suffered by blacks who had been brought to the New World against their will. Note particularly Frederick Douglass, William Wells Brown, and Harriet Jacobs.

9. It must be noted that Higginson took the occasion of writing this introduction to plug his own little volume, *Army Life in a Black Regiment.*

10. The few direct statements Keckley makes to her fellow blacks in *Behind the Scenes* are more pitying, at times almost ridiculing, than supportive: "Poor dusky children of slavery, men and women of my own race—the transition from slavery to freedom was too sudden for you! you were not prepared for the new life that opened before you, and the great masses of the North learned to look upon your helplessness with indifference" (112).

Chapter 8. Linkages: Continuation of a Tradition

1. Nelson describes a "niggerbitchfit" as the explosion of the rage that has built up in a black woman over a period of time. It is "a combination of a moment of absolute clarity, a psychotic episode, and a revolutionary action. It is an expression of rage out of control, the verbal rejection of the ever-accumulating invisibility, disrespect, and attack from all fronts that is a central part of what it means to be a black woman in America. It is finally voicing what you really think after an extended period of being reasonable, understanding, flexible, pleasant, a team player, a well-behaved colored woman, of going along to get along in a dying white culture and a very unhealthy black one that negates or minimizes our existence moment to moment. It is a frightening thing to experience for those on the receiving end" (201–2).

Afterword: Piecing It All Together

1. Geneva Smitherman's much-referenced *Talkin and Testifyin: The Language of Black America* is one of the first substantial texts that addresses the subversive use of English by black Americans wherein she often uses the language of black America. Note the following description of "playing the dozens": "What you do in playing the Dozens is sig on a person's kinfolk—usually the mother, the closest kin—instead of siggin on the person" (129).

2. Margaret Lindgren points out that "Harriet Jacobs and Harriet Wilson wrote in the context of a culture which demanded that they speak many 'dialects,' simply in order to survive" (21). This survival instinct supports their unaffected act of

speaking from and speaking through many voices in the textual and contextual representation of their autobiographies.

3. See Gates's *The Signifying Monkey*, xxxiii.

4. Gates briefly summarizes and simplifies the process: "To name our tradition is to rename each of its antecedents, no matter how pale they might seem. To rename is to revise, and to revise is to Signify" (*Signifying* xxxiii).

5. While Jacobs also employs aspects of the adventure novel, her primary literary paradigm was the sentimental narrative.

6. Perhaps expecting all newly free blacks to be as independent and self-reliant as herself, Keckley at times appears harsh in her assessment of these former slaves: "Thousands of the disappointed, huddled together in camps, fretted and pined like children for the 'good old times.' I believe they were sincere in these declarations, because dependence had become a part of their second nature, and independence brought with it the cares and vexations of poverty" (140).

Bibliography

Adams, Timothy Dow. *Telling Lies in Modern American Autobiography.* Chapel Hill: University of North Carolina Press, 1990.

Adell, Sandra. "Writing About Race." *American Literary History* 6, no. 3 (Fall 1994): 559–71.

Amadiume, Ifi. *Male Daughters, Female Husbands: Gender and Sex in an African Society.* London: Zed Books, 1987.

Ammons, Elizabeth. "Stowe's Dream of the Mother-Savior: *Uncle Tom's Cabin* and the American Women Writers Before the 1920s." In *New Essays on Uncle Tom's Cabin,* edited by Eric J. Sundquist, 155–95. Cambridge: Cambridge University Press, 1986.

Andrews, William L. "African American Autobiographical Criticism: Retrospect and Prospect." In *American Autobiography: Retrospect and Prospect,* edited by Paul John Eakin, 195–215. Madison: University of Wisconsin Press, 1991.

———. "The Changing Moral Discourse of Nineteenth-Century African American Women's Autobiography: Harriet Jacobs and Elizabeth Keckley." In *De/Colonizing the Subject: The Politics of Gender in Women's Autobiography,* edited by Sidonie Smith and Julia Watson, 225–41. Minneapolis: University of Minnesota Press, 1992.

———. *To Tell a Free Story; The First Century of Afro-American Autobiography, 1760–1865.* Urbana: University of Illinois Press, 1986.

———. "Toward a Poetics of Afro-American Autobiography." In *Afro-American Literary Study in the 1990s,* edited by Houston A. Baker Jr. and Patricia Redmon, 78–104. Chicago: University of Chicago Press, 1989.

———, ed. Introduction to *Classic American Autobiographies.* New York: Penguin Group, 1992.

Angelou, Maya. Foreword to *Dust Tracks on a Road,* by Zora Neale Hurston. New York: Harper Collins, 1996.

———. *I Know Why the Caged Bird Sings.* New York: Bantam Books, 1971.

Appiah, Kwame Anthony. "Race." In *Critical Terms for Literary Study,* edited by Frank Lentricchia and Thomas McLaughlin, 274–87. Chicago: University of Chicago Press, 1990.

Babb, Valerie. "Liberation Literacy: Literacy and Empowerment in Marginalized American Texts." In *Multicultural Literature and Literacies: Making Space for*

Difference, edited by Suzanne M. Miller and Barbara McCaskill, 37–53. Albany: State University of New York Press, 1993.

Baker, Houston A. *Blues, Ideology, and Afro-American Literature: A Vernacular Theory.* Chicago: University of Chicago Press, 1984.

———. "Figurations for a New American Literary History." In *Ideology and Classic American Literature,* edited by Sacvan Bercovitch and Myra Jehlen, 145–71. Cambridge: Harvard University Press, 1986.

———. *Long Black Song: Essays in Black American Literature and Culture.* Charlottesville: University Press of Virginia, 1972.

Bakhtin, Mikhail Mikhailovich. *The Dialogic Imagination: Four Essays.* Austin: University of Texas Press, 1981.

Barbee, David Rankin. "Bizarre Lincoln Story Is Traced. 'Sob Sister' Revealed as Writer of Tragic Tale of Widow." *Evening Star,* November 11, 1935, sec., A10.

Barnes, Elizabeth. "Affecting Relations: Pedagogy, Patriarchy, and the Politics of Sympathy." *American Literary History* 8, no. 4 (1996 Winter): 597–614.

Bascom, William. *The Yoruba of Southwestern Nigeria.* New York: Holt, Rinehart and Winston, 1969.

Bassard, Katherine Clay. *Spirited Interrogations: Culture, Gender, and Community in Early African American Women's Writing.* Princeton: Princeton University Press, 1999.

Belenky, Mary Field. Introduction to *Women's Ways of Knowing: The Development of Self, Voice, and Mind,* 3–20. New York: Basic Books, 1986.

Bell, Bernard. *The Afro-American Novel and its Tradition.* Amherst: University of Massachusetts Press, 1987.

Benstock, Shari. "Authorizing the Autobiographical." In *The Private Self: Theory and Practice of Women's Autobiographical Writings,* edited by Shari Benstock, 10–33. Chapel Hill: University of North Carolina Press, 1988.

Bentham, Jeremy. *A Bentham Reader.* Edited by Mary Park Mack. New York: Pegasus, 1969.

Braxton, Joanne M. *Black Women Writing Autobiography: A Tradition within a Tradition.* Philadelphia: Temple University Press, 1989.

Breau, Elizabeth. "Identifying Satire: *Our Nig.*" *Callaloo* 16, no. 2 (Spring 1993): 455–65.

Bredin, Renae Moore. "Theory in the Mirror." In *Other Sisterhoods: Literary Theory and U.S. Women of Color,* edited by Sandra Kumamoto, 23–43. Urbana: University of Illinois Press, 1998.

Brewer, Rose M. "Theorizing Race, Class and Gender: The New Scholarship of Black Feminist Intellectuals and Black Women's Labor." In *Theorizing Black Feminisms: The Visionary Pragmatism of Black Women,* edited by Stanlie M. James and Abena P. A. Busia, 13–30. London and New York: Routledge, 1993.

Brodzki, Bella, and Celeste Schenck. Introduction to *Life/Lines: Theorizing Women's Autobiography,* edited by Bella Brodzki and Celeste Schenck, 1–15. Ithaca: Cornell University Press, 1988.

Brown, William Wells. *Clotel; or, The President's Daughter.* 1853. In *The Norton*

Anthology of African American Literature, edited by Henry Louis Gates Jr. and Nellie Y. McKay, 255–76. New York: W. W. Norton and Company, 1997.

Busia, Abena P. A. "Silencing Sycorax: On African Colonial Discourse and the Unvoiced Female." *Cultural Critique* 14 (Winter 1989–90): 81–104.

Butterfield, Stephen. *Black Autobiography in America.* Amherst: University of Massachusetts Press, 1974.

Carby, Hazel V. *Reconstructing Womanhood: The Emergence of the Afro-American Woman Novelist.* New York: Oxford University Press, 1987.

Child, Lydia Maria, ed. Introduction to *Incidents in the Life of a Slave Girl, Written by Herself,* by Harriet A. Jacobs, 3–4. 1861. Edited and with introduction by Jean Fagan Yellin. Cambridge: Harvard University Press, 1987.

Cole, Phyllis. "Stowe, Jacobs, Wilson: White Plots and Black Counterplots." In *New Perspectives on Gender, Race, and Class in Society,* edited by Audrey T. McCluskey, 23–45. Women's Studies Program Occasional Papers Series: Indiana University Press, 1990.

Cooper, Anna Julia. *A Voice from the South by a Black Woman of the South.* 1892. New York: Oxford University Press, 1988.

Cutter, Martha J. *Unruly Tongue: Identity and Voice in American Women's Writing, 1850–1930.* Jackson: University Press of Mississippi, 1999.

Davies, Carole Boyce. *Black Women, Writing and Identity: Migrations of the Subject.* London and New York: Routledge, 1994.

Doriani, Beth Maclay. "Black Womanhood in Nineteenth-Century America: Subversion and Self-Construction in Two Women's Autobiographies." *American Quarterly* 43, no. 2 (June 1991): 199–222.

Douglass, Frederick. *Narrative of the Life of Frederick Douglass, An American Slave.* 1845. Boston and New York: Bedford Books, 1993.

DuBois, W.E.B. *The Souls of Black Folk.* 1903. New York: Dover Publications, 1994.

Dyer, Richard. "White." *Screen* 29, no. 4 (1988): 44–64.

Egan, Susanna. "Self-Conscious History: American Autobiography after the Civil War." In *American Autobiography: Retrospect and Prospect,* edited by Paul John Eakin, 70–94. Madison: University of Wisconsin Press, 1991.

Elliott, Emory, gen. ed. *The Columbia History of the American Novel.* New York: Columbia University Press, 1991.

Ellis, A. B. *The Yoruba-Speaking Peoples of the Slave Coast of West Africa.* Oosterhout, N.B., The Netherlands: Anthropological Publications, 1966.

Equiano, Olaudah. *The Interesting Narrative of the Life of Olaudah Equiano, or Gustavus Vassa, the African, Written by Himself.* 1789. New York: W. W. Norton and Company, 2001.

Etter-Lewis, Gwendolyn. "African American Women in the Work Place: Double Standards/Double Lives." In *Ethnic Women: A Multiple Status Reality,* edited by Vasilikie Demos and Marcia Texler Segal, 155–68. Dix Hills, N.Y.: General Hall, 1994.

———. "From the Inside Out: Survival and Continuity in African American Women's Oral Narratives." In *Unrelated Kin: Race and Gender in Women's*

Personal Narratives, edited by Gwendolyn Etter-Lewis and Michelle Foster, 169–79. London and New York: Routledge, 1996.

Fields, Barbara J. "Ideology and Race in American History." In *Region, Race, and Reconstruction: Essays in Honor of C. Vann Woodward,* edited by J. Morgan Kousser and James McPherson, 143–77. New York: Oxford University Press, 1982.

Fike, Michael A. "Jean Toomer and Okot p'Bitek in Alice Walker's 'In Search of Our Mothers' Gardens.'" *Multi-Ethnic Literature of the United States* 25, nos. 3/4 (Fall/Winter 2000): 141–60.

Finnegan, Ruth. *Oral Literature in Africa.* London: Clarendon Press, 1970.

Foreman, P. Gabrielle. "The Spoken and the Silenced in *Incidents in the Life of a Slave Girl* and *Our Nig.*" *Callaloo* 13, no. 2 (Spring 1990): 313–24.

Foster, Frances Smith. "Adding Color and Contour to Early American Self-Portraitures: Autobiographical Writings of Afro-American Women." In *Conjuring: Black Women, Fiction, and Literary Tradition,* edited by Marjorie Pryse and Hortense J. Spillers, 25–38. Bloomington: Indiana University Press, 1985.

———. "Autobiography after Emancipation: The Example of Elizabeth Keckley." In *Multicultural Autobiography: American Lives,* edited by James Robert Payne, 32–63. Knoxville: University of Tennessee Press, 1992.

———. "'In Respect to Females . . .': Differences in the Portrayals of Women by Male and Female Narrators." *Black American Literature Forum* 15, no. 2 (Summer 1981): 66–70.

———. "Neither Auction Block nor Pedestal: 'The Life and Religious Experiences of Jarena Lee, A Coloured Lady.'" *New York Literary Forum* 12–13 (1984): 143–69.

———. "Resisting *Incidents.*" In *Harriet Jacobs and "Incidents in the Life of a Slave Girl": New Critical Essays,* edited by Deborah M. Garfield and Rafia Zafar, 57–75. Cambridge: Cambridge University Press, 1996.

———. *Witnessing Slavery: The Development of Ante-bellum Slave Narratives.* Madison: University of Wisconsin Press, 1994.

———. *Written by Herself: Literary Production by African American Women, 1746–1892.* Bloomington: Indiana University Press, 1993.

Foucault, Michel. *The Archaeology of Knowledge.* New York: Pantheon Books, 1972.

———. *The History of Sexuality, Vol. I: An Introduction.* Translation by Robert Hurley. New York: Random House, 1978.

Fox-Genovese, Elizabeth. "My Statue, My Self: Autobiographical Writings of Afro-American Women." In *Reading Black, Reading Feminist: A Critical Anthology,* edited by Henry Louis Gates Jr., 176–203. New York: Penguin Group, 1990.

———. *Within the Plantation Household: Black and White Women of the Old South.* Chapel Hill: University of North Carolina Press, 1988.

Franklin, John Hope and Alfred A. Moss Jr. *From Slavery to Freedom: A History of Negro Americans.* New York: Alfred A. Knopf, 1988.

Gardner, Eric, "'This Attempt of Their Sister': Harriet Wilson's *Our Nig* from Printer to Readers." *The New England Quarterly* 66, no. 2 (June 1993): 226–46.

Garfield, Deborah M. "Conclusion: Vexed Alliances: Race and Female Collaborations in the Life of Harriet Jacobs." In *Harriet Jacobs and "Incidents in the Life of a*

Slave Girl": New Critical Essays, edited by Deborah M. Garfield and Rafia Zafar, 275–91. Cambridge: Cambridge University Press, 1996.

Garrison, William Lloyd, ed. Preface to *Narrative of the Life of Frederick Douglass, An American Slave, Written by Himself.* 1845. In *Classic American Autobiographers,* edited with introduction by William L. Andrews, 230–38. New York: Penguin Group, 1992.

Gates, Henry Louis, Jr. "'Ethnic and Minority' Studies." In *Introduction to Scholarship in Modern Languages and Literatures,* edited by Joseph Gibaldi, 289–302. New York: Modern Language Association, 1992.

———. *Figures in Black: Words, Signs, and the "Racial" Self.* New York: Oxford University Press, 1987.

———. Introduction to *Our Nig: or, Sketches from the Life of a Free Black, in a Two-Story White House, North. Showing that Slavery's Shadows Fall Even There,* by Harriet E. Wilson, xi–lv. 1859. London: Allison and Busby, 1984.

———. "James Gronniosaw and the Trope of the Talking Book." In *African American Autobiography: A Collection of Critical Essays,* edited by William L. Andrews, 8–25. Englewood Cliffs, N.J.: Prentice Hall, 1993.

———. *The Signifying Monkey: A Theory of Afro-American Literary Criticism.* New York: Oxford University Press, 1988.

Gates, Henry Louis, Jr., and Nellie Y. McKay, eds. *The Norton Anthology of African American Literature.* New York and London: W. W. Norton and Company, 1997.

Gilbert, Sandra M., and Susan Gubar. *The Madwoman in the Attic.* New Haven: Yale University Press, 1979.

———. "Sexual Linguistics: Women's Sentence, Men's Sentencing." In *No Man's Land: The Place of the Woman Writer in the Twentieth Century,* 227–71. New Haven: Yale University Press, 1988.

Gilman, Charlotte Perkins. *The Living of Charlotte Perkins Gilman: An Autobiography.* 1935. Madison: University of Wisconsin Press, 1990.

Gilman, Sander. "Black Bodies, White Bodies: Toward an Iconography of Female Sexuality in Late Nineteenth-Century Art, Medicine, and Literature." In *"Race," Writing, and Difference,* edited by Henry Louis Gates Jr., 223–61. Chicago: University of Chicago Press, 1986.

Gilmore, Leigh. *Autobiographics: A Feminist Theory of Women's Self-Representation.* Ithaca: Cornell University Press, 1994.

Gray, James L. "Culture, Gender, and Slave Narrative." *Proteus: A Journal of Ideas 7,* no. 1 (Spring 1990): 37–42.

Greene, Jack P. Prologue to *The Intellectual Construction of America: Exceptionalism and Identity from 1492 to 1800,* 1–7. Chapel Hill: University of North Carolina Press, 1993.

Grimke, Francis. Letter in *Journal of Negro History* (January 1936): 314.

Gwin, Minrose C. "Green-Eyed Monsters of the Slavocracy: Jealous Mistresses in Two Slave Narratives." In *Conjuring: Black Women, Fiction, and Literary Tradition,* edited by Marjorie Pryse and Hortense J. Spillers, 39–52. Bloomington: Indiana University Press, 1985.

Harper, Frances E. W. "Ethiopia." In *The Norton Anthology of African American*

Literature, edited by Henry Louis Gates Jr. and Nellie Y. McKay, 412. New York: W. W. Norton and Company, 1997.

Harpham, Geoffrey Galt. "Conversion and the Language of Autobiography." In *Studies in Autobiography,* edited by James Olney, 42–50. New York and Oxford: Oxford University Press, 1988.

Hemenway, Robert E. *Zora Neale Hurston: A Literary Biography.* Urbana and Chicago: University of Illinois Press, 1977.

Henderson, Mae Gwendolyn. "Speaking in Tongues: Dialogics, Dialectics, and the Black Woman Writer's Literary Tradition." In *Changing Our Own Words: Essays on Criticism, Theory, and Writing by Black Women,* edited by Cheryl A Wall, 16–37. New Brunswick, N.J.: Rutgers University Press, 1991.

Higginbotham, Evelyn Brooks. "African-American Women's History and the Metalanguage of Race." In *Revising the Word and the World: Essays in Feminist Literary Criticism,* edited by VeVe A. Clark, Ruth-Ellen B. Joeres, and Madelon Sprengnether, 91–114. Chicago: University of Chicago Press, 1993.

Higginson, Thomas Wentworth. Introduction to *Reminiscences of My Life in Camp, With the 33rd United States Colored Troops, Late 1st S.C. Volunteers,* by Susie King Taylor, xi–xii. Boston: Published by Author, 1902.

Hine, Darlene Clark. "Rape and the Inner Lives of Black Women in the Middle West: Preliminary Thoughts on the Culture of Dissemblance." *Signs* 14, no. 4 (Summer 1989): 912–20.

Holloway, Karla F. C. *Moorings and Metaphors: Figures of Culture and Gender in Black Women's Literature.* New Brunswick, N.J.: Rutgers University Press, 1992.

Holquist, Michael. Introduction to *The Dialogic Imagination,* by M. M. Bakhtin, xv–xxxiv. Austin: University of Texas Press, 1981.

hooks, bell. *Ain't I a Woman: Black Women and Feminism.* Boston: South End Press, 1981.

———. "Choosing the Margin as a Space of Radical Openness." In *Framework* 36 (1989): 15–23.

———. *Talking Back: Thinking Feminist, Thinking Black.* Boston: South End Press, 1989.

Hull, Gloria T., and Barbara Smith. "Introduction: The Politics of Black Women's Studies." In *All the Women Are White, All the Blacks Are Men; But Some of Us Are Brave,* edited by Gloria T. Hull, Patricia Bell Scott, and Barbara Smith, xvii–xxxi. Old Westbury, N.Y.: Feminist Press, 1982.

Hurston, Zora Neale. "Characteristics of Negro Expression." In *Voices From the Harlem Renaissance,* edited by Nathan Irvin Huggins, 224–36. New York and Oxford: Oxford University Press, 1995.

———. *Dust Tracks on a Road.* 1942. Reprint, New York: Harper Collins, 1996.

———. "The 'Pet' Negro System." In *I Love Myself When I Am Laughing . . . And Then Again When I Am Looking Mean and Impressive,* edited by Alice Walker, 156–62. New York: Feminist Press, 1979.

Jacobs, Harriet A. *Incidents in the Life of a Slave Girl, Written by Herself.* 1861. Edited and with introduction by Jean Fagan Yellin. Cambridge: Harvard University Press, 1987.

Jay, Gregory S. "The End of 'American' Literature: Toward a Multicultural Practice." *College English* 53 (1991): 264–81.

Johnson, Greg. "Gilman's Gothic Allegory: Rage and Redemption in *The Yellow Wallpaper.*" *Studies in Short Fiction* 26, no. 4 (Fall 1989): 521–30.

Johnson, Ronna C. "Said But Not Spoken: Elision and the Representation of Rape, Race, and Gender in Harriet E. Wilson's *Our Nig.*" In *Speaking the Other Self: American Women Writers,* edited by Jeanne Campbell Reesman, 96–116. Athens: University of Georgia Press, 1997.

Jones, Jacqueline. *Labor of Love, Labor of Sorrow: Black Women, Work, and the Family from Slavery to the Present.* New York: Basic Books, 1985.

Jones, Jill. "The Disappearing 'I' in *Our Nig.*" *Legacy* 13, no. 1 (1996): 38–53.

Kadar, Marlene. "Whose Life Is It Anyway? Out of the Bathtub and into the Narrative." In *Essays on Life Writing: From Genre to Critical Practice,* edited by Marlene Kadar, 152–61. Toronto: University of Toronto Press, 1992.

Kafka, Phillipa. *The Great White Way: African American Women Writers and American Success Mythologies.* New York: Garland Publishing, 1993.

Keating, Analouise. "(De)Centering the Margins? Identity Politics and Tactical (Re)Naming." In *Other Sisterhoods: Literary Theory and U.S. Women of Color,* edited by Sandra Kumamoto Stanley, 23–43. Urbana and Chicago: University of Illinois Press, 1998.

Keckley, Elizabeth. *Behind the Scenes. Or, Thirty Years a Slave, and Four Years in the White House.* 1868. New York: Oxford University Press, 1988.

Lang, Amy Schrager. "Class and Strategies of Sympathy." In *The Cultural Sentiment: Race, Gender, and Sentimentality in Nineteenth-Century America,* edited by Shirley Samuels, 128–42. New York: Oxford University Press, 1992.

Leatherman, Courtney. "English Curriculum Favors Morrison Over Swift, Report Says." *Chronicle of Higher Education* 46, no. 39 (June 2, 2000): A19–20.

Levine, Robert S. "*Uncle Tom's Cabin* in Frederick Douglass's Paper: An Analysis of Reception." *American Literature* 64, no. 1 (March 1991): 71–93.

Lindgren, Margaret. "Harriet Jacobs, Harriet Wilson and the Redoubled Voice in Black Autobiography." *Obsidian II* 8, no. 1 (Spring-Summer 1993): 18–38.

Lott, Eric. *Love and Theft: Blackface Minstrelsy and the American Working Class.* New York: Oxford University Press, 1993.

Mason, Mary G. "The Other Voice: Autobiographies of Women Writers." In *Life/ Lines: Theorizing Women's Autobiography,* edited by Bella Brodzki and Celeste Schenck, 19–44. Ithaca: Cornell University Press, 1988.

McDowell, Deborah E. *The Changing Same: Black Women's Literature, Criticism, and Theory.* Bloomington and Indianapolis: Indiana University Press, 1995.

McPherson, James M. Introduction to *Reminiscences of My Life in Camp,* by Susie King Taylor. 1902. New York: Arno Press, 1968.

Moody, Joycelyn K. "Twice Other, Once Shy: Nineteenth-Century Black Women Autobiographers and the American Literary Tradition of Effacement." *Auto/Biography Studies* 7, no. 1 (Spring 1992): 46–61.

Morrison, Toni. "The Site of Memory." In *Inventing the Truth: The Art and Craft of Memoir,* edited by William Zinsser, 103–24. Boston: Houghton Mifflin, 1987.

Mullen, Harryette. "Runaway Tongue: Resistant Orality in *Uncle Tom's Cabin, Our Nig, Incidents in the Life of a Slave Girl,* and *Beloved.*" In *The Cultural Sentiment: Race, Gender, and Sentimentality in Nineteenth-Century America,* edited by Shirley Samuels, 244–64. New York: Oxford University Press, 1992.

Mullings, Leith. "Images, Ideology, and Women of Color." In *Women of Color in U.S. Society,* edited by Maxine Baca Zinn and Bonnie Thornton, 265–89. Philadelphia: Temple University Press, 1994.

Nelson, Jill. *Straight, No Chaser: How I Became a Grown-up Black Woman.* New York: G. P. Putnam's Sons, 1997.

Ochiai, Akiko. "Ida B. Wells and Her Crusade for Justice: An African American Woman's Testimonial Autobiography." *Soundings: An Interdisciplinary Journal* 75, nos. 2/3 (Summer/Fall 1992): 365–81.

Olney, James. Introduction to *Behind the Scenes. Or, Thirty Years a Slave, and Four Years in the White House,* by Elizabeth Keckley, xxvii–xxxvi. New York: Oxford University Press, 1988.

———. *Metaphors of Self: The Meaning of Autobiography.* Princeton: Princeton University Press, 1972.

———. "Some Versions of Memory/Some Versions of 'Bios': The Ontology of Autobiography." In *Autobiography: Essays Theoretical and Critical,* edited by James Olney, 236–67. Princeton: Princeton University Press, 1980.

Omolade, Barbara. *The Rising Song of African American Women.* London and New York: Routledge, 1994.

Oyěwùmí, Oyèrónké. *The Invention of Women: Making an African Sense of Western Gender Discourses.* Minneapolis: University of Minnesota Press, 1997.

Pemberton, John, III. "The Dreadful God and the Divine King." In *Africa's Ogun: Old World and New,* edited by Sandra T. Barnes, 105–46. Bloomington: Indiana University Press, 1989.

Pemberton, John, III, and Funso S. Afolayan. *Yoruba Sacred Kingship: "A Power Like That of God."* Washington, D.C.: Smithsonian Institute Press, 1996.

Peterson, Carla L. *"Doers of the Word": African American Women Speakers and Writers in the North (1830–1880).* New York and Oxford: Oxford University Press, 1995.

———. "'Doers of the Word': Theorizing African American Women Writers in the Antebellum North." In *The (Other) American Traditions: Nineteenth-Century Women Writers,* edited by Joyce W. Warren, 183–202. New Brunswick, N.J.: Rutgers University Press, 1993.

Philip, Marlene NourbeSe. *She Tries Her Tongue: "Her Silence Softly Breaks."* Charlottetown, Canada: Ragweed Press, 1989.

Randall, Ruth Painter. *Mary Lincoln: Biography of a Marriage.* Boston: Little and Brown, 1953.

Reising, Russell J. *The Unusable Past: Theory and the Study of American Literature.* New York: Methuen, 1986.

Richardson, Marilyn, ed. *Maria W. Stewart, America's First Black Woman Political Writer: Essays and Speeches.* Bloomington: Indiana University Press, 1987.

Royster, Jacqueline Jones. *Traces of a Stream: Literacy and Social Change Among African American Women*. Pittsburgh: University of Pittsburgh Press, 2000.

Rutberg, Becky. *Mary Lincoln's Dressmaker: Elizabeth Keckley's Remarkable Rise From Slave to White House Confidante*. New York: Walker and Company, 1995.

Sale, Maggie. "Critiques from Within: Antebellum Projects of Resistance." *American Literature* 64, no. 4 (December 1992): 695–718.

Scott, Anne Firor. *Southern Lady: From Pedestal to Politics, 1830–1930*. Chicago: University of Chicago Press, 1970.

Sekora, John. "Red, White, and Black: Indian Captivities, Colonial Printers, and the Early African-American Narrative." In *A Mixed Race: Ethnicity in Early America*, edited by Frank Shuffelton, 92–104. New York: Oxford University Press, 1993.

Shaw, Thurstan. *Nigeria: Its Archaeology and Early History*. London: Thames and Hudson, 1978.

Smith, Barbara. "Toward a Black Feminist Criticism." In *All the Women Are White, All the Blacks Are Men; But Some of Us Are Brave*, edited by Gloria T. Hull, Patricia Bell Scott, and Barbara Smith, 157–75. Old Westbury, N.Y.: Feminist Press, 1982.

Smith, Sidonie. *A Poetics of Women's Autobiography: Marginality and the Fictions of Self-Representation*. Bloomington: Indiana University Press, 1987.

———. "Resisting the Gaze of Embodiment: Women's Autobiography in the Nineteenth Century." In *American Women's Autobiography: Fea(s)ts of Memory*, 75–107. Madison: University of Wisconsin Press, 1992.

Smith, Sidonie, and Julia Watson. "De/Colonizing and the Politics of Discourse in Women's Autobiographical Practices." In *De/Colonizing the Subject: The Politics of Gender in Women's Autobiography*, edited by Sidonie Smith and Julia Watson, xiii–xxxi. Minneapolis: University of Minnesota Press, 1992.

Smitherman, Geneva. *Talkin and Testifyin: The Language of Black America*. Boston: Houghton Mifflin Company, 1977.

Sollors, Werner. *Neither Black Nor White, Yet Both: Thematic Explorations of Interracial Literature*. Cambridge: Harvard University Press, 1999.

Sorisio, Carolyn. "'There is Might in Each': Conceptions of Self in Harriet Jacobs's *Incidents in the Life of a Slave Girl, Written by Herself*" *Legacy* 13, no. 1 (1996): 1–18.

———. "Unmasking the Genteel Performer: Elizabeth Keckley's *Behind the Scenes* and the Politics of Public Wrath." *African American Review* 34, no. 1 (Spring 2000): 19–38.

Soyinka, Wole. *Myth, Literature and the African World*. Cambridge: Cambridge University Press, 1976.

Sterling, Dorothy, ed. *We Are Your Sisters: Black Women in the Nineteenth Century*. New York: W. W. Norton and Company, 1984.

Stern, Julia. "Excavating Genre in *Our Nig*." *American Literature* 67, no. 3 (September 1995): 439–66.

Stewart, Maria W. *Maria W. Stewart, America's First Black Woman Political Writer:*

Essays and Speeches. Edited and with introduction by Marilyn Richardson. Bloomington: Indiana University Press, 1987.

Stover, Johnnie M. "African American 'Mother Tongue' Resistance in Nineteenth-Centure Postbellum Black Women's Autobiography: Elizabeth Keckley and Susie King Taylor." *a/b: Auto/Biography Studies.* Forthcoming.

———. "Nineteenth-Century African American Women's Autobiography as Social Discourse: The Example of Harriet Ann Jacobs." Forthcoming (November 2003).

Stowe, Harriet Beecher. *Uncle Tom's Cabin.* 1852. Edited by Elizabeth Ammons. New York: W. W. Norton and Company, 1994.

Tate, Claudia. "Allegories of Black Female Desire; or, Rereading Nineteenth-Century Sentimental Narratives of Black Female Authority." In *Changing Our Own Words: Essays on Criticism, Theory, and Writing by Black Women,* edited by Cheryl A. Wall, 98–126. New Brunswick, N.J.: Rutgers University Press, 1991.

———. *Domestic Allegories of Political Desire: The Black Heroine's Text at the Turn of the Century.* New York: Oxford University Press, 1992.

Taylor, Susie King. *Reminiscences of My Life in Camp, With the 33rd United States Colored Troops, Late 1st S. C. Volunteers.* Boston: Published by Author, 1902.

Tesfagiorgis, Freida High W. "In Search of a Discourse and Critique/s That Center the Art of Black Women Artists." In *Theorizing Black Feminisms: The Visionary Pragmatisms of Black Women,* edited by Stanlie M. James and Abena P. A. Busia, 228–66. London and New York: Routledge, 1993.

Thoreau, Henry David. *Walden.* 1854. In *Walden and Civil Disobedience,* edited and with introduction by Paul Lauter, 37–264. Boston and New York: Houghton Mifflin Company, 2000.

Tompkins, Jane. *Sensational Designs: The Cultural Work of American Fiction, 1790–1860.* New York: Oxford University Press, 1985.

Trowbridge, C. T. Letter in *Reminiscences of My Life in Camp, With the 33rd United States Colored Troops, Late 1st S.C. Volunteers,* by Susie King Taylor, xiii. Boston: Published by Author, 1902.

Turner, Justin G., and Linda Levitt. *Mary Todd Lincoln: Her Life and Letters.* New York: Alfred A. Knopf, 1972.

VanDerBeets, Richard. *The Indian Captivity Narrative: An American Genre.* Lanham, Md.: University Press of America, 1984.

Walker, Alice. *In Search of Our Mothers' Gardens.* New York: Harcourt Brace Jovanovich Publishers, 1983.

Washington, John E. "Ample Proof of Reality of Elizabeth Keckley." *Evening Star* (November 15, 1935): A12.

Washington, Mary Helen. "Zora Neale Hurston: A Woman Half in Shadow." In *I Love Myself When I'm Laughing . . . And Then Again When I'm Looking Mean and Impressive,* edited by Alice Walker, 7–25. New York: Feminist Press, 1979.

Watson, Carrie Elizabeth Syphax. Interview in *Journal of Negro History* (July 1936): 316.

Wells, Ida B. *Crusade for Justice: The Autobiography of Ida B. Wells.* Edited by Alfreda M. Duster. Chicago: University of Chicago Press, 1970.

Welter, Barbara. *Dimity Convictions: The American Woman in the Nineteenth Century.* Athens: Ohio University Press, 1976.

Wheatley, Phillis. "To Maecenas." In *The Norton Anthology of African American Literature,* edited by Henry Louis Gates Jr. and Nellie Y. McKay, 169–70. New York and London: W. W. Norton and Company, 1997.

White, Barbara A. "'Our Nig' and the She-Devil: New Information about Harriet Wilson and the 'Bellmont Family.'" *American Literature* 65, no. 1 (March 1993): 19–52.

White, Deborah Gray. *Ar'n't I a Woman: Female Slaves in the Plantation South.* New York and London: W. W. Norton and Company, 1999.

Williamson, Joel. *A Rage for Order: Black-White Relations in the American South Since Emancipation.* New York: Oxford University Press, 1984.

Wilson, Harriet E. *Our Nig: or, Sketches from the Life of a Free Black, in a Two-Story White House, North. Showing that Slavery's Shadows Fall Even There.* 1859. 2nd ed. London: Allison and Busby, 1984.

Woolf, Virginia. *A Room of One's Own.* 1929. Reprint, San Diego, New York, and London: Harcourt Brace and Company, 1989.

Yellin, Jean Fagan. Introduction to *Incidents in the Life of a Slave Girl, Written by Herself,* by Harriet Jacobs, xiii–xxxiv. 1861. Cambridge: Harvard University Press, 1987.

———. *Women and Sisters: The Antislavery Feminists in American Culture.* New Haven: Yale University Press, 1989.

Index

Johnnie M. Stover is associate professor of English specializing in American literatures at Florida Atlantic University. Her current research areas include African American autobiography, American Indian literature, and American literature of the late nineteenth and early twentieth centuries.

AEJ- 8823

WITHDRAWN

Gramley Library
Salem Academy and College
Winston-Salem, N.C. 27108